Modern Scholarship on European History

HENRY A. TURNER, JR.
Editor

NAZISM
AND THE
THIRD REICH

NAZISM
AND THE
THIRD REICH

Edited with an Introduction by
HENRY A. TURNER, JR.

Quadrangle Books
NYT

A New York Times Company
1972

NAZISM AND THE THIRD REICH. Copyright © 1972 by
Henry A. Turner, Jr. All rights reserved, including the right
to reproduce this book or portions thereof in any form. For
information, address: Quadrangle Books, Inc., 330 Madison
Avenue, New York 10017. Manufactured in the United
States of America. Published simultaneously in Canada by
Burns and MacEachern Ltd., Toronto.

Library of Congress Catalog Card Number: 70-130396

International Standard Book Number: cloth 0–8129–0253–X
paper 0–8129–6195–1

ACKNOWLEDGMENTS

The editor wishes to express his appreciation to the following for permission to translate and/or to publish the selections included in this volume: Reginald H. Phelps for "Hitler and the *Deutsche Arbeiterpartei*"; the editors of the *Political Science Quarterly* and Joseph L. Nyomarkay for "Factionalism in the National Socialist German Workers' Party, 1925–26: The Myth and Reality of the 'Northern Faction'"; Horst Gies for "The NSDAP and Agrarian Organizations in the Final Phase of the Weimar Republic"; Hans Mommsen for "The Political Effects of the Reichstag Fire"; the editors of the *American Political Science Review* and Robert Koehl for "Feudal Aspects of National Socialism"; the Graduate School of Contemporary European Studies, University of Reading, and T. W. Mason for "The Primacy of Politics— Politics and Economics in National Socialist Germany"; Wesleyan University Press and Eberhard Jäckel for "The Evolution of Hitler's Foreign Policy Aims," from *Hitlers Weltanschauung: Entwurf einer Herrschaft,* copyright © 1969 by Rainer Wunderlich Verlag Hermann Leins, Tübingen; the British Academy and Alan Bullock for "Hitler and the Origins of the Second World War."

CONTENTS

NAZISM
AND THE
THIRD REICH

Introduction

THE NATIONAL SOCIALIST German Workers' Party and the government it established in Germany between 1933 and 1945—the so-called Third Reich—rank among the most extraordinary and momentous political phenomena of recent times. To the astonishment of most contemporary observers, an obscure movement hostile to many basic aspects of modern civilization suddenly gained the support of millions and succeeded in capturing control of one of the world's most advanced nations. Once in power, it stamped out all vestiges of political freedom and civil equality, reducing Jewish Germans to an outcast status and imposing a remorseless totalitarian dictatorship on all those under its authority. After a series of reckless but successful diplomatic moves that undermined the equilibrium of forces established after the First World War, the foreign policy of the Nazi government plunged Europe into the second great military carnage in a quarter-century. In the course of that six-year conflict, the leaders of the Third Reich defiantly flouted internationally agreed-upon rules of warfare and embarked upon the most horrendous campaign of genocide in recorded history, systematically slaughtering millions of Jews.

The Third Reich perished in the military debacle of 1945, but it bequeathed to survivors and subsequent generations a bitter heritage. It left behind it millions of shattered and disrupted lives, vast residues of hatred and mistrust, and a devastated and divided Europe, caught in the grip of a stultifying and anxiety-ridden cold war. Today the impact of Nazism and the Third Reich is still felt in countless ways, but their deepest and most lasting effects may well derive from the staggering

3

blow they delivered to the once widespread confidence that western civilization represented an impregnable barrier to the forces of barbarism and bestiality. Since Auschwitz, the world has seemed a different place.

Nazism and the Third Reich have been of compelling interest for historians and social scientists. Concerned about the possible larger implications of Germany's experience, scholars in other countries have joined with a new generation of Germans in an effort to establish the historical record of Nazism, identify its causes, ascertain its nature, and assess its meaning. This undertaking has been facilitated by the availability of unprecedented amounts of documentary evidence. By virtue of the unconditional surrender of the Third Reich in 1945, for the only time in modern history vast quantities of the most recent state papers of a major nation were made available to scholars of all nations. Supplemented by the testimony and memoirs of survivors as well as much private and corporate documentation, this material has made it possible to examine in great detail not only the Third Reich but also the preceding period, during which Nazism was born and launched on the road to power.

Despite the plethora of studies dealing with Nazism and the Third Reich, those phenomena in no sense belong to a closed chapter of history. Instead, they remain the focus of a vigorous and ongoing body of international scholarship. Historians and social scientists have as yet far from plumbed the full depths of the sea of documentation they generated. Many basic questions are still unclarified while others remain the subjects of lively controversy. Moreover, new discoveries and insights constantly give rise to fresh avenues of inquiry and analysis. Much research is under way, but even more remains still to be done in what has become one of the most active areas of modern historical scholarship.

The selections in this volume have been gathered together in order to convey an impression of the variety and quality of recent scholarship on Nazism and the Third Reich. Most of them were published in learned journals, some in German, so that they would otherwise not be easily accessible to many interested readers. They are printed here complete with documentation, in part as a convenience to professional scholars but also as a means of acquainting interested students with the wealth of resources available for research on Nazism and the Third Reich. It is to be hoped that this volume will encourage still others to put their minds to the task of illuminating one of the most perplexing chapters in the recent experience of mankind.

1

REGINALD H. PHELPS

Hitler and
the *Deutsche Arbeiterpartei*

A major problem in the study of Nazism has been the obscurity of its origins. During the early years of its existence, the Nazi Party was merely one of several squabbling Bavarian right-wing extremist groups that carried on a precarious existence in seemingly hopeless isolation from the political mainstream of the new German republic created after the revolution of 1918. The party thus attracted little attention from the national press or from major political observers, leaving on the public record few traces of the sort that facilitate the task of the historian. The party's leaders were men of obscure background, including Adolf Hitler himself. The son of a minor Austrian customs official, Hitler was born in 1889 and grew up in a succession of towns in western Austria. Left fatherless at fourteen, he failed to complete a secondary education and went at the age of eighteen to Vienna, where he unsuccessfully sought admission to the Art Academy. For the next seven years, he lived a shiftless existence, first in Vienna, then, after 1912, in Munich, dropping at times into abject poverty. Although still an Austrian citizen, he enlisted in a Bavarian regiment of the German army at the outbreak of the First World War. Serving throughout the conflict as a messenger on the front lines of the western front, he was wounded, decorated for valor, and promoted to corporal. At the time of the Armistice of November 11, 1918, he lay in a hospital bed in North Germany, recuperating from temporary blindness caused by gas at the front a month earlier.

5

This study takes up Hitler's career at that point and examines the circumstances surrounding his fateful entry into politics. Utilizing a variety of evidence brought to light only since the fall of the Third Reich, the author exposes the misleading nature of the Nazi leader's own autobiographical version of his early political activities. This selection originally appeared in the American Historical Review, LXVIII *(1963), 974–986. It is reprinted by permission of the author, who is Associate Dean of the Graduate School of Arts and Sciences at Harvard University. He has published numerous articles on Nazism.*

IT IS NOT easy to squeeze out of that enormous sponge *Mein Kampf* a clear account of Hitler's first association with the Deutsche Arbeiterpartei in Munich. He tells nothing of the party's origins and little of the six months from his earliest contact with it in September 1919 until its first public triumph, his proclamation of its program in the Hofbräuhaus on February 24, 1920. To summarize his narrative:[1]

Coming from the hospital in Pasewalk, where his temporary blinding by gas had confined him, he reached Munich late in November 1918, joined a replacement battalion at Traunstein, and returned to Munich in March. He remained there under the short-lived Soviet republics set up in April and was assigned to an army "investigating commission"' shortly after the occupation of Munich by government troops early in May. He talked with comrades about founding a social revolutionary party. A lecture in an army citizenship course by Gottfried Feder on the dangers of international capitalism impressed him deeply. His energetic response to a participant who defended the Jews, in a discussion in one of these courses, led to his appointment as a "training officer" (*Bildungsoffizier*), and he found that he could "speak" to a crowd.[2]

One day Hitler was ordered to report on a meeting of the obscure Deutsche Arbeiterpartei, which, like any possibly subversive organization, interested the Reichswehr. In a dismal tavern, the Sterneckerbräu, Hitler found twenty or twenty-five men, chiefly of the lower classes, listening to Feder repeat the address he had already heard that spring. "My impression was neither good nor bad," he writes. He would gladly have left after listening to Feder for two hours, but chanced to stay for the ensuing discussion and rose to smite verbally a separatist speaker. As he went out, a man rushed after him to thrust into his hand a small pamphlet. Lying awake the next morning in his barracks room, he opened the pamphlet, *Mein politisches Erwachen,* and found that its author had experienced a change from internationalism to nationalism like that which he himself had undergone twelve years earlier in Vienna.[3]

Several days later he received a post card announcing that he was a member of the DAP and inviting him to its next committee meeting. In a back room of the Altes Rosenbad, ill-lit by a half-ruined gas lamp, he met the committee: four young men, shortly joined by the Reich chairman. At last Hitler gives names: the Reich chairman was Karl Harrer; the head of the Munich local group (no other existed) and the author of the pamphlet was Anton Drexler. The meeting was painful—"small-town club business [*Vereinsmeierei*] of the worst kind." Yet he detected "good faith and good will," a longing like his own for a new movement.[4]

Never could he, with his "lack of schooling," have gone to one of the larger parties to face the condescension of their educated leaders and the impossible task of altering their ideas, but in the Deutsche Arbeiterpartei, "this ridiculous little creation," he could change things and could shine among less than equals. After two days of troubled brooding, he made his decision and received a provisional membership card with the number seven.[5]

Hitler goes on to describe the depressing picture presented by the party: weekly sessions of the committee, which actually included the whole party membership; its "parliamentary" actions and its handwritten or typed invitations to meetings; the small triumph finally achieved when the use of mimeographed notices produced an audience of thirty-four. Then came more daring ventures: into the Hofbräukeller across the Isar, where Hitler spoke to over a hundred people; to larger halls, the Eberlbräu, and the Deutsches Reich in the Dachauerstrasse near the barracks. Over four hundred came to the party's seventh public meeting.[6] Now Hitler was in control, and after the resignation of the over-cautious Harrer, the decision was made to try a mass meeting on February 24 in the huge barrel-vaulted hall of the Hofbräuhaus. Red placards announced it; the hall was packed. After the first speaker (not named in *Mein Kampf*), Hitler rose to face an audience more than half hostile, elucidated the twenty-five points of the party's platform, and converted the crowd to unanimous support of every point. Thus, after nearly four hours they departed, and the fire was enkindled, Hitler declaims, to forge the sword that would give "Siegfried" his freedom and restore life to the German nation.[7]

What he offers is a heroic legend in half-naturalistic style, young

Siegfried warbling his wood-notes wild in Munich beer halls. Some of this interesting legend is true, but Hitler had an ability to forget, or ignore, or invent facts and incidents even over as short a period as that from 1919 to 1924, and to rearrange them for artistic effect. Despite gaps in the evidence, enough documents exist to correct this legend.

First, there are the origins of the movement that was to conquer Germany. Here Drexler and Harrer are the principals, and the Munich locomotive shops, the elegant Hotel Vier Jahreszeiten, and shabby back rooms in shabby taverns are the setting.[8]

Drexler, a native of Munich, started this particular phase of German national racism (though no serious discussion can ignore its forerunners, particularly Theodor Fritsch and his journal *Hammer,* in many societies and political groupings before 1914).[9] Like Hitler, Drexler refused to accept the Social Democrats as the voice of labor and consequently lost a job in Berlin. In 1902, back in Munich, he became a locksmith at the locomotive works. Physically unfit for the army, he found an outlet for his patriotism in the Vaterlandspartei and in founding at Munich in March 1918, as an offshoot of a national movement, the "Workers' Committee for a Good Peace."[10] A speech he delivered to colleagues from the locomotive shops on March 7 urged Bavarians, especially workers, to strengthen their will to victory and called for action against profiteers and speculators.[11]

Early in October he held a public meeting, calling for a new "national citizens' league," urging "Bourgeois, workers, unite!"[12] The audience was largely hostile. The November revolution discouraged him only temporarily; a week later he was approached by a curious emissary, Harrer, and asked to form with his friends a "Political Workers' Circle" (*Politischer Arbeiterzirkel*). The circle became the first cell of the National Socialist movement.[13]

Harrer represented a different line from Drexler's national-social-labor platform. A reporter on the Rightist *Münchner-Augsburger Abendzeitung,* he shared the murky ideas taught among "intellectual" racists and was a member of the Thule Gesellschaft, which served as ally and cover in Bavaria for the semisecret, activist, violently *völkisch Germanenorden.* An affluent adventurer, Rudolf von Sebottendorff, had reorganized this order in Bavaria during 1918 and acquired rooms for it in the Hotel Vier Jahreszeiten. Harrer was assigned to spread Thule ideas among the workers. He did not reach many, but he did reach Drexler.[14]

The circle, directed by Harrer, met from November 1918 at least until the following fall. Hitler could well have called these sessions

"Vereinsmeierei." Harrer regularly presented the evening's theme—
"Germany's greatest foe: The Jew," "Who is responsible for the World
War?" "Could we have won the war?" From three to seven members
(about a dozen different names appear)—artisans, small merchants,
colleagues from the shops, and for a time a gentleman named Von
Heimburg—sat about the table discussing the evening's topic. Bitter-
ness against the Jews, the need of "enlightening" the workers, hostility
to England marked the discussions.[15]

Clearly Drexler was the political figure in this assemblage. In December he proposed founding a party, and on January 5, at another small
tavern, the Fürstenfelder Hof, he launched his creation, the Deutsche
Arbeiterpartei, before an audience of twenty-four, mostly friends from
the shops.[16]

Even under the Leftist regimes in Munich that followed Kurt Eisner's
assassination in February, the DAP and the circle carried on their twilit
existence. An undated draft of a "discussion speech" by Drexler, possibly delivered at a Leftist meeting during this period, urged "the liber-
ation of the workers, yes, of all humanity" and, with anti-Semitic over-
tones, "the sovereignty of a government borne by the popular will."[17]
He barely missed arrest at the Thule rooms, where a DAP meeting was
scheduled for April 29, and thus perhaps escaped the fate of the seven
Thule members whose shooting the next day by the Reds was one of
the chief sources of anti-Leftist and anti-Semitic passion in Bavaria.[18]

Henceforth the omens were favorable for a movement like Drexler's,
under the rigid military regime and the prevailing hostility of the
Munich bourgeoisie to the Left and the Jews. Army and police reports
and minutes of cabinet meetings, to be sure, at first made little mention
of the latter in 1919.[19] But army intelligence reports from July on
showed an ominous undercurrent, breaking through in epidemics of
anti-Jewish stickers, or "general railing" (*Schimpfen*) at the Jews,
with the newly formed Deutschvölkischer Schutz- und Trutzbund and
the Thule Gesellschaft obviously fostering this mood and directing the
popular hatred against profiteers (*Wucherer* and *Schieber*) toward anti-
Semitism.[20] Ernst Pöhner, the Munich police president who became
one of Hitler's main allies, noted in his weekly survey early in September increasing economic anti-Semitism and in November reported that
the chief demand of anti-Semitic propaganda was for "breaking Jewish
loan capital and the disproportionate influence of the Jews in the leadership of the German people." Feder's dogmas of interest slavery were
obviously catching on. Racist "excesses and illegalities" must of course

be combatted, Pöhner wrote. A week later, on November 22, he stated that workers, too, were becoming interested in anti-Semitism, "especially the Deutsche Arbeiterpartei, founded only two months ago[!], already firmly established in Munich." "The anti-Semitic wave is only beginning," he noted.[21]

With this report, the DAP entered the ambiguous immortality of the police records. Its own records give an indication of how and when it grew. There are attendance lists for some eleven meetings in 1919, beginning on May 17, when ten members were present.[22] Hitler's close friend Dietrich Eckart spoke in August to an audience of thirty-eight; forty-two were present on September 12, when Hitler's signature first appears: "Gefreiter München 2. I. Rgt." His name appeared again on October 16, when the audience numbered over seventy, including Karl Brassler, contributor to the Rightist newspaper *Münchener Beobachter*. Finally the DAP achieved a long notice in the press. The *Beobachter*, not yet a party organ, reported on October 22 that Dr. Erich Kühn, editor of the Pan-German monthly *Deutschlands Erneuerung*, spoke on "The Jewish Question a German Question," and that afterward "Herr Hitler of the DAP discussed with passion the need for union against the common enemy of the nations, and gave reasons for supporting a German press, so the people can find out what is suppressed by the Jewish papers."

From this point, the *Beobachter*, the police intelligence reports published by Ernst Deuerlein, and a larger set of police reports in the Hauptarchiv help to check Hitler's memory.[23] His first formal performance for the party was in the Eberlbräu on November 12 (or 13), on a favorite theme, "Brest-Litovsk and Versailles." On November 26, before an audience of three hundred, he contrasted promises and reality under the Republic. Two weeks later, in the beer hall Deutsches Reich, an audience of equal size heard him declaim on "Germany facing her deepest degradation." After the Christmas recess, four hundred of the faithful gathered in mid-January to hear Feder; Hitler, following him, argued the justification for a workers' party opposed to Jews and capitalism. Dietrich Eckart drew a smaller crowd on February 5 (or 6). But Hitler's big push for a mass meeting had already begun.[24]

Hitler's stress on his affinity with the "ridiculous" little party has been noted above. He remarks that he was "impoverished and poor," "one of the nameless ones," "one of the millions that chance allows to live or die, without even their closest environment deigning to notice."[25]

This picture of the anonymous hero is of course part of his myth creation, for he was a rather well-known figure in Munich army circles when he first visited a meeting of the party, and he continued his activity for the Reichswehr—something he does not mention—during the months when, according to *Mein Kampf*, he was devoting himself to the party. Deuerlein's documentation[26] tells of Hitler's early participation in the courses organized by Captain Karl Mayr of the Munich Reichswehr, who, impressed by Hitler's rhetorical talents, assigned him to the *Kommando Beyschlag*, which indoctrinated returning prisoners of war at the transit camp Lechfeld. Here, late in August, Hitler lectured on "Peace Terms and Reconstruction" and "Social and Economic Slogans." The fan mail of the participants leaves no doubt of their enthusiasm for his "temperamentvolle Vorträge." The charisma was at work.

Thus it was not as the unknown soldier that Hitler joined the DAP. His two careers, army and politics, ran side by side. He is listed in January and February 1920 as a lecturer in the "citizenship continuation courses" conducted for soldiers by the Reichswehr: "Herr Hittler" besides such dignitaries as the Munich University historians K. A. von Müller and Paul Joachimsen.[27] He spoke on "The Peace of Versailles" and "The Political Parties and Their Significance," delivering one of his lectures on February 25, the afternoon following his presentation of the party program at the Hofbräuhaus. One month later he was discharged from the army, and Captain Mayr's strange plant was definitively transferred to even more fertile soil. None of this is in *Mein Kampf*.

What of the other side—the gloomy little group of members, always the same, according to Hitler, meeting as the "committee" of the DAP? Here the documents are less revealing. One difficulty is the unclear distinction between *Arbeiterzirkel* and committee. The former evidently remained as a secret inner circle, Harrer's pet, dutifully chewing its cud.[28] Drexler's draft of the minutes of the circle meeting of November 16 (a photostat was provided by Frau Anni Widmaier) records Hitler's first visit: "Present: Herr Harrer Drexler Hitler as new member. Introduction of Herr Hitler into the spirit of the circle, by Hr. Harrer. Reading of letters received, and replies to them. It was resolved to elect a committee to prepare for the setting up [*Aufstellung*, presumably of a program], with the following members: Harrer, Dr. Feder, Dr. [Paul] Tafel, Hitler, Drexler. Following this, discussion of the party program. Foundation of an anti-Semitic association [*Arbeitsgesellschaft?* word unclear]."[29] Evidently Hitler was also present at a circle meeting on November 24, where he consented to become director of a party speakers' school. It is still uncertain whether he was number 7 in the circle, as its first secretary, Lotter, contends, or number 7 of the party committee, as Drexler and Rudolph Schüssler, later business manager of the party, have it. The latter is more probable, considering the fluctuating membership of the circle and Drexler's precise statement. In any case, Hitler was never party member number 7. The attendance lists of meetings in 1919 consistently show more than seven present; Drexler indicates that there were nearly a hundred members before Hitler joined. His official number was 555 (no magic in that!) on the first party membership lists, set up alphabetically and beginning with number 501 to give the impression of greater size. To crown this legend, "555" was erased from his membership card and "7" inserted.[30]

The imperialist Hitler could of course tolerate no other leaders in the party. In December he drafted regulations for the committee, previously organized as a normal parliamentary body, to give it full authority and to ban any "side government" by a "circle or lodge"— obviously aimed at Harrer, who bowed out of office and party early in January 1920.[31]

Meanwhile horizons were broadening, and money, in driblets, but enough for some expansion, came in. Thus the peripatetic party late in December rented (for fifty marks a month, in advance, light and heat extra) a ground floor room in the Sternecker.[32] More important, Drexler and Hitler set to work on a platform. The circle had considered this subject in May, with Harrer proposing three [!] programs: a basic one, a "working program" adaptable to changing circumstances, and a "party program" defining exactly its goals.[33] An early version by Drexler of the basic program stresses "idealistic *Weltanschauung*," equal rights and duties, physical education, and "an open road for all talents for the common good." Much of it, except for the ominous phrase "Germany for the Germans," read like a nineteenth-century reformist document.[34]

The circle, with Hitler, discussed the program on November 16, and on December 14 Drexler had a new draft ready. It was idealistic and nationalistic, familiar refrains, but now with new emphases, on the unity of the Reich, the exclusion of Jews and foreigners from government, the union of all producers (*Schaffenden*) against loan capital and interest slavery, and on bridging the gap between physical and intellectual workers, and a plebiscite to decide between a republic and a *Volks-Kaisertum*.[35]

In his letter of January 1940, Drexler indignantly reminded his Führer that "following all the basic points already written down by me, Adolf Hitler composed *with* me—and with no one else—the 25 theses of National Socialism, in long nights in the workers' canteen at Burghausenerstrasse 6." Together, then, and with the larger contribution probably Drexler's, they worked over the draft of the twenty-five points. The final version has some changes of order and emphasis from Drexler's draft of February 9. Profit sharing, a pet thesis of Drexler, was stressed less, while "land reform" received fuller attention; the newly inserted and repeated "We demand" (*Wir fordern*) sounds distinctly like Hitler.[36]

And so, with a program in hand and the tide running favorably, all was set for the great coup, the first mass meeting, still under the old party name, though by the beginning of March "National Socialist" was prefixed to "German Workers' Party."[37] Drexler read at the large meeting of February 5 (or 6) the party's first propaganda leaflet— "Warum musste die DAP kommen? Was will sie?"—with "anti-Jesuitism" added to the familiar slogans.[38]

Hitler makes much of the dangers of the meeting of February 24, though large anti-Semitic gatherings in Munich were no rarity by then. He tells of his personal management of propaganda, placards, and handbills and his fear that the hall would not be full. Drexler's letter tells it differently. He, not Hitler, proposed a big public meeting in the Hofbräuhaus. In fact, he had to overcome Hitler's objections to it. Hitler does not mention that the red placards and the advertisement in the *Beobachter* neither listed his name nor alluded to the proclamation of the DAP program, nor that the "first speaker," proposed by Drexler, was a guest, not a party member—Dr. Johannes Dingfelder, a familiar *völkisch* and *Hammerbund* figure even before the war. Drexler tells of taking to Dingfelder a copy of the newly typed twenty-five points to explain what the DAP was about, "but one thing I did not tell Dingfelder was that a certain Adolf Hitler was speaking after him."[39]

The Hauptarchiv contains a manuscript of the speech "What We Need" (*Was uns not tut*) that Dingfelder had already delivered five times for the patriotic *Heimatdienst* and a carbon copy of Dingfelder's undated recollections of the meeting, entitled "Wie es kam!"[40] He recalls that on February 20 Drexler and Schüssler, both strangers to him, invited him to address the meeting; Drexler explained that no one else dared to. (Ten years later, Dingfelder adds, he found out that a Communist had threatened to shoot both Hitler and the chief speaker.)

He arrived in the overcrowded hall, learned that the expected chairman, Drexler, had had a nervous collapse, and that four hundred Reds were present. He decided to avoid trouble by not using the word "Jew." Marc Sesselmann, a member of Thule and the DSP and an editor of the *Beobachter,* opened the meeting. For acoustical reasons Dingfelder stood on a table beside the huge tiled stove at one side of the hall. He got through his speech with no trouble; indeed, Sesselmann thanked the Reds for keeping quiet. Then, after a few comments from the audience, Hitler, "a thin man with a small moustache," walked to the front of the hall, and the Reds' tumult began.

Dingfelder's speech, eloquent at times, found the cause of the war in the general lapse from natural law and religion. He quoted Shakespeare and Schiller to show the beauties of order and brought in recent history—the murder of the hostages in Munich, Bolshevism, "people of foreign race"—to demonstrate the horrors of disorder. "I am a Communist too," he announced, "but in the *Christian* sense." "Selfless leaders" were needed, not those "spiritually blind, who stand under the influence of foreign races." He praised Paul von Hindenburg and Erich Ludendorff and concluded, "For us too a savior is approaching!" If Germans once reawaken to order, work, and duty, "the world will—must—at last find health through the German spirit!"

Hitler's short narrative of the meeting in *Mein Kampf* describes it as his personal, overwhelming triumph: how he pronounced point after point of the program "amid ever-increasing jubilation," until the mass stood "united by a new conviction, a new faith, a new will." He concludes the first volume of his book with "So the hall slowly emptied. The movement took its course."[41]

The hero legend of the conquest of the Hofbräuhaus as archetype of the conquest of Germany! The *Beobachter,* to be sure, was less emotional.[42] On February 28 a notice perhaps five inches long appeared on an inside page, over half of it devoted to Dingfelder's speech. It continues: "Herr Hitler (DAP) presented some striking political points [*entwickelte einige treffende politische Bilder*], which evoked spirited applause, but also roused the numerous already prejudiced opponents present to contradiction; and he gave a survey of the party's program, which in its basic features comes close to that of the Deutschsozialistische Partei." This one sentence is all there is about Hitler. The report notes that the discussion following was very lively, "but toward the end strayed from the theme," and that the meeting left the impression of a movement "that will force its way through under all circumstances." But what has become of the revelation to the masses, the "shouts of applause" that drowned out objectors, the resolute hammering through of point after point until the hall was filled with men "united by a new conviction, a new faith, a new will"?

Fortunately other papers reported the meeting, though the accounts in four Munich "bourgeois" newspapers are so similar that they may well be from a single hand.[43] They concentrate on Dingfelder. Typically, the *Münchener Zeitung* of February 25 sums up the rest of the meeting: "The Committee member Hitler presented [*entwickelte*], following the lecture, the DAP program, which among other things stands for a Greater Germany, opposes the Jews, and demands the breaking of interest slavery. During the discussion—cut short because of the late hour, but in part stormy—the leader of the unemployed, Braig, supported by a group of opponents of the DAP, spoke, with the rest of the gathering objecting, against the new workers' party."

Finally, the author of the police report in the Hauptarchiv, the fullest contemporary account, tells in detail what happened after Dingfelder's speech. Hitler rose to ring the usual changes on Versailles, poverty, corruption, profiteering, and internationalism, and to read the program to a discordant audience: "Often there was such a tumult that I thought fighting [*Schlägereien*] would start any moment." After him, Sesselmann spoke, as did Braig, of the Independent Socialists, Ernst Ehrensperger of the DAP, and an opponent whose appeal for a Leftist dictatorship unloosed such an uproar that Hitler's final words were lost, and a hundred Independent Socialists and Communists thronged out on the street singing the "International," shouting "Down with Hindenburg, Ludendorff, and the German Nationalists!" This, and not the awed silence of a converted congregation, was the real conclusion of Hitler's first great public triumph.

Let us review the facts and fancies of Hitler's version of this crucial time. He stylizes his life into the *Märchen* pattern of the *Bärensohn* or *Starker Hans,* the male Cinderella, with the story of 1919–1920 as the central episode in his saga of the boy from Braunau who was to save Germany. As the coming savior, he must be unique; hence the dearth of reference to earlier, similar movements, the stress on the new *Weltanschauung* of the party, the omission of its early history and of its rivals, like the DSP, much more important at that time in Munich and Nuremberg and the north than the DAP. As the hero figure, he had to do everything great himself; hence the omission of the Reichswehr's continuing sponsorship, the condescension or hostility toward Drexler and

Harrer, the only early party colleagues he names, and the implication that he was the real creator of the program. As the player of the great role he must achieve things dramatically and suddenly; thus he obliterates traces of everything but himself in his fantastic story of the meeting of February 24.

But, with the exceptions noted, particularly regarding the party number and the Hofbräuhaus meeting, the myth is produced rather by stylization and omission than by invention. Most of the few facts he gives are no further removed from actuality than might be expected in the circumstances of writing *Mein Kampf*. But, in searching for the reality of Hitler, it is worth observing that the only scenes in the whole book sketched in full detail are those of his first visits to the Deutsche Arbeiterpartei. There, one can surmise, he found himself.

NOTES

1. Adolf Hitler, *Mein Kampf* (2 vols., Munich, 1930), I, Chaps. VIII, IX, XII; II, 518–525, 624–629. Among the innumerable secondary accounts of his early relations with the DAP, the following may be mentioned: Konrad Heiden, *Geschichte des Nationalsozialismus* (Berlin, 1932), pp. 18–27, and *Adolf Hilter, das Zeitalter der Verantwortungslosigkeit* (Zurich, 1936), pp. 76–84, 98–107; Walter Görlitz and H. A. Quint, *Adolf Hitler* (Stuttgart, 1952), pp. 101–137; the dissertation of Ulrich von Hasselbach, *Die Entstehung der Nationalsozialistischen Deutschen Arbeiterpartei* (Leipzig, 1931), *passim;* and, most recently, Georg Franz-Willing, *Die Hitlerbewegung,* I, *Der Ursprung 1919–1922* (Hamburg, 1962), pp. 66–75, 80ff., relying extensively on material in the NSDAP Hauptarchiv, formerly in the Berlin Document Center. See also, for some evidence of the army's role, the reminiscences of Ernst Röhm, *Die Geschichte eines Hochverräters* (2d ed., Munich, 1930), pp. 100–108.

2. Hitler, *Mein Kampf,* I, 226–229, 232–235. The best published documentation of Hitler's career from November 1918 until the summer of 1919 is in Ernst Deuerlein, "Hitlers Eintritt in die Politik und die Reichswehr," *Vierteljahrshefte für Zeitgeschichte,* 7 (1959), 179–185, 191–205. Feder, by profession an engineer, was already known in Bavaria as propagandist for "breaking the interest slavery" of "international capitalism," which became a major economic plank in the Nazi program.

3. Hitler, *Mein Kampf,* I, 236–239.

4. *Ibid.,* pp. 240–243.

5. *Ibid.,* pp. 243f.

6. *Ibid.,* pp. 389–394.

7. *Ibid.,* pp. 400–406.

8. The following brief sketch of Drexler and the DAP is a summation of an intended larger study of this subject. See also Reginald H. Phelps, "Anton Drexler, der Gründer der NSDAP," *Deutsche Rundschau,* LXXXVII (1961), 1134–43.

9. Reginald H. Phelps, "Theodor Fritsch und der Antisemitismus," *ibid.* (1961), 442–449.

10. Anton Drexler, *Mein politisches Erwachen* (2d ed., Munich, 1920), pp. 5–7, 12–15, 19–22, and "Lebenslauf," March 1935 (typescript copy available through courtesy of his daughter, Frau Anni Widmaier).

11. The Hauptarchiv of the NSDAP (hereafter cited as HA), No. 76, contains photostats of Drexler's outline of this speech, the resolution adopted after it, and the twenty-eight signatures of the participants. The Hauptarchiv and other material at the Berlin Document Center have been microfilmed by the Hoover Institution. The Hauptarchiv has recently been transferred from the center to the Bundesarchiv, Koblenz.

12. Drexler, *Erwachen*, pp. 23–26, and "Lebenslauf."

13. Drexler, "Lebenslauf." Franz-Willing, *Hitlerbewegung*, p. 63, erroneously states that the circle was founded in October.

14. Rudolf von Sebottendorff, *Bevor Hitler kam* (2d ed., Munich, 1934), gives a highly seasoned account of the Thule Gesellschaft and its relation to the DAP and the competing Deutschsozialistische Partei. Sebottendorff bought the foundering newspaper *Münchener Beobachter* in the summer of 1918, thus providing various *völkisch* groups with an organ. Thule was active in April 1919 against the Soviet rulers of Munich, and seven of its members were shot by the Reds as "hostages" on April 30. HA, No. 1497a, contains a copy of a report of Drexler's interrogation after the Hitler putsch (PD VIa, *Vorführungs-Note*, November 30, 1923), with information on the circle and the DAP; documents of Johannes Hering in HA, No. 865, provide much material on Thule. See also *ibid.*, No. 78, typescript of a speech by Michael Lotter, secretary of the circle, "Der Beginn meines politischen Denkens," delivered on October 19, 1935.

15. HA, No. 76, *Protokolle* of the circle, December 5, 1918–September 9, 1919, photostats, mostly in Drexler's hand, of fourteen meetings, with names of those present from December 30, 1918 on; photostats of minutes of three further meetings, supplied to me by Frau Widmaier.

16. Drexler, "Lebenslauf"; HA, No. 76, *Protokoll* for December 30, 1918; *ibid.*, No. 78, Lotter, "Der Beginn."

17. *Ibid.*, No. 76, has a photostat of the manuscript; *ibid.*, No. 77, one of the typescript of this draft.

18. *Ibid.*, No. 78, Lotter, "Der Beginn."

19. The minutes of cabinet meetings from March 19, 1919, to the end of the year contain only one passing allusion to anti-Semitism. The minutes are in the Bavarian State Archives, Munich (Hauptstaatsarchiv) (hereafter cited as BHStA) : *Ministerratsprotokolle, MA* 1946 B1, B2.

20. The intelligence reports are found in BHStA, files of *Reichswehr Gruppenkommando* 4 (hereafter cited as GK4). See, for the following, GK4, Band XI, Akt I, *Lagebeurteilungen*, May 1919–July 1920; Band XXXVI, Akt 7, *Judenhetze*, July 1919–January 1920, a mixed file of Reichswehr and police reports; Band XLII, Akt 2, the weekly *Nachrichtenblatt* of the *Polizeidirektion München*, May 24, 1919–December 1921. Weekly reports of the *Regierungspräsidenten* of the governmental districts of Bavaria for the period April 1919–April 1920 are found in BHStA, MA 1943 I. V. IXC/20 I and II. They are valuable indicators of public opinion. A report on a nationalist workers' party appears in GK4, Band I, Akt 4, headed GK4, Abt. Ib, No. 468 *geh.*, October 31: "Die Lage am 30. Okt. 19." It may refer to the DAP, but more probably concerns the rival Deutschsozialistische Partei.

21. BHStA, GK4, Band XLII, Akt 2, *Nachrichtenblatt*, July 12, September 6, November 15, 22, 1919.

22. HA, No. 80, contains the attendance lists. Since occupation and residence are usually given by those signing, they are very important evidence of the decline of the old guard of Drexler's colleagues and the influx of intellectuals and the military from the summer of 1919 on.

23. Deuerlein, "Hitlers Eintritt," pp. 205–211. HA, No. 81, contains police reports—only one of them identical with those cited by Deuerlein from the Bavarian State Archives—of the meetings of November 26, and December 10, 1919, and January 16, and February 6, 24, 1920; the series continues through December 3, 1920. The dates given for the meetings sometimes vary slightly (and inexplicably) in different sources.

24. Hitler, *Mein Kampf*, I, 400f.

25. *Ibid.*, p. 243.

26. For the following, see Deuerlein, "Hitlers Eintritt," pp. 179, 182–184, 191–193, 196–198, 200–205.

27. BHStA, GK4, Band VII, Akt 2: RWGK4/*Leitung der staatsbürgerlichen Fortbildungskurse, Zeiteinteilung für den 1. Kurs (13.I. bis 31.I.20)*, January 8, 1920, and a similar schedule for the second course, dated February 5, 1920.

28. HA, No. 77, *Politischer Arbeiterzirkel/Satzungen*, n.d., one page, carbon copy; they were distributed at the circle meeting of May 13 (HA, No. 76, *Protokolle*).

29. *Ibid.*, No. 78, Lotter, "Der Beginn"; *idem*, letter to Hauptarchiv, October 17, 1941. Both state that Hitler attended a circle meeting in September, but the minutes quoted and Drexler's evidence (see note 30, below) outweigh these statements.

30. See HA, No. 78, Lotter, "Der Beginn," and *ibid.*, No. 1372, letter of Schüssler to Dr. Uetrecht of the Hauptarchiv, typescript, November 20, 1941. In January 1936 Drexler told Dr. Damann of the Hauptarchiv (HA, No. 81, *Aktennotiz* Damann) that Hitler first attended a circle meeting on November 16. This agrees with the minutes of that meeting. Drexler, outraged by distorted official radio "history" of the party's origin, drafted a long, angry letter to Hitler late in January 1940, of which Frau Widmaier has made available a carbon copy. In it he stated: "No one knows better than you yourself, my Führer, that you were never the seventh member of the party, but at most the seventh member of the committee, which I asked you to join as propaganda chief (*Werbeobmann*)." In this letter—never sent, since Drexler planned to forward it to Hitler after the war—are also the statements about the size of the party in September 1919 and about the "forging" of Hitler's party card.

31. HA, No. 76, "Organisation des Ausschusses der Ortsgruppe München und seiner Geschäftsordnung," photostat of typescript (in pencil at top: "Dezember 1919/Geschäftsordnung Entwurf Hitler zur Ausschaltung Harrers"). See also *ibid.*, No. 77, "Der Ausschuss der Ortsgruppe München," typescript, n.d. Lotter, "Der Beginn," mentions the disagreement with Harrer.

32. HA, No. 80, "Sternecker Mietsvertrag," December 22, 1919.

33. *Ibid.*, No. 76, *Protokoll* of May 13, 1919.

34. *Ibid.*, No. 77, *DAP: Grundsätze*, typescript, copy, n.d.

35. *Ibid.*, No. 76, *Entwurf DAP Programm 14.XII.19*, photostat of a Drexler manuscript.

36. *Ibid., Auszug aus Programm vom 9. Feb. 20,* photostat of typescript, signed by Drexler. Hasselbach, *Entstehung,* pp. 12, 19, 26–36, evidently relying on information from Drexler, discusses the development of the program.

37. Curiously, the Hauptarchiv seems to have no account of this important change, which may have been explained by hopes of closer association with older German National Socialist parties in Austria and Czechoslovakia.

38. HA, No. 111, has the text of the leaflet; see also Drexler's letter of January 1940.

39. HA, No. 884, correspondence of Dingfelder with Julius Rüttinger of the *Hammerbund;* Hitler, *Mein Kampf,* I, 400–405; Drexler, letter of January 1940.

40. HA, No. 1214, file of Dingfelder. The only significant discrepancy from the police report of the meeting (see above, p. 15) is Dingfelder's statement that Sesselmann, not Hitler, presided. Here Dingfelder errs; not only the account in *Mein Kampf,* but an earlier article, "Zur Erinnerung an die Versammlung vom 24. Februar 1920 im Münchner Hofbräu," published anonymously in the *Beobachter* (February 22, 1922), but clearly by Hitler, confirms the logical assumption that Hitler, not Sesselmann, ran the meeting. The *Beobachter* article, which to be sure mentions Dingfelder, already shows the legend formation at work: the "storm of jubilation" of the crowd, the hammering through of the program "point by point," and—a striking metaphor, missing from *Mein Kampf*—the feeling at the end "that now a wolf has been born, destined to burst in upon the herd of seducers and deceivers of the people."

41. Hitler, *Mein Kampf,* I, 405f.

42. The paper, which changed its name during 1919 from *Münchener* to *Völkischer Beobachter,* was still officially a nonpartisan *völkisch* organ, though in fact it stood closest to the Deutschsozialistische Partei. Only after political and financial crises, solved in part by the famous "loan" by Franz Ritter von Epp to Dietrich Eckart in December 1920, did the *Beobachter* appear as the NSDAP organ.

43. Copies of the several press accounts are in the Friedrich J. M. Rehse Collection, Acc. No. 11,564: "Berichte der Presse über obenstehend angekündigte Versammlung," Manuscript Division, Library of Congress. The Independent Socialist *Der Kampf* and most of the "bourgeois" press reported the meeting; the *Bayerischer Kurier* and the Social Democratic *Münchener Post* evidently ignored it. HA, No. 78, Lotter, "Der Beginn," states that over 100 new members, swept away by Hitler and the program, joined the party in the Hofbräuhaus at the meeting. Probably the most authentic membership list from 1920, however (photostat of typescript, by courtesy of Frau Widmaier), records no new members that day, 36 for February 25 (37 for February 5, and 92 for May 1, 1920).

2

JOSEPH L. NYOMARKAY

Factionalism in the National Socialist German Workers' Party, 1925–26: The Myth and Reality of the "Northern Faction"

In the months following his less than auspicious appearance at the Hofbräuhaus, Hitler did in fact come to be the most successful agitator of the party, now the NSDAP. By the summer of 1921 he had established himself as its unchallenged leader. The next two years were devoted to strengthening the fledgling organization and extending it beyond Munich to other parts of Bavaria. Special emphasis was placed on the party's stormtroop adjunct, the SA (Sturmabteilung), *since Hitler aimed at an overthrow of the republican state, either by force or threat of force (as in Mussolini's "March on Rome"). That approach was effectively discredited by the attempted beerhall putsch of November 1923, which was easily suppressed by forces loyal to the Bavarian government. Arrested, tried for treason, and sentenced to a prison term, Hitler was removed from active political life for more than a year. When he was released in December 1924 he had new plans for reconstructing the party, which still recognized him as its leader. But during his absence changes had taken place that were to complicate those plans. The result was the first major internal crisis of the NSDAP.*

The author of this selection, an Associate Professor of Political Science at the University of Southern California, examines that crisis in the light of new documentary evidence. And by analyzing the forces

*that determined the outcome of the crisis, he seeks to establish the basic
institutional nature of the NSDAP. Professor Nyomarkay has dealt
with the latter question more extensively in his book,* Charisma and
Factionalism in the Nazi Party *(Minneapolis, 1967). This selection
first appeared in the* Political Science Quarterly, LXXX *(1965), 22–47.
It is reprinted by permission of the publisher and the author.*

Few ASPECTS of the history of the German Nazi party have received
such scant scholarly attention as the nature of its factional[1] conflicts.
Although references to intraparty conflicts may be found in most accounts dealing with the movement, no attempt has yet been made to
make factional conflicts the subject of a thorough academic research.

Admittedly, factionalism was only of marginal significance in the
history of the Nazi movement and this may well account for the lagging
academic interest in the subject. In striking contrast to Socialist and
Communist movements where factional conflicts have raised dramatic
issues, frequently to the point of splitting these movements, and have
been of lasting significance, the history of Nazi factionalism was neither
so dramatic nor so enduring in its effects. The several Nazi factions
passed out of existence without seriously affecting the course of party
history. Factionalism did not split the movement, did not give rise to
competing sets of leaders, did not seriously compromise Hitler's leadership and authority at any time, did not raise important questions of
theory, and, with the exception of 1934, did not result in mass purges.

But the failure of the Nazi factions can hardly justify the lack of
academic interest in the subject. Indeed, it is exactly the impotence of
the Nazi factions which should have raised some fundamental questions
about the nature of factionalism in the movement. How, after all, can
this failure be explained in view of the considerable organizational
strength and able leaders that these factions possessed? The Working
Association of North and West (the Northern Faction) in 1925–1926,
the *Kampfverlag* circle in 1926–1930, and the Stormtroops (SA) until
1934 represented the most dynamic and powerful segments of the
movement, yet when Hitler turned against them they dissolved without
a trace. Why did these factions capitulate to Hitler so easily? Why did
they not give rise to splinter movements? Why were the leaders of these
factions, apparently so popular and powerful, abandoned by their followers at the crucial moment? Why were there no mass purges and why

were Hitler's authority and leadership never in serious jeopardy? Why, in short, was the factional experience in the Nazi party so radically different from the factional conflicts in the Socialist and Communist parties?

Answers to these questions presuppose an extensive comparative study, a requirement which cannot be satisfied in an article. The present essay is merely the first step in this direction and constitutes only a part of a more comprehensive study of factionalism. The purpose of this article is partly historical, partly conceptual and comparative. In the first sense, it attempts to fill a neglected aspect of historical research. The character and nature of the Northern Faction has long been the subject of facile and superficial generalizations which have obscured most of the peculiarities of Nazi factionalism. This has been partly due to the lack of available primary source materials on the internal aspects of the Nazi movement in the post-1925 period. The American Historical Association's Berlin Document Center microfilm project has made such material available in this country and has made this study possible.

The second objective of this essay is to suggest hypotheses concerning the pattern of factional behavior in the Nazi party on the basis of this research[2] in the hope that these might yield useful analytical tools for comparative studies. In particular, this essay will suggest a direct relationship between the pattern of intragroup conflicts and the nature of legitimacy operative in the group. The charismatic principle of legitimacy appears to have had a direct influence on the nature of factionalism in the Nazi party, while the ideological nature of legitimacy in Socialist and Communist movements seems to have influenced the character of factional conflicts in those movements. If this hypothesis is valid, a study of factional conflicts might be a promising back-door approach to a comparative study of political movements.

I

The year 1924 marks the passing of a distinct phase of National Socialism. Prior to that date the movement was regional, largely restricted to Bavaria and to the southern part of Germany. Its political orientation was strongly identified with the nationalism of the forces of the Right and the military. Its propaganda and organizational activities were predicated on the idea of a putsch.[3]

Beginning with 1924 a considerable shift of emphasis took place in each of these concerns of the party. As a result of Gregor Strasser's organizational talents and his alliances with the *völkisch* groups of

North Germany, National Socialism made considerable headway in the north after 1924, as Table 1 illustrates.

TABLE 1[4]

THE DEVELOPMENT OF LOCAL PARTY ORGANIZATIONS, 1923–1925

Districts	Number of Local Party Organizations 1923	1925
A. Southern Districts:		
Bayerische Ostmark	75	57
Oberbayern	22	16
Württemberg-Hohenzollern	37	20
Schwaben	32	16
Mainfranken	24	13
Franken	22	18
B. Northern Districts:		
Düsseldorf	10	20
Essen	3	9
Berlin	1	9
Kurhessen	5	15
Mecklenburg	0	14
Osthannover	0	11
Pommern	3	10
Sachsen	27	88
Südhannover	8	40
Thüringen	14	46

The decline in the number of local party organizations in the south was due to the problems inherent in Hitler's determination to organize a new party out of the remnants of the old. The functioning local party organizations were informed early in March 1925 that as of that moment old membership cards became invalid and new applications for membership had to be submitted to the Munich headquarters.[5] This created grave problems for the local party leaders, who found it difficult to make the old party members understand why they should be paying new initiation fees.[6] The other factor that created difficulties on the local level was Hitler's demand that local party organizations rupture their ties with all *völkisch* groups and that no party member should be allowed to maintain simultaneous membership in any *völkisch* association.[7] This was a bitter pill to swallow for many local party leaders who had traditionally identified the Nazi party with the *völkisch* idea. Many of the local leaders refused to make the break and declined to subordinate themselves unconditionally to Hitler's personal leadership in the early months of 1925. As a consequence of these factors, several local party organizations seceded or were dissolved during these early months, especially in the southern areas where most of the Nazi party organizations existed prior to 1925.[8] In the north most of the local organizations were being built from the bottom up; hence that area was not correspondingly affected by these problems.

Fortunately for Hitler, because of the organizational weakness of the *völkisch* movement most of the dissident Nazi leaders were forced to realize in the following months or years that they had no future outside the Hitler party. Soon they were to bow to Hitler's point of view, one by one capitulating unconditionally to his demands.[9] Thus the decline of the local party organizations in the south was only a temporary phenomenon; by 1928 they had overcome their setback of 1925 (Table 2).

TABLE 2[10]

THE DEVELOPMENT OF LOCAL PARTY ORGANIZATIONS, 1925–1928

| Districts | Number of Local Party Organizations | |
	1925	1928
A. Southern Districts:		
Baden	31	62
Bayerische Ostmark	57	115
Franken	18	36
Oberbayern	16	32
B. Northern Districts:		
Düsseldorf	20	21
Essen	9	11
Berlin	9	28

It is important to note that while these shifts were impressive on paper, they did not represent any corresponding shifts in the real balance of party power in the south and the north. Although the northern districts underwent a period of relative stagnation in terms of membership in the latter part of the 1920's, for some time after 1925 they still remained the most promising part of the movement.[11] Their promise lay in their attempts to identify themselves with the working classes, while the southern districts still tended to cling for the most part to the bourgeois, antisocialist, racist idea of National Socialism.[12] Munich remained the business and spiritual stronghold of the movement, but there was little question that the dynamic part of the organization lay in the north.

The socialistic, working-class orientation of the movement in the north after 1925 cannot be conclusively supported by the available statistical data.[13] However, ample evidence to this effect can be gathered from the available party correspondence from the year 1925–1926, which appears to be persuasive. In their frequent (almost daily) reports to headquarters, the local party leaders of the north tended to stress the importance of associating their movement with the Left in order to attract members of the working classes.[14] Thus, the local leader of the city of Lübeck stressed the importance of "going to the workers." If we can get only fifty Social Democrats," he asserted, "we are better off and are more secure than if we had a battalion of the Tannenberg League with seven officers and sixty men." In conclusion he affirmed that "Playing soldiers won't help here."[15] District leader Josef Klant of Hamburg reported to headquarters: "We have won fifty workers, which pleases us more than fifty doctors."[16] Reports from Danzig,[17] Halle,[18] East-Hannover,[19] South-Hannover,[20] Elbe-Havel district,[21] Anhalt-Dessau,[22] Mecklenburg,[23] and Schleswig-Holstein[24] contained similar sentiments and listed with great pride and self-satisfaction the party's successes in industrial districts. Many of these districts suggested the formation of National Socialist trade unions in order to attract the manual workers.[25]

Thus the Socialist element became a prominent part of Nazi appeals in the north after 1924. Social justice, nationalization of the economy, "bread community," and other socialistic tenets were prominent in the speeches of Gregor Strasser.[26] That these principles were not ends in themselves but means to the establishment of an organic national community was of crucial significance, but a distinction too subtle to be noticed by those to whom the speeches were addressed. What was important for Strasser's audiences was the expression of and emphasis on these principles; for what ends they were to be used was of secondary importance.

The post-1924 tendencies in the north introduced significant changes in the organizational base of the movement as well. The keystones of the northern part of the movement were the local organizations which sprang up on the initiative of local citizens and were financed from membership dues and private contributions.[27] The network of local organizations put the movement on a more secure foundation and was important during the period of relative economic prosperity and international peace of the late 1920's. These local cells became indispensable nuclei around which the great masses of new party members could be organized after 1929.

These changes were by no means contrary to the ideas that Hitler had developed while in prison. Indeed, they implemented those concepts of the party as laid down in *Mein Kampf:* the necessity of a mass base, dissociation from the right-wing bourgeois forces, and systematic party organization based on the principle of absolute leadership.[28] What produced the differences between the northerners and Hitler were not issues of substance but the principle of absolute leadership and issues of tactics.

II

Upon his release from prison in 1924, Hitler set out to forge a strongly disciplined party out of the loose association of local organizations which was all that remained of the old party.[29] By the end of that year there was no effective central leadership in Munich, and the local organizations, having been left to their own devices for so long, were beginning to develop independent attitudes.

Many entered into close relationships with other groups, *völkisch* or Socialist (depending on the local circumstances), without bothering to keep Munich informed about their activities. Meanwhile, a corresponding confusion reigned in Munich. Hermann Esser, Gottfried Feder, Alfred Rosenberg, Philip Bouhler, and Franz X. Schwarz were in Munich but had hardly more in common than their physical proximity. Gregor Strasser spent most of his time in Berlin or traveling around North Germany trying to organize Nazism in the north. Ernst Röhm was involved with his *Frontbann* activities and seemed to care little about the problems of the "politicians."

In the first issue of the new *Völkischer Beobachter* (February 26, 1925) Hitler published his "Fundamental Directives" for the new party, and on the next day he convened his first party meeting at Munich. On this public occasion he appealed to all Nazis o bury their personal differences[30] and to unite behind him for the sake of the movement. According to one observer, the result verged on the ridiculous: "Singly and in pairs, men who had been bitter enemies mounted the platform and shook hands, some of them unable to restrain the tears which Hitler's magic voice had worked up. In groups they vowed their forgiveness of each other and swore undying loyalty to the Fuehrer."[31]

The unity of February 1925 remained confined to the leadership of the party for several months to come.[32] It took Hitler and Bouhler several months to bring the great majority of the independent-minded local leaders into line and impose on them unitary party discipline. The party of 1925 was anything but disciplined and well organized. Conflicting sets of local leaders competed for recognition in numerous districts, and it was sometimes difficult for those sitting in Munich to know which faction would turn out to be more trustworthy in the future.[33] By the end of the year, however, most of the local leaders had achieved official recognition and the centralizing authority of Munich was beginning to be effectively exerted on the local levels.

As a consequence of cleverly designed policies, the Party Central Office in Munich under the effective direction of its business manager, Philip Bouhler, successfully extended its supervision and control over the minute details of local and district party organizations.[34] The exclusive right of Munich to issue membership cards enabled the Central Office to keep accurate accounts of party membership in each district. Since the number of members determined the financial obligations of the local organizations to Munich, this knowledge enabled Bouhler to exercise strict control over local party finances. Local party organizations were required to collect one Reichsmark for each new member and one-half a Reichsmark each month thereafter. The initiation fees as well as a quarter of the monthly membership dues were to be forwarded by the local organizations to the district offices whenever these were in existence; in other instances these funds were to be forwarded directly to Munich. The district party leaders were required also to forward to Munich the initiation fees and one-tenth of the monthly membership dues. In addition, all extra contributions which local and district party leaders may have received from private individuals or groups were to be sent in toto to Munich.[35]

It is easy to appreciate why many local party leaders began to resent the progressive imposition of such central controls and supervision. The delays involved in the issuance of membership cards exasperated local leaders who found themselves besieged by individual applicants demanding their cards upon having paid their fees. Such local difficulties do not seem to have impressed the people in Munich who adamantly insisted on the scrupulous examination of each application regardless of the delay involved.

However, the delay was only the lesser part of the problem from the local point of view. The real source of irritation was the financial obligation imposed by Munich on the district and local party organizations. Regardless of local circumstances, Bouhler demanded one Reichsmark for each new applicant and ten Pfennig each month for every registered member. The arguments of local party leaders that many of their members were unemployed workers, students, old people, or disabled veterans who did not have the money to pay failed to impress Bouhler.

He answered these complaints by monotonously repeating the official regulations and reminding the local leaders that their situation was not unique but shared by most of the other local organizations. In order to extract the money due to Munich, Bouhler frequently went so far as to refuse issuance of new membership cards for the local districts and to deny them speakers until financial affairs had been straightened out. This was of great importance for the local leaders who were dependent on Munich for literate speakers. The big prize, of course, was Hitler, and this was duly recognized by Bouhler who declared on one occasion that Hitler would not visit districts which owed money to Munich.[36]

Some exasperated local leaders, Josef Goebbels and Karl Kaufmann among them,[37] issued their own membership cards in open defiance of party regulations. When called to account by Bouhler, they defiantly admitted their actions. They accused Bouhler of having no idea of local party affairs, and declared with amazing audacity that they had yet to see the contributions of the Munich headquarters to the development of the movement. They argued for the impossibility of requiring old Nazis to pay another initiation fee, especially when many of them had spent time in prison for having been Nazis. Similarly, it was impossible to collect dues from the unemployed.[38]

Such sentiments were more typical than unusual and were rooted in the attitudes of the man-in-the-field toward the members of the general staff. There was widespread feeling among local leaders that while they were carrying the lion's share of the work, the headquarters got the lion's share of the dues. There were dissatisfactions with the efficiency of the Munich office as well as with the occasionally conflicting directives coming from Munich.[39]

Such dissatisfactions on the local level were aggravated in the north by the quite perceptible differences in ideological orientation between the north and the Munich leadership.[40] As a result, by the summer of 1925 some northern leaders wanted to assume the ideological offensive against the "reactionary-bureaucratic" elements in the party.[41] By late November discussions had reached the point where Gregor Strasser and Goebbels set out to draft a new party program which they planned to present for adoption at a conference of northern party leaders scheduled to meet in January 1926.

III

Much has been made of this program and of the Hannover conference of January 25, 1926.[42] It has been alleged that this movement was secessionist, primarily ideologically oriented, and directed against Hitler's leadership.[43] However, the party correspondence of the period tends to refute such interpretations, as do contemporary diaries and documents. Available primary sources show persuasively that the northern districts never developed into a "separate party,"[44] but worked under very effective control throughout the period. Contemporary documents also reveal that the ideological division between north and south was not as sharp as it has usually been portrayed.[45] It can also be shown that while several of these leaders resented the firm hand of Bouhler, nothing was further from their minds than to challenge Hitler's leadership. Hitler remained the only concrete point of unity in the heterogeneous movement. He was above the conflicts, and he was regarded "as something mystical, unreal."[46]

On January 25, 1926, the Hannover conference was convened. At this important meeting twenty-four northern party leaders were present representing seven northern party districts. The conference resolved to organize the "Working Association of the North and West," elected its officers, approved its propaganda organ, and adopted the draft program. The unanimity of the conference was broken only by Gottfried Feder and Robert Ley.[47]

The conference elected Gregor Strasser as the leader of the Association. As its propaganda chief and editor of the *National Socialist Letters,* the conference elected Otto Strasser, while Goebbels was appointed editorial writer. The editorial offices and the press of the Association were to be known thereafter as the *Kampfverlag,* indicating the revolutionary sentiments of its founders.

The program of the Association stressed socialistic reforms in domestic politics and advocated a pro-Russian foreign policy. It proposed nationalization of heavy industry, distribution of unearned land holdings, and expropriation of royal properties. According to Otto Strasser, sentiments were expressed against the idea of the absolute authority of the leader. "We acknowledge no Pope who can claim infallibility," Bernhard Rust is reported to have exclaimed.[48] Such exclamations, however, assuming that they really were made, should not obscure the crucial fact that the conference was not directed against Hitler, but was organized to impress upon him the necessity of redefining the party program along socialistic lines. The conference did not repudiate Hitler's leadership, but sought to capture his charismatic symbol for their cause. That this may have been their mistake was argued by Otto Strasser at a later date: "Perhaps we should have acted at that moment, made Hitler *honorary* president and thus prevented him from doing any damage by depriving him of all effective power in the Party. We did nothing, because we thought we were much more powerful than he. This was our error and it must be recognized."[49]

Strasser, however, distorted the circumstances of 1925. The reason that they did not depose Hitler was not because they overestimated their power but because they knew that without Hitler the party could not survive. They needed Hitler's name and authority. Besides, if they had wanted to get rid of Hitler, they should have done so in December or January before Hitler had reestablished his authority. At that time Gregor Strasser decided for Hitler and with this decision the last chance was given up to continue without him. The point is that they did not think of getting rid of him. On the contrary, they thought him to be on their side and they were sure that they would capture him for their positions, as Goebbels's diary makes clear.[50]

The Hannover conference of January 1926 brought into the open the disagreements between the two camps. What made Hitler intervene and summon the Bamberg conference for February 14 was not the basic ideological disagreements which had existed for some time (and which were to continue to exist), but the direct challenge that the Hannover conference implied to the principle of absolute leadership.

IV

Many of the accounts published about the Bamberg conference can safely be classified as fiction. They have not only misrepresented the ascertainable facts concerning the conference, but have been predicated on the mistaken assumption that the Bamberg meeting was called to put an end to the Association which was organized against Hitler. A representative account may be quoted from one of the most authoritative studies on the history of Nazism: "On 14 February 1926, he [Hitler] summoned a conference in his turn, this time in the South German town of Bamberg. Hitler deliberately avoided a Sunday, when the North German leaders would have been free to attend in strength. As a result the Strasser wing of the Party was represented only by Gregor Strasser and Goebbels."[51]

In contrast to such accounts, the contemporary police report shows that the meeting was held on Sunday (February 14), and was attended by sixty to sixty-five party leaders. Several of these were from the north: Ernst Schlange (Berlin), Walter Ernst (Halle), Friedrich Hildebrandt (Mecklenburg), Glans (Hamburg), Bernhard Rust (Hannover), as well as Gregor Strasser and Goebbels.[52] It is not known how many other northern party leaders were present, since the police report does not include a complete list of the participants, but it is obvious that several of the most important leaders from the north were able to attend.[53]

In the absence of documentary evidence, the rest of the speculation contained in Bullock's account cannot be challenged with equal certainty. It can be argued, however, that the site of the conference was not chosen in order to make the cost of travel prohibitive for northern leaders. Had this been Hitler's intention, the logical site of the conference would have been Munich, the party headquarters, which lies some 150 miles farther south. Indeed, it may be argued that it was in Hitler's interest to have as many northerners at the meeting as possible.[54] Hitler's purpose for calling the Bamberg conference was not to defeat the northern leaders, but to convince them of the necessity for party unity. He did not regard the northerners as his opponents but as subordinates who had to be brought back to the right track. Besides, it was not the purpose of Nazi party meetings to make decisions on the basis of majority rule. Thus, the number of northern leaders present was quite irrelevant to the outcome of the conference. To maintain that the reason for Hitler's "victory" at Bamberg was a packed conference reveals a basic misunderstanding not only of Hitler's relationship with the northern leaders, but also of the nature of decision-making in the Nazi party.

There are no known official records of the proceedings of the conference.[55] The account of the conference which appeared in the official party newspaper indicates clearly enough, however, the major points of Hitler's concern. According to the *Völkischer Beobachter* (February 25, 1926), Hitler addressed himself to three main topics. First, he rejected Strasser's idea of a Russian entente; that, according to Hitler, would have meant the bolshevization of Germany. Instead, he suggested that British and Italian alliances offered the most promising possibilities for Germany. The East he regarded as an area of colonization. Second, he rejected the northerners' position with respect to the expropriation of royal properties on the principle that "nothing should be given to them [princes] which does not belong to them," but also that nothing should be taken away from them which belongs to them. "We are for rights," he declared. "We know only Germans, not princes." Third, he prohibited anyone from raising religious issues in the party because these "have no place in National Socialism."

This is the extent of the newspaper's report of the meeting. It ends with the following statement: "The rest of the meeting was taken up by programmatic discussions in which several people participated besides Hitler, especially Feder, Strasser, and Streicher. Complete agreement was achieved."

Otto Strasser's account goes beyond this report and states that the conference adopted the following resolutions: (1) abandonment of the Hannover program and reaffirmation of the Twenty-five Points, (2) dissolution of the Association and the establishment of a unified party organization; (3) nomination of all district leaders by Hitler; (4) creation of a party tribunal to regulate intraparty disputes with the power to expel members and to dissolve local organizations; the members of this tribunal were to be nominated by Hitler; and (5) establishment of the SA.[56]

The outcome of the conference is generally referred to as a victory for Hitler. It is submitted here that this is a misinterpretation, since there existed no movement against Hitler. At the conference Hitler refused to go along with the northern point of view, and this was a great blow to Strasser and Goebbels.[57] However, Hitler did not handle them as defeated enemies; although the Association had to be dissolved, its propaganda organ in Berlin was allowed to continue. Gregor Strasser was put in charge of party propaganda, and just a few months later Goebbels was named district leader in Berlin-Brandenburg.[58]

The decisions of the conference proved to be conclusive. The Association of the North and West was immediately dissolved;[59] Gregor Strasser went to Munich to assume his new position while continuing his association with his brother in the *Kampfverlag*. If the Northern Association had been directed against Hitler, however, the decision of a "packed" conference would not have been accepted as a matter of course. In fact, there was not a single resignation or expulsion. Herbert Blank's argument that the district leaders and Gregor Strasser abided by Hitler's decision in early 1926 because they were financially dependent on their party offices is not convincing; four years later it may have been a more important factor.[60]

V

The readiness with which Hitler's decisions were followed by the northern leaders, who only three weeks before had manifested such remarkable unity and strength of conviction in adopting their draft program and founding their Association, is not puzzling if one recognizes that their actions had not been directed against Hitler, but were predicated on his support. When Hitler pronounced the Hannover program wrong, the northerners, disappointed as they were, accepted his verdict. It is important to note, however, that Hitler did not attack the substance of the Hannover program. He did not try to enforce an ideological uniformity in the movement. Indeed, his factotum, Goebbels, whom he had sent to Berlin in late 1926, assumed a position there just as socialistic and anticapitalistic as that of the other northern leaders. Ideological heterogeneity was a characteristic of the Nazi movement from its inception; it was of no concern to Hitler. There was no orthodoxy in Nazi ideology; the only orthodoxy was the totalitarian principle of absolute obedience to an absolute leader.

Hitler called the Bamberg conference to ward off possible threats to his leadership. The quasi-independent organization of the northern districts implicitly challenged the Nazi principle that the leader was the sole center of the movement. No other institution or body of persons was to have an all-encompassing competence. Questions affecting the movement as a whole pertained to the leader alone. Others were allowed only limited authority delegated by the leader; they could act only within the spheres of their limited competence.

The Hannover conference challenged this principle of party organization by assuming the right to decide questions pertinent to the movement as a whole. That the conference meant only to guide Hitler back to the "true path" was immaterial to the issue.

The second threat to Hitler's absolute leadership was the proposed party program adopted in Hannover. Again, it was not the substance of the program that was important, but the mere existence of it. A program is by definition incompatible with the idea of absolute leadership. Its principles tend to bind the leader to certain courses of action and may be used as standards by which to evaluate the actions of the leader. A program gives every member of the political party an opportunity (if not an obligation) to judge the actions of the leader and to call him to account. The leader becomes an executive and ceases to be a "philosopher"; his responsibility will be to implement the principles of the program rather than to formulate the principles themselves.

It is not certain to what extent the members of the Hannover conference were aware of these implications of their actions. Certainly, the idea of a democratic party organization was far removed from their minds. Their concern was simple and immediate. What they wanted was to set down the "true" principles of Nazism, or, rather, those which promised the greatest political success. They did not think that these principles would be necessarily incompatible with the idea of absolute leadership which they understood only imperfectly. The participants in the Hannover conference did not mean to challenge Hitler's authority; they only meant to fight the people who surrounded Hitler in Munich. It was a conflict between the men-in-the-field, the local party leaders, and the courtiers of the party headquarters. The Hannoverians were not aware, as Hitler was, of the implications of their resolutions for the principles of charismatic authority. Had they been aware that they were challenging Hitler's authority, they hardly would have counted on his support in Bamberg.

However, the motivations of the northern leaders were immaterial from Hitler's point of view, for he realized immediately the implications of the draft program. At the Bamberg conference Hitler rejected the Hannover program; in May he declared the 1920 program as unalterable.[61] This placed all discussion about the program out of order, and the party took another step toward the program's ultimate totalitarian ideological emptiness.

The aim of the founders of the Working Association of North and West from 1925 to 1926 was to liberate Hitler from his Munich surroundings, not to challenge his leadership of the movement. Their purpose was to impress upon Hitler the necessity of a programmatic approach based on socialistic principles if the movement were to meet with success in working-class circles. When they called the Hannover meeting to form the Association and to adopt the draft program, they appeared to be sincerely convinced that they were acting in good faith and in the best interests of the movement. They believed that their draft program incorporated the true principles of National Socialism, which had been corrupted by the Munich clique composed of Streicher, Esser, Rosenberg, Amann, and others. They thought that Hitler had been misled by this group which had managed to isolate him from the outside world. The northerners wanted to establish contact with Hitler and tended to be confident that once Hitler learned of their position he also would accept it.

The most authentic evidence in support of these observations is Goebbels's diary for the years 1925 and 1926. This diary, which was never intended for publication, was discovered in its original form after the end of the war. The entries represent Goebbels's feelings and attitudes in those years and provide interesting insights into party affairs.

On August 21, 1925, Goebbels noted, "Hitler is surrounded by the wrong people." Goebbels went on to state that the organization which Strasser and he were working on in the north would provide a weapon against the stale bureaucrats in Munich. On September 11 he noted that Hitler appeared to be between the two camps (the north which believed that socialism had to be achieved first in order to provide a broad basis for nationalism, and the south which believed that the worker had to be won over to the "National Idea" directly), but that in principle he had already decided for the north. The continuing problem was Hitler's inaccessibility. "We have to get to Hitler," Goebbels wrote on October 19; and again, he noted on November 2, "perhaps it will be possible to have a longer discussion with Hitler."[62]

Goebbels looked forward to the Bamberg meeting with great hopes and expectations. He thought that Feder would be defeated and Hitler would adopt their point of view.[63] Then came the blow; Hitler turned against them. "I feel as if I had been beaten," Goebbels wrote after the conference. "My heart aches. . . . A sad journey home. . . . I hardly say a word. A horrible night! Surely one of the greatest disappointments of my life. I do not believe Hitler without reservations any more. That is what is terrible: I have been deprived of my inner self. I am only half."[64]

Goebbels idolized Hitler from the beginning, and to find himself in opposition to his leader was an unbearable burden for him.[65] Hardly a week after the Bamberg meeting he wrote to Hitler protesting against Streicher's attacks upon him. He spent the next weeks in anxious waiting for Hitler's answer. On March 29 it finally arrived; Hitler invited him to speak in Munich. Goebbels spoke in Munich and at the end of the speech he was embraced by Hitler. "I am terribly happy," he noted.[66]

Goebbels was one of the leaders of the northern group in 1925–1926, the principal collaborator of Gregor Strasser, and the co-author of the draft program submitted at the Hannover conference. His recorded attitudes are certainly significant indications of the aims and purposes of the northerners in 1925–1926. They never considered moving against Hitler, but hoped to the very end to gain his support.[67] Otto Strasser's biographer summed up the 1926 crisis correctly when he wrote: "They [the Strasser brothers] did not see the struggle in that light, they did not feel themselves to be working against Hitler. They only saw that Hitler was betraying the things he claimed to represent, the promise he had made, and sought to bring him back to them."[68]

The factional experience of 1925–1926 also demonstrates the pattern of Hitler's tactics. During 1925 he refused to take a stand in the dispute between the northern party leaders and the Munich office, to the great disappointment of Goebbels.[69] However, this tactic of neutrality tended to strengthen Hitler's position. As the issues sharpened, Hitler's arbitration became increasingly important for both sides. Consequently both had to depend on his mercy.

Although Hitler was informed in November 1925 of the intention of the northern leaders to form an association at the Hannover meeting in January of the next year, he did not voice any displeasure. He easily could have prevented the meeting at that time, but he remained silent. He allowed the meeting because he did not consider the ideological arguments of Goebbels and Strasser to be threats to his authority. When, however, the second Hannover conference passed resolutions contradicting his policy on the expropriation issue, he immediately convened the Bamberg conference.

When he finally made his move at Bamberg, there was no question of a party split. His decision was accepted in the north without the resignation of a single northern leader. Under the circumstances there was no need to punish a single member of the Association. He promoted the leader of the Association, Gregor Strasser, and a few months later appointed Goebbels as district leader of Brandenburg-Berlin. Participation in the Association did not affect the careers of such prominent functionaries as Erich Koch, Karl Kaufmann, Bernhard Rust, Victor Lutze, and many other lesser figures. The actions of the charismatic leader were not those of a victor, but of a benevolent and forgiving arbiter.

VI

There remains to suggest some explanations for the factional experience of 1925–1926. As the fundamental hypothesis the proposition is advanced here that the nature and characteristics of intragroup divisions are determined by the nature of legitimacy of the group. Legitimacy in totalitarian movements may be either ideological or charismatic; it is either dogma or person that justifies the existence of the group. The existential requirement of both ideology and leader in totalitarian movements should not obscure the important realization that behind any organization there exists an idea which legitimizes or justifies the existence of the group. This idea may be expressed in an ideology or it may adhere to a person and, accordingly, the group may be termed ideological or charismatic. In ideological movements the leaders will claim authority on the basis of the dogma, and will always represent themselves as its representatives and carriers. Thus, for instance, Communist leaders have always been careful to give their power an ideological justification and not to appear more than instruments of the revealed faith.[70] In charismatic movements, on the other hand, the leader claims authority because he incorporates the idea in his person. Thus, Hitler could identify the idea of National Socialism with his person instead of representing himself as an instrument of it. By definition, the leader and the idea were the same in Nazism; the idea was not something external and independent of the person of the leader, but was incarnated in the leader.

It is suggested here that the difference between ideological and charismatic legitimacy is of crucial importance for the pattern of factional behavior because legitimacy not only defines the cohesive force in the group but also represents the basis of intragroup conflict. That is, in an ideological movement it is the dogma which ultimately holds the group together and which lends authority to the leader. It is, however, also the dogma which can give rise to various interpretations which can in turn become the bases of factional conflicts. The dogma legitimizes the group, but it can also lend legitimacy to factions. Hence, in ideological movements factions will always base themselves on some interpretation of the ideology and will challenge the existing leadership on ideological grounds.

In charismatic movements, the identification of leader and dogma deprives the factions of an ideological base. Legitimacy inheres in the leader, hence an attack on the leader in a charismatic movement would be analogous to an attack on the dogma in an ideological movement. Yet the legitimizing idea of the movement can never be challenged, otherwise the dissenters would place themselves immediately outside the movement and as such would not compose factions which assume the framework of a group. In that case the conflict would be intergroup, not intragroup. For this reason, factions in ideological movements will always avoid attacks on dogma. In charismatic movements, for the same reasons, factions will always avoid attacks on the leader. In both cases the legitimizing idea will remain above factional strife, but while it will continue to bind the movement together, it can also provide the basis for intragroup conflict. This explains why Hitler managed to stay above the conflict in 1925 and 1926; why the factions, instead of challenging his authority, strove to gain his support. It was the personal nature of legitimacy which forced both the northerners and the Munich group to claim to be the representatives of Hitler and his truest followers. This also explains why Hitler could so easily put an end to the Association of the North and West at Bamberg. By turning against them, he deprived them of their legitimacy. From then on they could not claim to be Hitler's representatives; they had no choice but to surrender, since opposition to Hitler would have meant opposition to National Socialism.

Thus, the 1925–1926 factional conflict, taking place on the secondary level of leadership, not only preserved and enhanced Hitler's authority and power, but also ensured the unity of the movement. Hitler was the ultimate arbiter to whom all factions appealed; he remained the only point of unity, the only force of cohesion in the ideologically and sociologically heterogeneous movement. That Hitler was an arbiter rather than a participant in the conflict was also reflected in the way in which he dealt with the members of the northern faction after the Bamberg meeting—not as a victor, but as the benevolent judge. He did not punish them, but continued to keep them in positions of authority and power. Indeed, there would have been no reason to punish men who, though misguided, acted in good faith.

Thus the unity of the movement was preserved; the leaders retained their positions of authority while the rank-and-file remained basically unaffected by the whole crisis. For the ordinary party member or follower there was no crisis of conscience; those who were loyal followers of the northern leaders never assumed any conflict between these leaders and Hitler. They followed the northern orientation because they thought that they were following Hitler. There was no reason for Hitler to doubt the loyalty of the rank-and-file, and there is no evidence that he did. The Bamberg conference did not necessitate mass purges; the rank-and-file membership was hardly affected by that leaders' conference.

Why, then, was the Bamberg conference necessary? Why did Hitler consider it imperative to intervene when there were no threats to his leadership? In the absence of relevant data, the answers to these questions will have to remain conjectural. It may be plausible to suggest that while Hitler realized the fundamental loyalty of the northerners to his person, he may have felt instinctively that what the northerners attempted to do was ultimately incompatible with the nature of his movement. The attempt to define National Socialism programmatically would have challenged the charismatic nature of its legitimacy and ipso facto Hitler's absolute leadership. The ideology of a charismatic movement has to remain sufficiently vague so as not to become the basis of legitimacy. The attempt at Hannover to draw up a program was a step to make the movement an ideological one. This is what Hitler could not tolerate and that is what made the Bamberg conference necessary.

NOTES

1. The term "faction" is used here as a group of individuals joined together to further some particular goal in opposition to other groups belonging to the same association. "Faction" implies a certain degree of permanence resting on some

organizational basis which tends to lend it a degree of independence and power as well. Finally, "faction" also tends to involve some basic issue, thereby calling into question the purpose of the group as a whole. This definition serves to distinguish factional conflicts from other kinds of intragroup disagreements which are personal in character and involve issues of no more consequence than the status of a particular individual in the association.

2. Although the *Kampfverlag* was the creation of the Northern Faction and also served to perpetuate some of the ideas and aspirations of the northern leaders of 1925–1926, it constituted a separate experience in the history of the movement and will be, therefore, excluded from this analysis.

3. The obsolescence of "putschist" tactics had already been pointed out by Feder in August 1923. In his letter to Hitler of August 10, he urged Hitler to pay greater attention to organizational matters. "The times of the *condottieri* have passed," he warned (Oron James Hale, "Gottfried Feder Calls Hitler to Order. An Unpublished Letter on Nazi Party Affairs," *Journal of Modern History*, XXX [1958], 359).

4. Wolfgang Schaefer, *NSDAP. Entwicklung und Struktur der Staatspartei des dritten Reiches* (Hannover and Frankfurt/M., 1957), p. 11.

5. See party business manager Philip Bouhler's correspondence with local party leaders in: Washington, D.C., The National Archives, *Captured German Documents Filmed at Berlin* (Microfilming Program at the Berlin Document Center, American Historical Association), Microcopy No. T-580, Reels 20–26 (hereafter cited as *Berlin Document Center*).

6. The party correspondence provides ample evidence for this. See, for instance, the letter of the district leader of Lueneburg-Stade to Bouhler, May 15, 1925 (*ibid.,* Reel 21).

7. See Hitler's "Aufruf an die alten Parteigenossen der NSDAP," and "Grundsätzliche Richtlinien für die Wiederbegründung der NSDAP," *Völkischer Beobachter,* February 26, 1925.

8. Hitler's tactics toward the dissident local party leaders varied according to the local circumstances. Some he dismissed outright by dissolving their local organizations; in other instances he merged several local organizations and thereby forced the dissident leaders to bow to the will of the majority of their followers. See, for example, the Württemberg case in the Bavarian police reports, Stanford, Hoover Library, *Documents from the NSDAP Hauptarchiv,* Reel 70, Folder 1515 (hereafter cited as *Hoover Microfilm Collection*); and the Cologne district reports in *Berlin Document Center,* Reel 21.

9. See Professor Mergenthaler's capitulation to Hitler in June 1927 (*Hoover Microfilm Collection,* Reel 70, Folder 1515).

10. Schaefer, *NSDAP,* p. 12.

11. Kurt G. W. Ludecke, *I Knew Hitler* (London, 1938), p. 341.

12. Ideologically, National Socialism in Bavaria remained basically a lower-middle-class affair closely allied with the forces of the Right. The typical concerns of Bavarian local party meetings in the 1920's were the Jews, international capital, and religion. See Joseph Goebbels's remark in Rudolf Semmler, *Goebbels—The Man Next to Hitler* (London, 1947), pp. 56–57; Hitler's *Secret Conversations, 1941–1944* (New York, 1953), p. 67; Police Reports on the meetings of the Ansbach local organization, *Hoover Microfilm Collection,* Reel 5, Folder 134.

13. Only fragmentary lists of members are available. The Berlin Document Center files contain initial membership lists for only seven districts comprising a total of about two hundred members. Roughly about one-third of them can be classified as workers; the rest were members of the "middle classes," students, and professionals. Their average age in 1925 was twenty-nine years. See *Berlin Document Center,* Reels 20–26.

14. In some districts this had been achieved to such an extent that the Nazis were regarded as standing shoulder to shoulder with the Communists on economic matters (Report from Danzig, March 20, 1926, *Berlin Document Center,* Reel 20). In other districts the leaders warned against identification with the Right (Report from Hamburg, November 11, 1925, *ibid.,* Reel 21; Report from East-Hannover, January 29, 1926, *ibid.,* Reel 21). The Berlin Nazis called themselves "Hitlerproleten," or Hitler's proletariat, thus indicating their socialistic, lower-class origins and ideology (Reinhold Muchow's report from Berlin, August 1926, *Hoover Microfilm Collection,* Reel 5, Folder 133).

15. Report from Luebeck, December 14, 1925 (*Berlin Document Center,* Reel 23).

16. Report from Hamburg, March 24, 1925 (*ibid.,* Reel 20).

17. Reports of October 6, 1925, January 15, 1926 (*ibid.,* Reel 20).

18. Report of October 11, 1926 (*ibid.,* Reel 20).

19. Otto Telschow to Goebbels, October 23, 1925 (*ibid.,* Reel 21).

20. Report of May 15, 1925 (*ibid.,* Reel 21).

21. Reports of December 18, 1925, December 27, 1925, February 1926 (*ibid.,* Reel 22).

22. Report of November 3, 1925 (*ibid.,* Reel 22).

23. Reports of April 8, 1925, June 18, 1925, December 14, 1925 (*ibid.,* Reel 23).

24. Reports of March 1, 1925, May 5, 1925 (*ibid.,* Reel 25).

25. The party headquarters was besieged by local organizations for directions on the subject of trade unions, but their pleas remained unanswered. "The trade union question is under consideration and is to be decided shortly," was Bouhler's usual reply. See Reports from Elbe-Havel district, February 1926 (*Berlin Document Center,* Reel 22); from Danzig, January 15, 1926 (*ibid.,* Reel 20); Anhalt-Dessau, November 3, 1925 (*ibid.,* Reel 22); and Bouhler's replies on succeeding dates.

26. See the collection of Gregor Strasser's speeches in his books: *Freiheit und Brot* (Berlin, n.d.); *Hammer und Schwert* (Berlin, n.d.); *Kampf um Deutschland, Reden und Aufsätze eines National-sozialisten* (Munich, 1932).

27. Theodore Abel, *Why Hitler Came Into Power* (New York, 1938), pp. 78–81; Albert Krebs, *Tendenzen und Gestalten der NSDAP* (Stuttgart, 1959), p. 41. Not only did the local organizations not receive any help from Munich, but they were required to send to Munich a substantial portion of their hard-earned funds.

28. During his imprisonment and in the years immediately following his release from Landsberg, Hitler was bitterly opposed to the bourgeoisie. He blamed the bourgeoisie and the bourgeois spirit for the failure of the November putsch. This contempt comes forth with particular intensity in the pages of *Mein Kampf* and was also evident in his speeches of this period. See Adolf Hitler, *Mein Kampf* (New York, 1939), pp. 59, 225, 567, 612; *Hoover Microfilm Collection,* Reel 70, Folder 1515

29. On the character of the Nazi party in 1924, see Munich Police Report (*Hoover Microfilm Collection*, Reel 68, Folder 1497A).

30. Hitler's motto throughout the "years of fighting" was "let bygones be bygones." As he stated in the first issue of the *Völkischer Beobachter*, the first and overriding task of the leader was to achieve unity in the party.

31. Ludecke, *I Knew Hitler*, p. 258. See also Munich Police Reports (*Hoover Microfilm Collection*, Reel 69, Folder 1509 and Reel 87, Folder 1835). Three important party personalities were absent from this meeting, but two of them responded favorably to Hitler's appeal for unity. Gregor Strasser and Rosenberg accepted the new party principles, but Röhm refused to accede to Hitler's wish to subordinate the *Frontbann* to the party. He resigned from his offices two months later.

32. The unity was more apparent than real even on the highest levels. The mortal enemies of 1924 were friends in 1925 only on public occasions and in the presence of Hitler. Personality conflicts and rivalries continued, but since they did not affect Hitler's leadership they were allowed to persist.

33. Conflicts were particularly evident in Berlin during the summer of 1926 (*Berlin Document Center*, Reel 19); Halle during the summer of 1925 through the summer of 1926 (*ibid.*, Reel 20); Hamburg in the spring of 1926 (*ibid.*, Reel 21); Rhineland-South in the spring of 1925 (*ibid.*, Reel 22); and in East Prussia in the spring of 1925 (*ibid.*, Reel 24).

34. During 1925 and 1926 many local organizations were directly subordinated to Munich pending the establishment of district organizations. Considerable confusion existed in organizational nomenclature at this time.

35. See these requirements as stated in Bouhler's letter to district leader Walter Ernst in Halle, September 25, 1925 (*Berlin Document Center*, Reel 20).

36. Bouhler to the Nuremberg local, July 26, 1926 (*Berlin Document Center*, Reel 20).

37. District leaders Bernhard Rust (Hannover), Hermann Fobke (Göttingen), Prof. D. Schultz (Hessen-Nassau-North), and Hinrich Lohse (Schleswig-Holstein) proposed in a joint letter to Bouhler (April 15, 1925) that membership cards be issued by district leaders in order to save time and paperwork and to escape the problem of undue centralization (*ibid.*, Reel 21).

38. Correspondence, Rhineland-North district, October 22, 1925 (*ibid.*, Reel 22).

39. Ernst (Halle district) to Hess, September 18, 1925: ". . . there seem to be two orders, one from you and one from the party office. Which should be followed?" (*ibid.*, Reel 20).

40. The presidential elections of March–April 1925 exhibited these ideological differences when, after much vacillation, Hitler decided to support Hindenburg on the second ballot. Hitler's action associated the party with the monarchist, conservative-*völkisch* groups of Graefe and constituted a serious embarrassment for the northerners who were aligned with Ludendorff's Tannenberg League —a *völkisch*, anticapitalistic organization. See the *Völkischer Beobachter* of March 14, March 21, and April 10, 1925, and Ludecke, *I Knew Hitler*, p. 264. Weigand von Miltenberg (pseud.), *Adolf Hitler—Wilhelm III* (Berlin, 1931), p. 64; Otto Strasser, *Hitler und Ich* (Konstanz, 1948), p. 81.

41. Helmut Heiber, ed., *Das Tagebuch von Joseph Goebbels, 1925/26* (Stuttgart, n.d.), p. 21.

42. There were two conferences in Hannover. One was held in November 1925, the other in January 1926. The confusion about the date of "the" Hannover conference is discussed by Heiber, p. 56.

43. Alan Bullock, *Hitler: A Study in Tyranny* (London, 1959), pp. 120ff.; Walter Görlitz and Herbert A. Quint, *Adolf Hitler. Eine Biographie* (Stuttgart, 1952), pp. 256ff.; Konrad Heiden, *Der Fuehrer* (Boston, 1944), pp. 286ff.; Konrad Heiden, *A History of National Socialism* (New York, 1935), pp. 113ff.; and several books by Otto Strasser.

44. Bullock, *Hitler*, p. 121.

45. Had the ideological division been as sharp as some writers maintain, there would hardly have been such demand on the part of northern leaders to have Esser, Rosenberg, Streicher, and other representatives of the "south" as speakers in their districts. Nor would the southern districts have been so anxious to have Gregor Strasser speak at their meetings (*Berlin Document Center*, Reels 19–26).

46. According to Goebbels, it was in Hitler's presence that Strasser and he decided to draft a new program (Heiber, *Das Tagebuch*, p. 43; Görlitz and Quint, *Adolf Hitler*, p. 253).

47. Feder was the twenty-fifth member of the conference. He was an outsider who had been sent by Hitler to observe the proceedings. The accounts of this meeting are fragmentary. See Otto Strasser and Michael Stern, *Flight from Terror* (New York, 1943), pp. 115ff.; Heiber, *Das Tagebuch*, pp. 55–56; Miltenberg, *Adolf Hitler*, p. 70; Heiden, *A History of National Socialism*, p. 287; Görlitz and Quint, *Adolf Hitler*, p. 257.

48. Strasser and Stern, *Flight from Terror*, pp. 115–116.

49. Otto Strasser, *L'aigle Prussien sur L'Allemagne* (Montreal and New York, 1941), p. 189.

50. "We shall put on a nice act in Bamberg and shall win over Hitler," wrote Goebbels in his diary on February 11, 1926 (Heiber, *Das Tagebuch*, p. 59). It now seems fairly certain that Goebbels never expressed the wish at the conference that Hitler should be expelled from the party, as reported by Strasser and Stern, *Flight from Terror*, pp. 115–116. His diaries show unwavering support and loyalty to Hitler.

51. Bullock, *Hitler*, pp. 122–123. See also the accounts of Heiden, *A History of National Socialism*, pp. 287–289; Rudolf Olden, *Hitler* (New York, 1936), pp. 202–203; and Otto Strasser, *L'aigle Prussien*, pp. 191–203; *Flight from Terror*, pp. 121–123; *Hitler und Ich*, pp. 88–91, 100–101.

52. *Hoover Microfilm Collection*, Reel 33A, Folder 1788. The meeting on February 14 was secret; no party members other than leaders were allowed to attend. The next day there was a public meeting of six to seven hundred persons at which the agreements reached the previous day were publicly announced.

53. It can be seen from the party correspondence that more leaders were invited from the north than were actually present. District leaders Fobke (South-Hannover-Braunschweig) and Viereck (Elbe-Havel) declined the invitation (*Berlin Document Center*, Fobke's letter to Hess, February 2, 1926, Reel 21; Viereck's letter to Bouhler, February 11, 1926, Reel 23). While most party leaders received invitations, some did not. Kaufmann (Rhineland-South) complained to Bouhler that he had not received an invitation, although to his knowledge everybody else had. Bouhler informed him that not all district leaders had been invited (*ibid.*, Reel 22).

54. "Bamberg was chosen as the site of the conference in order to enable those living far away to come" (Bouhler's correspondence to Viereck, February 9, 1926, *Berlin Document Center,* Reel 22).

55. "There is no agenda for the conference. Hitler wants to discuss a series of important questions" (Bouhler's letter to Viereck, February 6, 1926, *Berlin Document Center,* Reel 22).

56. Strasser, *L'aigle Prussien,* p. 193.

57. See Goebbels's entry in his diary for February 15, 1926, in Heiber, *Das Tagebuch,* pp. 59–61.

58. It is not true that Goebbels deserted Gregor Strasser at the conference, as was reported by Otto Strasser and repeated by others. It was not until several weeks later that Goebbels was offered and accepted the district leadership in Berlin. On March 26 he notes in his diary the receipt of Hitler's letter and the invitation to speak in Munich, which he eagerly accepted. Heiber, *Das Tagebuch,* p. 68. On Otto Strasser's account see *Hitler und Ich,* p. 90; *Flight from Terror,* pp. 122–123.

59. The "Working Association of North and West" was dissolved when its Hannover program was repudiated by Hitler. But there is no evidence that any association ever existed in the strict organizational sense of the term. After all, only three weeks elapsed between Hannover and Bamberg.

60. Miltenberg, *Adolf Hitler,* pp. 78–79.

61. Hans Volz, *Daten der Geschichte der NSDAP* (Berlin and Leipzig, 1934), p. 14.

62. Heiber, *Das Tagebuch,* pp. 21–22, 27, 35, 39.

63. "Wir werden in Bamberg die spröde Schöne sein und Hitler auf unser Terrain locken" (*ibid.,* p. 59).

64. *Ibid.,* p. 60.

65. Goebbels's adoration of Hitler is evident throughout his entries. See *ibid.,* pp. 27, 33–34, 39, 40, 43, 65, 71.

66. *Ibid.,* pp. 61, 68, 71.

67. That they had no intention of deposing Hitler was illustrated vividly by their continued use of "Heil Hitler" in the 1925–1926 period (Görlitz and Quint, *Adolf Hitler,* p. 256).

68. Douglas Reed, *Nemesis? The Story of Otto Strasser* (London, 1940), p. 80.

69. Heiber, *Das Tagebuch,* p. 27.

70. Hence the "cult of personality" tends to be a continuing problem in ideological movements since it contradicts ideological legitimacy.

3

HORST GIES

The NSDAP and Agrarian Organizations in the Final Phase of the Weimar Republic

[TRANSLATED BY JOYCE CRUMMEY]

The charismatic personality of Hitler and his undeniably central role in the NSDAP have led some writers to pay inadequate attention to the part played in his rise to power by the Nazi party machine. In the light of recent scholarship, the NSDAP emerges as a remarkably well-structured and effective political organization, staffed, at least in its upper echelons, by extremely able, if unscrupulous, men. Without its organizational achievements, Hitler's personal demagogic talents would not have sufficed to exploit fully the opportunity presented to Nazism by the onset of the World Depression in 1929. Only through the efforts of a formidable party organization could the appeals of Hitler and the Nazi doctrine be translated into the millions of votes that enabled the NSDAP to increase its representation in the national parliament from 12 to 107 in 1930 and to become the largest party two years later, with 230 seats. Nazism's triumphs, it seems clear in retrospect, were the product of a remarkably successful combination of two organizational principles previously regarded as antithetical: charisma and bureaucracy.

The author of this selection, who teaches modern history at the University of Münster, uses fresh evidence to reconstruct and analyze the operations of a hitherto neglected but vitally important component of the Nazi party machinery. He has extended his study to cover the period after the appointment of Hitler as Chancellor in 1933 in another article: "Die nationalsozialistische Machtergreifung auf dem agrarpolitischen Sektor," in Zeitschrift für Agrargeschichte und Agrarsoziologie, *XVI (1968), 210–232. This selection was originally published as "NSDAP und landwirtschaftliche Organisationen in der Endphase der Weimarer Republik," in* Vierteljahrshefte für Zeitgeschichte, *XV (1967), 341–376. It is reprinted by permission of the author.*

I

Prior to 1930 the National Socialist Party made little headway in the countryside other than in Schleswig-Holstein, where because of special circumstances, especially the failure of the Rural People's Movement (*Landvolkbewegung*), it had become "a reservoir of the dissatisfied and disappointed, of failed revolutionaries and indignant philistines."[1] At the beginning, the NSDAP was more likely to repel than to attract agrarian groups. It had originated in the urban milieu of the working and lower-middle classes; it attracted other new followers among veterans without political affiliation. There were markedly socialist planks in its platform. The demand for "land reform," derived from Adolf Damaschke's ideas, and still more that for "expropriation without remuneration of land for public uses" revealed an essentially hostile attitude toward private property which frightened the farmers away.[2] Thus in 1928 the party leadership felt it necessary, in an explanation of Point 17 of the party program, to "correct" what were termed "malicious distortions and ugly insinuations" about the policy of the NSDAP concerning agrarian land ownership.[3] Now, by means of an interpretation that drastically altered the basic text, "expropriation without remuneration" was restricted to land "which was obtained illegitimately or administered without regard for the good of the people." With this change in its party program, which in 1926 had been designated as "unalterable," the NSDAP followed Hitler's tactics of employing statements of policy purely as instruments of opportunist political propaganda.[4]

To be sure, deepening economic depression and widespread material need made the NSDAP increasingly aware of the rural population.[5] Even in his Vienna days, Hitler had admired Karl Lueger's practice of "putting the main emphasis of his political activity on winning over those strata of society whose existence was threatened."[6] This tactical formula for success bore its first fruit in Schleswig-Holstein.[7] But party organization and personnel were far from adequate for a broad agrarian policy. Although Werner Willikens, who had represented the NSDAP in agrarian questions in the Reichstag since 1928, was the center of a small circle of National Socialist rural agitators, their activity in the field of agrarian policy inside and outside the party was of almost no significance.[8] Not until the beginning of 1930 was there a recognizable attempt on the part of the NSDAP to crystallize its own theory of agrarian policy and include the rural population in its propagandistic calculations. This tendency is evidenced by the attempt on the part of the *Reichsleitung* (National Leadership) to open up a new reservoir of voters for the NSDAP in rural areas by issuing an "Official Proclamation Concerning the Policy of the National Socialist Party on the Rural Population and Agriculture."[9]

A little later, in May 1930, there was further indication of increasing Nazi interest in agrarian policy: the appointment of R. Walther Darré as advisor on agricultural questions to the *Reichsleitung* of the NSDAP. Hitler's new agrarian expert, a certified graduate of an agricultural institute who had made a name for himself with publications in the field of race theory,[10] not only made a new—and in fact dazzling—addition to the Nazi *Weltanschauung* by means of his "blood and soil ideology"; he also had a clear notion as to how the NSDAP could gain an organizational foothold in rural areas. Within a year, Darré succeeded in building for the Nazis a rural organization—the Agrarian Apparatus (*agrarpolitischer Apparat,* hereafter aA)—extending over the whole Reich and enjoying considerable influence over the policies of existing farmers' associations. Of all the politically active pressure groups during the period of rule by presidential decree, agriculture enjoyed the advantage of being able to count on a favorable hearing for its problems and needs from President Hindenburg, especially where the interests of the eastern regions were involved. Thus it was all the more fatal for the Weimar Republic when the aA of the NSDAP succeeded in gaining influence over the policy of agrarian organizations.

Building on the successes of the NSDAP in the election of September 1930, Darré managed, by means of propaganda and agitation, not only to increase still further his party's share of the rural votes;[10a] the radicalization of the agrarian occupational organizations was also consciously encouraged and adapted to Hitler's political goals. By infiltrating the ideology and personnel of the Rural League (*Reichslandbund,* hereafter RLB), the leader of the aA succeeded in enlisting the largest and most influential farm organization of that time in the service of National Socialism.

II

The plan which led to the aA of the NSDAP was created not by Darré, but by A. Georg Kenstler. Kenstler, the founder and publisher of the racist periodical, *Blut und Boden* (Blood and Soil), advocated the "advancement and extension of the active national revolutionary agrarian movement of Schleswig-Holstein throughout the Reich."

The rural movement was to be extended beyond the region of Schleswig-Holstein and made into a nationwide movement so that its political goals and revolutionary aspirations might be pursued more effectively.[11] Kenstler saw in National Socialism a suitable instrument for this "political and cultural awakening of Germany's farmers" (*Bauerntum*).* In 1929 Kenstler, Darré, and Dr. Hans Ziegler, the editor of the NSDAP organ in Thuringia, cooperated closely on plans for a central office for agrarian policy in Weimar. It was to be the organizational focus of a rural movement extending over the entire Reich.[12] Supported financially by the NSDAP and directed by Darré, the projected organization was to "make an up-to-the-minute survey of the situation available at all times, so that appropriate measures could be taken as necessary."[13] However, since the *Reichsleitung* of the NSDAP in Munich, while indicating interest in the project, was not at first convinced of the necessity of such an organization,[14] the negotiations and discussions dragged on until the early summer of 1930. Meanwhile, Darré had been named advisor on agricultural questions to the NSDAP and commissioned to develop a Department of Agrarian Affairs within the *Reichsleitung* in Munich.[15]

Only two weeks after he began his work in Munich, on August 15, 1930, Darré presented the *Reichsleitung* with two memoranda. In these he set forth his ideas on the subject of the party's "mission to the farmers of Germany," and his plans for carrying it out.[16] The first of the two memoranda was concerned with the place of agriculture in a future Nazi state; Darré explored in detail the significance of agriculture in the coming struggle for control of Germany and the farmers' role as revolutionaries in this struggle. Darré's point of departure was the obvious one that the urban population was dependent for its nourish-

---

Bauerntum is often translated into English as "peasantry," but because the latter carries with it connotations that are anachronistic when applied to most of Germany's rural population in the twentieth century, *Bauer* will be translated here as "farmer." So will *Landwirt,* usually, though not always, employed to indicate the owner of a larger quantity of land and/or livestock; where *Landwirt* appears in the original German text, it will be included in parentheses.—ED.

ment on rural food production. Therefore it would do the Nazis little good to win over only the cities. On the other hand, once in control of the food producers, that is the farmers, they would have the advantage in power politics. "Thus it is of vital importance to the NSDAP to gain control of the agrarian sector in Germany. For an action to withhold the urban food supply, if organized hand in hand with National Socialist groups in the cities, would in the long run prevail over the machine-gun fire of police or army."

Significantly, this chain of reasoning was set forth in August 1930, when Darré counted on the election to the Reichstag of about 60 National Socialist deputies in the September 14 balloting.[17] At that point it seemed to him utopian to think of a power seizure by legal means, that is, through the democratic, parliamentary process. He thus thought in terms of a militant confrontation. However, the situation was changed by the results of the September election, which gave the NSDAP 107 Reichstag mandates as compared to its previous twelve. Now, for the first time, Nazi infiltration of existing state institutions and professional organizations seemed both possible and promising. Adapting his tactics to Hitler's, Darré set out on this path.

In the second memorandum, Darré made concrete suggestions as to how the party could gain an organizational foothold in the countryside.[18] In this memorandum, also dated August 15, 1930, and entitled "Outline of the Plan to Develop an Agrarian Organizational Network Throughout the Reich," Darré presented ideas largely derived from those of A. Georg Kenstler, mentioned above. The mentality of the German farmers could only be understood by someone himself from the countryside, "with a feel for the homeland and for blood," and not by urban agitators. Moreover, because Germany's farmers differed ethnically and in agricultural practices from one region to another, Darré proposed to the party an organization "capable of embracing the widely divergent elements of agrarian life but still so firmly under the control of the *Reichsleitung* that the latter will be assured that the programmatic guidelines of the party will be uniformly followed, even in the most far-flung corners of the Reich." In his planning, Darré, whose Department of Agrarian Affairs was subordinate to Konstantin Hierl's Department II of the Reich Organization of the NSDAP, availed himself of the political organization of the party led by Gregor Strasser: every political leader of the NSDAP from the *Gau* (regional division) to the *Ort* (local unit) was to be assigned a *landwirtschaftlicher Fachberater* (expert consultant on agriculture), who had a twofold task.[19] First, he was to support his immediate superior in the political organization in the day-by-day political struggle. In addition, however, he was to be in direct contact with the central office for agrarian policy of the NSDAP in Munich. From there the *Fachberater* were to be trained and instructed according to unified guidelines; but their most important responsibility would be to report their observations and experiences to Munich, where this incoming material would be "sifted" and made "available to all agricultural consultants in the Reich as intelligence regarding agrarian policy for the political struggle on the home front."

Darré's plan thus provided for a communications system fanning out over the entire Reich which would supply the central office with information and receive instructions from it. The aA was conceived as a cadre of functionaries which was to enable the party to carry out "well-considered, coordinated attacks and prompt defensive measures" in the day-by-day political struggle in rural areas. It was to provide the NSDAP with a new tool for capturing power in the state, "a weapon to be employed swiftly and forcefully in the offensive and defensive struggle over agrarian policy." Propaganda and agitation were the organization's primary tasks. Not only was it charged with obtaining new farm votes for the NSDAP, but through it the party was also to be provided with additional revolutionary forces that could be called upon in the event of power struggles with its opponents. There was as yet no thought of infiltrating established agricultural organizations.

The zeal of the new party agrarian expert as well as the plan of action he brought to Munich had obviously not been expected there. It seems reasonable to believe Darré's report that his memoranda aroused "consternation," while nevertheless convincing Hierl and the *Reichsleitung* of the "necessity and appropriateness" of the measures he suggested.[20] Only a week after Darré had presented the plan, its realization was begun. On August 21, 1930, the Agricultural Department of the *Reichsleitung*'s Organizational Department II ordered all *Gauleiter* (leaders of the NSDAP within a *Gau*) to name a *Fachberater* for agrarian affairs by the first day of October.[21] "As far as possible," the *Bezirksleiter* (district leaders) were to follow suit. The rationale and details of the proposed organization corresponded almost verbatim to Darré's memoranda of August 15, 1930. There was only one small discrepancy; in one memorandum Darré had stated that the "ideal solution" would be for each *Gau* to hire a full-time agricultural *Fachberater*. The *Reichsleitung* did not follow this suggestion, probably mainly for financial reasons. Each *Gauleiter* was instructed to recruit "a farmer

(*Landwirt*) of reliable reputation" as a "volunteer consultant." At the same time, Hierl and Darré provided precise "guidelines" for the selection of the new co-workers. They had to have the confidence of the local political leadership of the party as well as that of their fellow farmers. Furthermore, the consultants had to be in touch with agrarian life, although the degree of expertise required in this regard could vary on a scale according to the importance of the jurisdiction, i.e., *Ort* (local unit), *Kreis* (subdistrict), *Bezirk* (district), or *Gau* (regional district). Through "mental alertness" and "effectiveness in public appearances," he must "represent the party convincingly to his fellow farmers." He must in addition "explain agricultural matters to the party." Furthermore, "a certain skill in writing" was recommended, so that the *Fachberater* would be able to answer attacks in the press promptly. Darré's specifications for his future co-workers also make it perfectly clear that, at the time aA was organized, he was more concerned with the mass of farmers than with their organizations.

In the ensuing months, these directives for implementation of Darré's plans were augmented and made more precise. There were no further changes in the goal, the purpose, or the organizational principle of the NSDAP's network of agrarian functionaries. An instruction sheet issued on November 17, 1930, emphasized unambiguously what was expected of the *Fachberater*.[22] "Every consultant must feel that he is a kind of 'eye and ear' of the *Reichsleitung*," that is, he must try to find out "which needs and anxieties oppress the rural population of his region, which hopes and wishes they cherish, which local, ethnic, and geographical peculiarities of theirs are to be taken into consideration in formulating the agrarian propaganda of the NSDAP." Furthermore, the aA should "penetrate into all rural affairs like a finely intertwined root system," should "embed itself deeply in them and seek to embrace every element of agrarian life so thoroughly that eventually nothing will be able to occur in the realm of agriculture anywhere in the Reich which we do not observe and whose basis we do not understand. Let there be no farm, no estate, no village, no cooperative, no agricultural industry, no local organization of the RLB, no rural equestrian association, etc., etc., where we have not—at the least—placed our LVL (*Landwirtschaftliche Vertrauensleute,* or "agrarian agents") in such numbers that we could paralyze at one blow the total political life of these structures."[23]

Here it is clear for the first time that with the success of the NSDAP in the September 1930 elections the goals of the aA of the party had changed. Now, not only were the farmers specified as a target for agitation in rural areas by Darré to his co-workers; it was also explained unmistakably to the *Fachberater* that a second object of attack must be kept in view: the farmers' associations. "Every consultant must without fail regard every non-National Socialist rural organization, regardless of its nature, as a fortress to be conquered and one day transformed into a National Socialist group."[23a] An asset in the pursuit of this goal was Darré's insistence, in one memorandum of August 15, 1930, on the importance of keeping secret from the general public the structure—and the very existence—of the new organization of the party.[24]

These were far-reaching aims limited neither to propaganda in rural areas for the wooing of new NSDAP voters nor to the ideological schooling of Nazi rural agitators. Their fulfillment required a coherently constructed, broadly-based organization; "a network of loyal people." According to Darré's plan, the aA was in the main composed of the *Reichsleitungsfachberater* for agriculture [Darré himself] and the respective *Gaufachberater, Bezirksfachberater, Kreisfachberater,* and *Ortsgruppenfachberater.* There were in addition the aA's agrarian agents (LVL) in other agricultural organizations and leagues, as well as estates. As the organizational network began to tighten, practical necessity determined the deployment of *Abschnittsfachberater* (intermediary section consultants) for communication between the *Gaufachberater* and the *Bezirksfachberater.*[25] To facilitate cooperation between the various *Gaufachberater, Landesfachberater* (consultants responsible for several regional divisions) were introduced in 1932. All consultants were subordinated to their respective political leaders in matters of party activity. But in order to provide for a unified line on agrarian policy and for the tough discipline needed in a hard-hitting organization, Darré insisted on a direct line of authority within the aA. Thus the chain of command —and accountability—extended downward from the National Leadership through the *Gaufachberater* all the way to the aA's agents within other agricultural organizations (LVL). The agricultural consultants of the NSDAP were thus accountable both to a political leader and to an immediate superior in the hierarchy of the aA.[26] Instructions and information from the *Reichsleitungsfachberater* (Darré) were sent out in directives to the *Gaufachberater,* who then instructed the subdivisions of the aA within his *Gau.* A full-time official, Richard Arauner, a former fellow student of Darré's and like him a certified graduate of an agricultural institute, directed the main office of the aA at the Munich headquarters of the *Reichsleitung.*[27]

In view of the extent of the political organization of the NSDAP by the end of 1930—35 *Gaue*—the dimensions of the task Darré had set himself become clear. It is all the more astonishing that he was able by January 9, 1931, to report in a detailed account of his activities that he had "managed to achieve extensive development of the aA in almost every *Gau*."[28] By then, Darré had brought together a tightly-knit cadre of party agrarian functionaries which won him admiration and respect within the party,[29] although it demanded great exertions and often occasioned discord.[30] As the crowning achievement of this period of development, the agricultural *Fachberater* of the NSDAP National Leadership wanted to attract public attention with a large farmers' rally. "The goal of the meeting must be to destroy with one blow the widespread myth that the NSDAP has no more than a lukewarm interest in agricultural problems and pursues them only halfheartedly."[31] This was the motivation for the first convention of the NSDAP *Landwirtschaftliche Gaufachberater* in Weimar on February 8, 1931. The finale of the convention was a farmers' rally (*Bauernkundgebung*) in which Hitler and other leading representatives of the party participated.[32]

Not only in setting up the aA but also later, Darré put heavy emphasis on knowing his co-workers in rural areas personally as well as on cultivating a sense of camaraderie and a consciously militant esprit de corps patterned after the practices of the SA. His aim was to increase both the political effectiveness of the organization and the readiness of individual co-workers for action.[33] All activity in this area was directed at making of the aA a well-tuned and pliant instrument of battle for the party.[34] This aim, despite the strictly enforced leadership principle (*Führerprinzip*), did not rule out a critical evaluation of work accomplished. Darré may have directed his aA with instructions issued from a central point, but he left their execution to the initiative, adaptability, and sound common sense of the *Gaufachberater,* as indeed regional peculiarities required. Thus he soon came to know the personal characteristics of his co-workers. He was sparing neither with praise[35] nor with blame. Lethargy, lack of understanding, carelessness, and indifference were criticized, sometimes openly.[36] "The necessity of sorting out and eliminating unsuitable personnel" was repeatedly emphasized[37] and in some cases actually put into practice.[38] To this evidence of concern for the dependability of the aA and the tightness of its inner structure should be added Darré's frequent orders to investigate all agricultural agents (LVL) and weed out "dubious elements."[39] In August 1932, moreover, a "surveillance service" (*Überwachungsdienst*) was established in the aA to protect the organization against opportunists (*Konjunkturritter*) within its own ranks and against attempts from without to gain influence over it and infiltrate it.[40]

One of the most important tasks which Darré had set himself in his memoranda of August 15, 1930, was that of schooling his aA co-workers according to uniform guidelines.[41] At the outset, he was less concerned with informing the NSDAP propagandists about NSDAP economic policy than with instructing the agricultural consultants in agitational techniques. "The aA is an agrarian political arm of the party, with at most limited concern for the technical and economic aspects of agriculture."[42] In his opinion the NSDAP's advantage over its competitors in rural politics lay precisely in its lack of a firm commitment to any particular agricultural policies.[43] Several methods were employed for the training of the agricultural consultants. Darré regularly provided his co-workers with material in the form of directives,[44] which were supplemented with brochures and other publications written by leading Nazi rural politicians.[45] However, from September 1931 on, the most important source of guidance for agrarian functionaries of the NSDAP was a weekly national newspaper published by Darré, the *Nationalsozialistische Landpost.*

The outward extension of the aA ran parallel to this inner consolidation until, by the end of 1932, when the NSDAP's fight for control in Germany entered its decisive phase, the agricultural organization had become one of the most successful and most dependable branches of the party. The annual report of the agricultural department of the NSDAP in the *Gau* of Saxony for 1932 provides information on the growth and activities of the aA at that time.[46] Led by *Gaufachberater* Helmut Körner, the Saxon aA consisted of: 34 *Kreisfachberater*, about 1100 agrarian agents (LVL), about 40 speakers on agriculture, 22 deputies in the Chamber of Agriculture, and four parliamentarians in the Saxon Landtag and the Reichstag. The department for agriculture within the *Gau* leadership employed nine staff members (*Hilfsreferenten*) and seven aides (*Sachbearbeiter*). One *Sachbearbeiter* was responsible for agricultural cooperatives, one for Chamber of Agriculture affairs, one for the RLB, and one for the Rural Youth League (*Junglandbund*). A *Hilfsrefent* was made responsible for a day-by-day propaganda campaign in the press, i.e. providing the provincial newspapers with agitational contributions and, in case of hostile attacks in the press, taking suitable countermeasures in the form of corrections, "contributions," and so forth. In the closing remarks of his report, the *Gaufachberater* for Saxony included the following: "The entire apparatus is highly centralized, and

I can say without exaggeration that nothing happens in the agrarian life of Saxony about which I would not be immediately informed. Thus, constant watch is kept over our opponents. Furthermore, within twenty-four hours I can pass on a particular news item to the entire agrarian population of Saxony with appropriate comment. The good connections which I have made allow me insight into the activities of all agrarian organizations in Saxony, even as high up as the Ministry of Economic Affairs, Agricultural Division." With this, Körner had no doubt fulfilled completely the task assigned to him by Darré.

At the same time, by the end of 1932, Darré had achieved a marked improvement in the position of the aA in the party structure. Taking advantage of the organizational reshuffling occasioned by the removal of Gregor Strasser, he succeeded in disentangling his aA from the underbrush of the party organization; as chief of the newly-created Office for Agrarian Policy in the *Reichsleitung* of the NSDAP, from which the entire work of the aA was directed, Darré was from now on directly subordinate to Hitler alone.[47]

III

One of the two main tasks of the agrarian apparatus of the NSDAP, gaining votes in rural areas, was of a propagandistic and agitational nature. At countless meetings of farmers, at discussion evenings, and in the press, Darré and his colleagues worked to portray in the brightest and most attractive hues the relationship of National Socialism to agriculture, a relationship previously enveloped in enticing shadows.[48] Since 1931 the agrarian press organ of the NSDAP, the *Nationalsozialistische Landpost,* had been supplemented by pages devoted specifically to agriculture in almost all National Socialist regional newspapers; starting in April of that year, even the *Völkischer Beobachter* had reserved a fortnightly page for agrarian affairs.[49] Darré himself undertook extensive lecture tours in order to "give the rural population . . . an objective picture of National Socialism's stand on agriculture and to explain the logic of the movement's support for agriculture."[50]

National Socialist agitators in rural areas had no greater scruples than those elsewhere about the tactics they employed against political opponents. They valued neither honesty in making demands nor objectivity in discussions. Their aim was to exploit the success in the September 1930 elections, primarily by encouraging dissatisfaction, in order to align the farmers behind the Swastika banner. At the same time, Darré's goal was to prove in elections that the NSDAP was a "farmers' party," so as to be able to demand appropriate representation in the leadership ranks of the legitimate agrarian occupational organizations. The growing economic distress of the farmers, their alienation from the democratic state and the "Berlin" governments, the dissatisfaction of the rural populace with the incomprehensible policies of their occupational organizations, the suicidal factional struggles among the agricultural organizations—all this was fuel for the fire which Darré and his *Fachberater* were now igniting in rural areas.

The three most successful themes of this agitation were anti-Semitism, the fight against liberalism, and fear of Bolshevism. The polemic of slogans, general phrases, and demogogic oversimplification was trump. In the language of the Nazis, this was expressed as the necessity of conflict with political opponents "on a philosophical (*weltanschaulich*) basis."[51] "Hot potato" issues were to be kept as far as possible out of the debate, since the Nazis must at all costs avoid "writing a check on the future," the cashing of which might conceivably become dangerous.[52] Here Darré was merely drawing the consequences from Hitler's tactics; for after the NSDAP had made the decision to seek power not as a revolutionary cadre party, but as an evolutionary popular party aided by the ballots of voters of all classes and all interests, nothing was more dangerous than identification with the one-sided demands of interest groups. Since Hitler's "movement" as a "party above parties"[53] postulated the "ideal national community" (*Volksgemeinschaft*) and raised no demands in agricultural questions which differed from those of other more or less right-wing parties and agrarian organizations, Nazi support for the interests of one occupational sector had to be made palatable with a general "philosophical" (*weltanschaulich*) phraseology.[54]

The method of using slogans to discredit opponents was employed especially against the Christian National Farmers' and Rural People's Party (*Christlich-Nationale Bauern- und Landvolkpartei;* hereafter CNBLP), the only purely farmer-oriented interest group active in party politics. For this rural party, which was reinforced in 1928 by secessionists from the German National People's Party (DNVP) and in 1930 had gained nineteen seats in the Reichstag, it was especially easy to take advantage of the NSDAP's vulnerability as a "people's party" representing the most heterogenous interests.[55] On the other hand, Darré had selected precisely this party as the primary target of his campaign for conquests in rural areas. Via the CNBLP he hoped to penetrate into the bastion of the Rural League (RLB), which was much more important for the aA. His scheme succeeded. In a year—from autumn 1931 to November 1932—an unprecedented agitational campaign by the aA decimated the CNBLP; it lost its entire representation in the Reichstag.[56]

In vain the rural press, especially in Thuringia, sought to alert the RLB to its danger. ". . . the CNBLP is being flogged, but the blows are aimed at the RLB as an autonomous agrarian organization independent of the Nazis. The aim is to make of the RLB the rural party organization which the Nazis lack."[57] The efforts of the CNBLP to arouse the leadership of the largest German rural organization were unsuccessful. On the contrary, after the RLB had dissociated itself in early 1931 from the agrarian policy of the Brüning government and its Minister of Agriculture, Martin Schiele (who had run in the 1930 elections as the top candidate of the CNBLP),[58] a rapprochement began to take shape between the NSDAP and the RLB.[59] This was first evidenced in a joint action in September 1931 which led to the downfall of Baron Tilo von Wilmowsky, a member of CNBLP. After Wilmowsky had withdrawn from the RLB national leadership, he was defeated in a bid for reelection as chairman of the Saxon provincial branch of the RLB. The RLB had turned "with a trusting plea for help" to Darré, who mobilized the aA in Saxony against Wilmowsky, the "business tycoon, director of the *Danatbank,* and member of the National Railway Council."[60] The convention of the "national opposition" in Bad Harzburg on October 11, 1931, provided further opportunity for an alignment of DNVP/RLB and NSDAP against the CNBLP.[61]

The dissension in the ranks of the agrarian parties and organizations revealed by these developments was without question of great importance for the Nazi successes in the sphere of agrarian politics. The agitational frontal attacks of the Nazis and Darré's infiltration tactics were not the only reasons why the CNBLP, and somewhat later the occupational organizations of German agriculture, were decimated or fell into the hands of the functionary cadres of the aA. Also of vital importance was the disunited and multiform nature of the rural occupational and political organizations, which mirrored the philosophical and structural diversity of German agriculture. The influence exerted by the "East Elbian Group," thanks to their extensive familial, social, and political connections, was especially evident in the fall of the Brüning government in May 1932. Undoubtedly the plan for placing settlers on estates no longer capable of operating profitably, a project passionately opposed by the East German estate-holders, played a significant part at that time.[62] The Junker estate owners were particularly successful in mobilizing the RLB on behalf of their interests in connection with the official agrarian policy of the Weimar Republic. The RLB had been created in 1921 through the merger of the old Agrarian League (*Bund der Landwirte*) and a coordinating organization for regional farm organizations founded in 1919, the *Deutscher Landbund*.[63] The RLB had taken over the decentralized structure of the latter organization, which accorded financial autonomy to its corporatively associated state and provincial affiliates.

Whereas the RLB represented mainly the interests of large-scale agriculture, small and intermediate units of the livestock and processing branches were organized in the *Deutsche Bauernschaft*. In alliance with the "Union of German Christian Farmers' Associations" (*Vereinigung der deutschen christlichen Bauernvereine*), the *Bauernschaft* protested against the one-sided favoritism shown to the interests of the RLB by the government.[64]

These conflicts of interest were not removed when, in March 1929, all three associations, together with the *Deutscher Landwirtschaftsrat*, the central organization of the Chambers of Agriculture, joined ranks as the "Green Front." In taking this step, the leadership ranks of the associations had grudgingly given in to pressure from their various regional subdivisions.[65] They also acted out of concern for the intensified competitive struggle with industry, commerce, and trade unions, joining in with the chorus: "Build the National Farmers' Front!" for a more unified representation of agricultural interests.[66] The Green Front, however, was purely a coordinating organization which did not at all curtail the autonomy of the various associations, since these were prepared only for joint action, not for unification. The President of the Union of German Christian Farmers' Associations, Andreas Hermes, gave expression to this in a revealing slogan: "Unity in well-organized diversity."[67] After some initial successes in dealings with the government, primarily in fulfilling the wishes of large estate owners,[68] the Green Front came under the domination of heterogeneous interests which crushed all tendencies toward a real unification. When moderate RLB President Martin Schiele entered Brüning's cabinet as Minister of Agriculture, he was replaced shortly thereafter as Executive President by Count Eberhard von Kalckreuth—a change of leadership which resulted in a more radical course for the largest occupational organization in German agriculture. The old conflicts of interest, which were especially pronounced in the case of the *Deutsche Bauernschaft* and the RLB, broke out again. Since February 1930, in fact, the Green Front had gradually been losing the unified strength it needed to influence economic policy and had been exploited by the RLB to serve the aims of the large estate owners.[69]

The struggle within German agriculture for a better place at the governmental feed trough was evident not only in the press, but also in a continual flow of proposals to the government. In a brochure, "Der Bauer im Kampf gegen den Landbund" (The Farmer's Fight Against the RLB), the *Wirtschaftsverband bäuerlicher Veredlungsarbeit,* a coordinating organization for farm organizations in northwest Germany, charged that official agricultural policy had forced farmers to pay to bail the great estates of the East out of bankruptcy.[70] Protective tariffs and subsidies for rye had, it was alleged, caused a rise in the price of fodder and thus ruthlessly injured the small cattle-breeders and processors. A revision of German agricultural policy was urgently needed. "Maintaining heavily indebted large estates which cling to obsolete farming practices is a function inappropriate to German agricultural policy. It takes no heed of the sons of farmers eager to establish farms."[71] The brochure closed by pointing out that the interests of urban consumers and the farmers were more closely bound together than those of the farmers and the East Elbian owners of large estates.

The farmers' organizations emphasized especially that by favoring the RLB the government was supporting elements whose negative attitude toward the state represented a permanent danger to the Weimar Republic.[72] On August 5, 1931, Heinrich Lübke, the business manager of the *Deutsche Bauernschaft,* emphasized in a letter to the Chancellor that the real aim of the RLB was "to make demagogic promises while concealing their unfeasibility from the farmers, and thereby discrediting the government in the eyes of the farmers [*Landwirte*] and making it appear hostile to agriculture. The ever more rapid gravitation of the farmers to the radical right and left is the product of these policies of the RLB."[73]

Such conflicts of interest within German agriculture, together with—and greatly augmented by—material want, prepared the way for an advance by National Socialism into rural areas. They were accompanied by an increasing politicization of the occupational organizations, which further intensified the conflicts and also fed suspicion and dissatisfaction within German agriculture. The *Deutsche Bauernschaft* and the *Vereinigung der deutschen christlichen Bauernvereine* were rivals for the favors of the Center Party. Within the RLB there were differences of opinion between followers of the CNBLP and the DNVP. Moreover, the farm vote was further splintered by a number of additional "farmers' parties" on the regional level.[74] An illustration of the confused political behavior of some agricultural organizations and their leaders is provided by the case of RLB President Schiele, who had joined the Brüning government as Agricultural Minister. Dissatisfied with the radical course of the DNVP under Hugenberg's leadership, which was receptive to the interests of industrial tycoons, Schiele left the party and ran for the Reichstag in 1930 on the CNBLP ticket. After the election, however, he refused to assume his seat, and the agrarian policy of the Brüning government was left without a political foundation.[75]

In a critical analysis of the representation of the agrarian sector in the final phase of the Weimar Republic, former state secretary Dr. Wilhelm Peters found major faults not only in the Chambers of Agriculture, but also in the occupational organizations.[76] "Economic distress has rendered the farmer [*Landwirt*] not only unable but also unwilling to maintain production. Although he recognizes the efforts of the Chambers . . . he regards them as bodies that exact taxes but with which he is out of touch; he regards the organizations which otherwise represent his occupation as groups which are expensive to maintain and accomplish little in proportion to this expense."[77] Peters stated that large sums were squandered and much labor unnecessarily expended as a result of organizational waste motion, failure to apportion the tasks at hand, and general bureaucratization. "In the extra-governmental occupational organizations . . . there is not only great confusion, not only division and thus squandering of energies, but the people involved there also work against one another—often with vulgar, hateful tactics; economic policy tends increasingly to degenerate into party politics, leaving further and further behind the necessary premise of every occupational organization: to stand above party politics."[78]

Material distress and economic depression were thus compounded by the rural population's dissatisfaction with their occupational organizations, which were entangled in political differences of opinion and conflicts of interest. The resulting hostility of farmers toward these organizations first became evident in the Rural People's Movement (*Landvolkbewegung*) in Schleswig-Holstein, an emergency protest movement based on the principle of self-help. Klaus Heim, one of its leaders, clearly expressed this general dissatisfaction. "The fact is that the state, the parties, the national agricultural organizations, the Chambers of Agriculture and cooperatives have failed. The fact is that the farmer has been paying his dues everywhere for years and has heard for years how much has been achieved for him—yet he sees that he is faring worse and worse."[79]

Thus the agricultural organizations presented a fertile field to Nazi rural propaganda, which was able to point to them as examples of the "decimating results of liberal thought." Not only had "the agrarian sector in Germany been reduced to a herd of special interest groups,"[80] but one could also observe—all the way from the cooperatives through the occupational organizations and even up to the ministries—a lack of structural cohesion, unnecessary paper-shuffling, lethargy on the part of leaders, and a sterile duplication of effort. The administration of Germany's agricultural affairs, the Nazis claimed, was among the worst in the world.[81] Naturally the National Socialists did not lack agitational material in this area: the scandals arising from aid to the eastern regions (*Osthilfe*), corruption within agricultural organizations, excessive salaries for agrarian officials—paid for by the farmers' contributions—conflicts of interest between farmers' unions and branches of the RLB. All these were presented to the farmers as faults of the "liberalistic system"—with appropriate propagandistic distortion, often enough totally unfounded, but usually based on a grain of truth. National Socialism, by way of contrast, offered not only a simplification of agricultural administration but also a new unity among the farmers' organizations. According to Nazi propagandists, the agrarian sector could thus be internally strengthened and fitted into a state with an "organic" structure supported by the basic concept of "folk community" (*Volksgemeinschaft*).

IV

These developments cleared the way for the second main task of the aA of the NSDAP: infiltration of German agrarian occupational organizations. Of all these associations, the RLB cooperated most closely with Darré in this respect. Especially in the preceding two years, this agrarian organization had pursued a highly unstable policy. "First the German Nationals (DNVP) and, in Middle Germany, the People's Party (DVP), had been in alliance with the RLB. For years, ever since the beginning of the 'leftward defections' from the Hugenberg party, there had been a struggle over the question of whether electioneering should be carried on with Hugenberg or with the secessionists, or whether it was better to proceed independently. After trying the first, the second, and the third, ties to the Hitler party were eventually formed."[82] This characterization of the policy of the RLB is confirmed by a memorandum which one of its members wrote for Darré. The author had worked long years in a key post in the organization and now pointed to the embitterment of many provincial branches of the RLB about the vacillating political attitude of the national leadership.[83] Even in the *Bundesvorstand* (Federal Directorate) of the RLB, many officials hoped for "salvation from this chaos in an alignment with the NSDAP." By the late summer of 1931, in fact, Heinrich von Sybel, one of the two directors of the organization, had already established the first contacts with National Socialism.[84]

In one memorandum of August 15, 1930, Darré had spoken of the future attitude of the NSDAP toward the RLB: "The RLB today is a powerful organization, possessing considerable means of direct and indirect manipulation for keeping the farmers in line. However, the RLB is obviously an organization created in order to nip in the bud every sign of rebellion on the part of the farmers. The influence of the RLB can only be eliminated both by waging against it an ideological (*weltanschaulich*) war (for it is liberalistic), and by consigning it to its proper place among organizations concerned with the economic aspects of affairs."[85] The tactics outlined here were put into practice in the ensuing months and their application was broadened through ideological and personnel infiltration. On the "ideological level" the RLB was attacked via the CNBLP. The effort to depoliticize the RLB—that is, to curtail the influence within it of the DNVP and the CNBLP—was carried on not only by means of peaceful competition but also through systematic infiltration by the NSDAP. Darré had at first hesitated over whether to attempt "taking over existing agricultural organizations from within," that is, employing a kind of "factory cell tactics,"[86] or whether it would be better "to attack the RLB from without."[87] The latter course of action, however, had only "maneuvered the RLB leaders into a defensive position."[88] Thus, after the rural successes of the NSDAP in the September 1930 elections, the political course of the aA was charted solely with an eye to infiltrating the RLB's ideology and personnel. To his functionaries Darré presented this task purely as one of "conquering one position after another from within," and this, according to a retrospective report by a member of the aA, was relatively easy wherever the branches of the RLB were not firmly aligned with a political party. "But where the RLB identified with the CNBLP, in Hesse and Thuringia, the fight was harder, for there party opposed party, each claiming to represent the farmers best."[89]

While the struggle between the NSDAP and the CNBLP was becoming increasingly rough, there was no lack in rural areas of National Socialist demands for an amalgamation of the RLB and National Socialism. But the branches of the RLB refused to cooperate.[90] Instead their leadership ranks stood by and watched the barrage of Nazi agitation directed at the CNBLP, trusting in the invulnerability of their own secure position. "The leaders of the RLB did not believe the National Socialists would be able to shake the foundations of their organization. They contented themselves with a defensive posture. . . ."[91] At first, the NSDAP was interested in collaboration with individual provincial branches of the RLB, since this would have been valuable in terms of propaganda and general betterment of the Nazis' position.[92] However, as these efforts quickly proved futile, the tactic of infiltration was tenaciously pursued. On April 18, 1931, the *Gaufachberater* of Baden wrote to his *Bezirksfachberater:* "Thus, our aim is no longer demolition of the RLB, but rather the maintenance of its organization. The inescapably logical conclusion leads us to the necessity of acquiring influence in the RLB through party comrades. We must establish ourselves in its lower ranks, so that we can later take it firmly in hand by installing party comrades in the leadership positions."[93]

Progress along this path was easy for the NSDAP, thanks to the defensive tactics of the RLB and the rivalry between the CNBLP and the DNVP for positions of leadership. The DNVP was not unhappy over the erosion of the CNBLP by the NSDAP.[94] Thus, the DNVP was little concerned about the fact that the aA subjected to extremely hostile agitation those provincial branches of the RLB in which the CNBLP was dominant.[95] For example, Werner Willikens, Darré's deputy, excused the behavior of the NSDAP toward the Thuringian branch of the RLB with this comment: "We acknowledge the Rural League fully, but we must fight against it if it disregards its tasks by aligning itself with any political parties whatever."[96] Hugenberg's colleagues, with confidence in their own strength, obviously did not understand that this could hold true for the German National People's Party just as well as for others.

Meanwhile, Darré and Hierl attempted to lull the RLB national leadership into a feeling of security. An inquiry into policy was answered in a letter of September 26, 1931: "The NSDAP seeks a state in which, beneath the state authority (*Staatsleitung*), there will be, alongside an advisory board for political matters, an economic advisory board for economic matters. . . . The NSDAP regards the RLB as the organization which, with some restructuring, would be suited to provide top leadership for the occupational representation of the agrarian sector in the economic parliament."[97]

In opposing the CNBLP while sparing the DNVP, Darré and his co-workers were thus forcing the RLB into the "neutral" position of an organization concerned solely with agricultural interests, so that possible resistance to a Nazi claim for representation in RLB leadership ranks might be paralyzed. Meanwhile, Hitler himself issued the slogan for the rural members of the NSDAP: "Now the great organization of the Rural League is fighting for the soil. We acknowledge without question the unconditional necessity of a strong farm organization to influence economic policy and we demand of our party comrades who are farmers (*Landwirte*): Join the Rural League! Unquestionably valuable forces are at work in this great organization, which, once put to work in the proper places, will also be able to accomplish much in the Third Reich. . . ."[98] While thus issuing an obvious invitation to the opportunists in the RLB, Hitler also identified the common enemy of both organizations, the "Marxist plague," not only playing skillfully on the old fears of RLB members,[99] but also conjuring up the necessity of a unified front. "Therefore the appeal to all National Socialist farmers: Join the Rural League."

To be sure, the Nazis by this time already possessed many footholds in the leadership ranks of district and provincial branches of the RLB,[100] including the director of the RLB national office, von Sybel. Now it was a question of obtaining mass support in the organization by "legal" means. Darré faithfully applied to the agrarian sector the tactics employed by Hitler against state and Parliament. For him, "the existing situation made it necessary for the NSDAP to view the Rural League, like the state, as an instrument of power, which must be taken up and used for the good of the cause which we serve. Thus it became necessary for the NSDAP to penetrate the RLB and to try to take over one power stronghold after another within it, step by step. . . ."[101] The instructions given to RLB members in the aA by Darré employ equally clear language. The goal was to "rid" the organization "of undesirable elements and pockets of resistance";[102] in fact, the *Reichsleitungsfachberater* openly asked his *Gaufachberater:* "Which personalities must, in your opinion, be removed in order to achieve as soon as possible a really sincere neutrality toward us on the part of the RLB or the organizations related to it?"[103] A further directive by Darré urged the National Socialist members of the agrarian organization to "nibble away at its official apparatus; then, along with this mortar, the big stones will fall out on their own."[104]

Despite Darré's unambiguous tactical concept and the equally clear directives for its implementation, it seems to have been necessary to clear up differences of opinion among the provincial co-workers of the aA. By the slogan "Join the Rural League," Hitler had not meant "that the farmer should belong to the RLB rather than to the NSDAP as a political organization, or that RLB leaders belonging to the CNBLP or the DNVP should lead us by the nose."[105] In September 1931, Darré addressed to his *Gaufachberater* a long directive elaborating in great detail the tactics of the NSDAP toward the RLB.[106] The Nazis were not advocating an insipid policy of compromise, he wrote. Instead, the RLB was simply to be employed as a political and economic organization serving the National Socialists' goals. "The NSDAP is not a party, but a movement employing the means of party politics to reach its goal: this is stipulated in the National Socialist constitution." Thus, the NSDAP's role as "organ of the German movement for freedom" required the infiltration of the Rural League, i.e. the largest German agricultural organization. Darré regarded the neutralization of the RLB as the most important stage in this process. First, this would eliminate the possibility of open enmity toward the Nazis on the part of the League; moreover, it would enable the party to compete "equally against the other parties" for the farm vote, "free from any obstruction on the part of the Rural League leadership. Furthermore, this development would automatically enable NSDAP personnel to get a foothold in the RLB." At the close of his letter, Darré gave his co-workers additional practical directives: "The *Gaufachberater,* when they agree on neutrality with the individual branches of the Rural League, must observe this neutrality scrupulously until they actually possess the power to eliminate or otherwise checkmate any noxious element in the RLB."

Later Darré was to employ this same tactical concept down to the smallest detail in his dealings with the RLB's national leadership. But even in 1931 some of his co-workers on the lower level of the provincial branches of the RLB succeeded in carrying out to the letter the instructions of the *Reichsleitung*. For example, negotiations on April 1, 1931, between the Rural League of Baden and the NSDAP resulted in the following agreement: the Rural League would give up all partisan political activity and regard itself purely as an organization for protecting the farmers' economic interests; the period of mutual hostility was over, the economic demands of the Rural League would be represented in the Parliaments by the NSDAP; every NSDAP farmer was free to join the Rural League, which for its part posed no obstacles to those of its members wishing to join the NSDAP.[107]

Of decisive significance, however, for the successes the aA was able to record against the Rural League by the end of 1931 were the elections to the Chambers of Agriculture in Prussia during the autumn and winter of 1931–1932. Darré prepared for them carefully during the summer. With the help of questionnaires directed to all *Gaufachberater,* he gathered information about individual Chambers of Agriculture, their personnel and political makeup, and so forth.[108] In August 1931 he had even appointed his own "specialist for Chamber affairs," who was to carry out organizational and tactical preparation for the election.[109] The previous practice of regarding the Chambers of Agriculture as unpolitical or suprapolitical institutions was rigorously countermanded by Darré: "We want to make all elections to Chambers of Agriculture into political campaigns in order to get these fighting weapons of agriculture into our hands."[110]

To be sure, certain difficulties arose in August and September, when various provincial branches of the Rural League wanted to present merged slates of candidates, as they had done in previous elections.[111] Certain *Gauleiter* apparently supported this wish.[112] Darré, who had obtained in advance the advice of various experts,[113] rejected such slates on behalf of the entire aA. He sensed an attempt to absorb his party; in spite of official acknowledgment of the RLB as an organization of the agrarian sector and despite the call to all NSDAP farmers to join the League, he ordered the NSDAP to put up its own lists of candidates. This circumvented the danger that the relative voter strength of the two factions might be concealed by means of joint slates. In the approaching *Landtag* elections in Prussia, it could be of decisive significance for undecided voters if the NSDAP recorded a spectacular success—as Darré believed it would—in the elections to the Chambers of Agriculture.[114] However, the primary motive for Darré's decision was "that, owing to the results of elections to the Chambers of Agriculture, we shall no longer be satisfied with a camouflaged neutrality on the part of the Rural League, but shall instead lay claim, based on the proportion of rural votes, to a share of influence over the RLB—a claim we shall then ruthlessly make good on."[115]

National Socialist agitation in rural areas in September and October 1931 was directed against alleged mismanagement and corruption in the Chambers of Agriculture.[116] Darré instructed his functionaries to keep an eye out for Chamber officials who could be useful in uncovering irregularities.[117] According to the instructions, information concerning per diem and expense account payments to Chamber members would be welcomed as valuable propaganda material. Darré himself made use of his experiences as an employee of the Königsberg Chamber of Agriculture in 1928–1929 and of written evidence he had collected there to launch a large-scale campaign against representatives of that Chamber.[118] He was relentless in goading on those within the aA as well: playing on his officials' ambition, he allowed them to hope for personal advancement as a reward for success; in other cases, he resorted to open threats.[119]

On December 3, 1931, the National Socialist rural publication (*Landpost*) could announce a significant success for the aA in eleven Prussian provinces: the NSDAP had obtained a considerable proportion of seats in each Chamber.[120] Three days earlier, Dr. Hans Erich Winter, Darré's advisor for Chamber affairs, had published an article in the *Völkischer Beobachter* on the necessary consequences of the already completed Prussian Chamber elections. But even before that, on December 8, the National Leadership of the RLB had met in Berlin to discuss the NSDAP's demand—now an ultimatum—for Nazi participation in the leadership of that organization.

The latter development was the outgrowth of a discussion between Darré and Director Arno Kriegsheim of the RLB at the beginning of November 1931. Darré had assured Kriegsheim that the NSDAP would keep the agreement made with Hugenberg in Bad Harzburg and that it was still willing to acknowledge the RLB as an occupational organization.[121] However, Darré had added, he was compelled to point out that of the two right-wing parties of the national opposition only the DNVP was represented in the RLB. Since the CNBLP had lost almost all its importance, this meant that the DNVP enjoyed a monopolistic position in the largest organization of the agricultural sector, the RLB. Yet those election results for the Prussian Chambers of Agriculture which had become known up to that point showed "that far more than half the members of the RLB belonged to the NSDAP." To be sure, Kriegsheim objected that the leadership of the branches of the Rural League could not adapt so quickly to the rapidly changing mood of the rural population. Darré played openly on the power of the aA, however, threatening an organized exodus of members from the branches of the Rural League: "The *Reichsleitung* does not feel capable of preventing the rebellious farmers from deserting or destroying those Rural League organizations which do not grant them the desired influence in leadership circles."[122] The chief of the aA of the NSDAP indicated to his partner in the discussion that a rejection of his demands for representation in the leadership of the RLB would force the NSDAP leadership to develop its own agricultural organization.[123] At the close of the discussion, Darré brought up the subject of the revolutionary mood among the farmers. He suggested to Kriegsheim that the leadership of the RLB be divided on a basis of parity between the DNVP and the NSDAP. Kriegsheim assured him that as a preliminary step along this path he would in the near future propose the establishment of an additional presidency in the RLB for the NSDAP.

Darré informed his various *Gaufachberater* of this discussion without delay, making it known that in the meantime the Executive President, Count Kalckreuth, had indicated his basic approval of a restructuring of the previous RLB leadership.[123a] Darré then directed his functionaries to take measures aimed at mobilizing support for the Nazi demands within the provincial branches of the RLB.[124]

Accordingly, at the aforementioned meeting of the *Bundesvorstand* (Federal Directorate) of the RLB on December 8, 1931, in which Hitler and Darré participated on behalf of the NSDAP, it was resolved to propose to the delegates' assembly of the RLB that a fourth presidential post be created, and filled by a National Socialist.[125] On December 18, 1931, the delegates of the state and provincial branches of the RLB, at the suggestion of the RLB *Bundesvorstand,* chose Darré's deputy in the aA, Werner Willikens, to be one of the four presidents of the RLB. This development represented a noteworthy success for the aA in its first year of work. In three ways it greatly strengthened the position of Darré and his party in the approaching election year of 1932. First, the RLB was now neutralized as a potential opponent of the NSDAP, so that the farmers could no longer be mobilized against the party. Second, the NSDAP was now officially recognized as a "farmers' party" by the country's largest rural organization.[126] Finally, the NSDAP was now in a position to exert direct influence on RLB policy.

Realization of this last goal required a continuation, with the same intensity as before, of Nazi efforts to infiltrate the lower levels of the RLB.[127] By placing a National Socialist in the RLB praesidium, Darré had succeeded in "setting an example for the state and provincial

Rural Leagues."[128] Now, with the protection afforded by this beach-head at the top, the immediate task was to push further with the previous tactic of storming the RLB bastion from below. Pointing, by way of encouragement, to the altered power relationships among the political parties in the countryside and to the successful election of Willikens to the national leadership, Darré instructed his co-workers to press for the election of new officers in the lower units of the RLB.[129]

V

The goal of aA activity in 1932 was not only the infiltration previously discussed; there were a number of election campaigns to be fought during that year. To be sure, as Darré pointed out in retrospect,[130] the RLB could no longer "attack the NSDAP from the rear at the time of the elections." Instead, its drawing power was useful in attracting voters to the NSDAP.

After the election of Werner Willikens to the RLB praesidium, the largest organization of the agricultural sector, under the leadership of Count Kalckreuth, turned increasingly away from the DNVP and toward the NSDAP. The *Völkischer Beobachter* reported on January 9, 1932, that the Executive President of the RLB, Kalckreuth, had made some serious accusations against Hindenburg. Kalckreuth accused the *Reichspräsident* of an indecisiveness which deprived Germany of a government with "the will and the strength to take into its own hands the fate of the German people, rather than regarding the grave consequences of its own sins of omission as the inescapable decree of fate."

If it was not already clear in this statement, the progressive radicalization of the RLB was especially evident during the presidential election campaigns of March and April 1932. Although various provincial and county Rural League branches had endorsed Hindenburg or Düsterberg [the candidate of the DNVP],[131] the RLB rejected Hindenburg, who was an honorary member, as the candidate of the current "system," "independently of the national opposition's resolution of the candidacy question."[132] After the first round of balloting, the RLB national leadership congratulated Hitler on his success and encouraged him "to continue our battle with determination all the way to the final victory."[133]

In the meantime Darré did all he could to obtain a further positive endorsement for Hitler at a meeting of the *Bundesvorstand* of the RLB planned for March 22. He mobilized his functionaries to attend this meeting in full force "to support our party comrade Willikens," recommending that county branches of the Rural League exert sufficient pressure on uncooperative provincial branches so that the latter would present no obstacles to an endorsement of Hitler by the RLB.[134] The action was a complete success. In the second round of presidential balloting, the RLB openly supported Hitler.[135] Although Hitler's bid was again unsuccessful, Darré thanked the RLB for its help in the campaign and gave assurances that the organization was "no longer an opponent, but our friend, thanks to the wise leadership of Count Kalckreuth."[136]

In most provincial branches of the Rural League, just as in the RLB central office, those members who were active National Socialists were decisive in the adoption of a radicalized political course toward the last cabinets of the old "system." After the concessions granted by Chancellor Franz von Papen to the NSDAP—including suspension of the ban on the SA—Darré advised his aA "to avoid" for the time being "harassment of the Papen cabinet."[137] Direct attacks on the Papen cabinet on the part of the NSDAP began only in mid-August, after Hitler had persisted in his claim to "unlimited power" despite all of Papen's and Schleicher's plans for taming the Nazis by giving them a share of authority.[138] The target of the large-scale, centrally-directed propaganda campaign of the aA was Papen's Minister of Agriculture, Baron Magnus von Braun.[139] In attempting to represent the interests of agricultural processors in the question of import quotas, Braun was fighting a losing battle against industrial, commercial, and trade-union pressure groups.[140] Although the farmers' organizations loosely united in the "Green Front" had up to then tolerated the Papen cabinet, they now joined the chorus of dissatisfaction led by the National Socialists.[141] In unison with the NSDAP, they now charged in their telegrams and resolutions that the government was deliberately delaying import quota negotiations.[142]

When General von Schleicher replaced Papen in early December 1932, conflicts in the NSDAP[143] brought a brief pause in Nazi attacks on the government. But they were soon resumed with full intensity. Agricultural organizations led by National Socialists protested in numerous telegrams intended to make known "how the entire nation judges the actions of Schleicher's cabinet."[144] The Chancellor was criticized for a "gap-ridden," "inorganic" agrarian program. "Deeds—not words!" were demanded; a further decline in the price of butter was attributed to the "inactivity" of the government. Only the assumption of power by Hitler could save the situation. "The National Socialist rural population has recognized that genuine relief can come neither from Schleicher's cabinet nor from another cabinet with the same basic outlook."[145] The fact that the government was severely crippled by the conflict between export interests, represented by Economic Minister Warmbold, and agricultural interests, represented by Baron von Braun,[146] provided National Socialist agitators with a splendid argument in support of their call for a radical upheaval.

At this point even agricultural organizations not previously the target of Nazi infiltration joined in the NSDAP's ceaselessly repeated demand for the resignation of the "incompetent" Schleicher cabinet. All of German agriculture, within which a ruinous struggle was being waged among proponents of different interests,[147] seemed to be united under the direct and indirect leadership of Darré's aA against the last spokesmen of the Weimar Republic.

In 1932, despite Baron von Braun's attempts "to help the previously neglected small-scale processing interests,"[148] there were numerous complaints among farm groups, especially in northwest Germany, that the large estate owners east of the Elbe were given preferential treatment in official agrarian policy.[149] But it was not only agriculture which was divided by internal quarrels in the pursuit of divergent interests; entrepreneurs, trade unions, skilled craftsmen, farmers, and large-scale agricultural producers—in brief, every branch of the economy—expected aid and relief for its material need from the state. Since Parliament was largely eliminated from the power struggle, the Office of the Chancellor became the forum for the struggles and disputes among the various pressure groups.[150] The organizations of the individual segments of the economy "regretted having to state" that their "objective suggestions and requests" had in no way been "given a hearing" by the government. They even urged the government to suppress their economic competitors with force.[151] With no sense of responsibility for constitutional order and the good of the state, the organization of each economic sector sought its own advancement, almost invariably invoking "responsibility toward the entirety of the people on the part of the national government."[152] Every branch of the economy sought to save for itself what could still be rescued, naturally at the cost of some other segment.[153] Heinz Haushofer's analysis of the attitude of agriculture applies with equal validity to all sectors of the economy: "German agriculture assessed attitudes toward its vital concerns largely as a simple friend-enemy problem; the individual farmer regarded the necessity of survival in terms of the formula 'you or I.'"[154]

The din of the all-encompassing strife drowned out those few voices calling for moderation and restraint in demands. In 1932 Hans Schlange-Schöningen pleaded with the agricultural organizations: "It is not right to preach incessantly to the farmer (*Landwirt*) that he is constantly threatened by ill will on the part of the other economic sectors, that they are all conspiring against him."[155] Schlange-Schöningen observed that freedom from state paternalism was a demand irreconcilable with that for "willingness on the part of the state—invoked as its sacred duty and obligation—to answer with the reserves of the nation any call for aid whatsoever."[156] These words were as ineffectual as Schlange-Schöningen's expressions of his fear that the one-sided politics of the agricultural pressure groups had led to the deplorable isolation of this sector: "If, instead of unrealistically mixing day-to-day politics with long-term policy planning, there had been some undertaking of practical efforts! If only attention had been paid to the badly neglected commercial aspect of agriculture! If only there had been more detailed work on market regulation! . . ."[157]

These regrets were already too late. By the end of 1932 there was a general clamor for a "strong statesman" who would provide leadership by decisively intervening and settling the seemingly irresolvable conflicts between the various branches of the economy, which had by then reached the cabinet level.[158]

The government, confronted with the wishes, demands, and mutual struggles of the pressure groups in the agricultural sphere, seems to have fallen victim to feelings of helplessness and resignation.[159] "There are no further grounds for state measures with regard to agriculture. There is now no possibility of helping agriculture through state aid—it must be left to itself; we shall see what develops in a few years, perhaps after further catastrophes and painful losses."[160]

It is understandable that the agricultural organizations should not have been appeased by such an attitude. They were all united in demanding the recall of Schleicher's cabinet, and in the forefront of the agitation for Hitler as his replacement marched the RLB, spurred on by those of its members who were National Socialists and part of Darré's aA. The dismissal of the last Chancellor of the Weimar period, even more obviously than the downfall of the Brüning government, can in large measure be attributed to the political influence of the RLB under Count Kalckreuth's leadership. Once again government plans for placing settlers on the East Elbian estates summoned their owners to the battle against "agrarian Bolshevism."[161] A threatened parliamentary investigation of the scandals arising from the program for aid to the East must also have been unpleasant for many of the large estate owners. Thus the interests of large-scale agriculture and the intentions of the National Socialist members of the RLB brought them together in a joint action against the Schleicher government. On January 11, 1933, a meeting of the Directorate of the RLB issued a resolution reminiscent, in its demagogic form, of the press jargon of the NSDAP.[162] On that day representatives of the government and of the RLB had conferred in Hindenburg's presence and the President had clearly taken the side of his friends, the large estate owners. Schleicher sought to save his position by brusquely terminating relations between the government and the RLB.[163] The result was a further move on Hindenburg's part toward dissociating himself from his Chancellor.[164] The dissension between the RLB and General von Schleicher was significant in opening the door to Hitler's achieving the Chancellorship.

Although Darré by no means held completely aloof from these developments,[165] he was forced to restrain his ambition to become Agricultural Minister in order to facilitate Hitler's legal acquisition of power.[166] When the "government of national concentration" was formed under Hitler's leadership on January 30, 1933, there was no way to avoid giving most of the ministries to non-Nazis. For Darré, this meant conceding the office he had sought to the DNVP leader Alfred Hugenberg, who was also appointed Minister of Economics. But by capitalizing on the mounting "national revolution" and by effecting a complete subordination of the various agricultural organizations to the NSDAP, Darré finally succeeded in routing his opponent from the DNVP. On June 30, 1933, R. Walther Darré, as National Farmers' Leader (*Reichsbauernführer*), took over the Ministry for Food and Agriculture.

VI

Although the NSDAP began its activity in the agricultural sphere relatively late, during the decisive years 1930–1933 it achieved especially great successes in that sector. The activization of the National Socialist agrarian policy was mainly the work of Darré. As director of the newly-created Department of Agricultural Affairs in the *Reichsleitung* of the NSDAP, he was able to develop the party's own farm organization and in addition, through his cadre of functionaries, to exert effective influence on German politics. By means of a permanent propaganda campaign, the aA of the NSDAP was able to weaken considerably the prestige and authority of the Weimar State among the rural population. The aA was an instrument of agitation and campaign propaganda, a system of communications for the NSDAP extending throughout the Reich, and an organization through which Hitler was able to bring the agricultural organizations into line. As such, it chalked up considerable successes which contributed not a little to the National Socialists' acquisition of power.

Prior to the September elections of 1930, Darré's calculations were largely determined by the overall tactics of exploiting dissatisfaction and unrest in rural areas to gain new voters for the NSDAP. In addition, he wanted to augment the striking power of the party in anticipation of confrontations of a revolutionary, power-political variety. But this latter consideration was consigned to the background after the September 1930 elections brought the Nazis gains that were greater in predominantly rural regions than in the cities. The watchword now was infiltration, not destruction, of the established organizational structure of agriculture.

The existing organizations representing the agrarian sector in Germany were in no position to adapt to the shifting economic and political conditions of the last phase of the Weimar Republic. That they were torn by disunity and dissension was bad enough. But the door was thrown open to the Nazis by the largest and most influential organization of all, the RLB, which continued in the well-worn paths of intrigueridden opposition politics, overestimating its own strength and holding fast to traditional economic ideas and to inherited organizational forms. Once the organization had been allowed to fall under increasing political influence, it was not easy to counter the argument that it would violate its statutory neutrality in party politics unless it allowed the NSDAP, like other parties, to be represented in its councils. Against the determined will to power and the vigorous combat methods of the Nazis, the leading spokesmen of the farmers were armed only with ill-founded self-confidence, political naïveté, and illusionary opportunism.[167] In addition, the RLB was to a certain extent ideologically susceptible to the tenets of Nazi propaganda. Aspirations to economic autarky and glorification of the *Bauerntum*—typical of Darré's "blood and soil ideology"—had for a long time been goals pursued politically by the RLB and its adherents.

By the end of 1932, when the agony of the Weimar State was at its acute stage, the aA of the NSDAP had achieved an effectiveness which made possible its active intervention in political developments of decisive importance. The attitude of the agricultural organizations toward the Papen and Schleicher governments was in large measure determined by the National Socialists. Their call for a "strong statesman" found ears whose attentiveness was increased by the government's obvious inability to quiet the tumultuous strife of pressure groups seeking state subsidies and aid. The Schleicher cabinet's loss of the last remnant of Hindenburg's confidence—its only basis of support—was in no small degree the work of the RLB, which was in turn spurred on by the Nazis.

NOTES

1. Erwin Topf, *Die Grüne Front. Der Kampf um den deutschen Acker* (Berlin, 1933), p. 41.

2. For example, in the Reichstag elections of May 1928, the NSDAP received a proportion of votes below its national average in the predominantly rural voting districts of East Prussia (55.7% of the work force employed in agriculture), Pomerania (50.7% in agriculture), East Hannover (42% in agriculture), and Hesse-Darmstadt (34% in agriculture). In the German Reich (30.5% of the population in agriculture) the NSDAP received 2.6% of the vote (*Statistisches Jahrbuch für das Deutsche Reich 1928*, pp. 25 and 580f.). Cf. also W. Seipels's comment: "Doubtless the Rural League leaders found an excellent propaganda weapon against us in the accusation that the National Socialists wanted to expropriate land. For the farmers' hatred of Marxism was derived not least from its attacks on private property. . . . Herein lay an enormous danger for the development of the National Socialist movement, and we had great difficulty in overcoming the mistrust which was aroused within the agrarian sector in this way." See E. Schmahl–W. Seipel, *Entwicklung der völkischen Bewegung. Die antisemitische Bauernbewegung in Hessen von der Böckelzeit bis zum Nationalsozialismus* (Giessen, n.d. [1933]), p. 158.

3. Cf. Gottfried Feder, *Das Programm der NSDAP und seine weltanschaulichen Grundlagen* (Munich, 1931), p. 4.

4. Cf. Hitler, *Mein Kampf* (Munich, 1936), p. 234: "Any idea, even the best one, becomes dangerous if taken for an end in itself when it is in reality only the means to an end."

5. From 1924 to the end of 1931 almost two and a half million acres of land were sold at auction; whereas in the two years 1926–1928, the number of forced auction sales of agricultural enterprises had risen to 4,896 (with a total arable area of 182,500 acres), the figures for the year 1931 alone are 5,765 agricultural enterprises and 441,655 acres; see H. Beyer, "Die Landvolkbewegung Schleswig-Holsteins und Niedersachsens 1928–32," *Jahrbuch der Heimatgemeinde des Kreises Eckernförde*, xv (1957), 174; *Statistisches Jahrbuch für das Deutsche Reich 1932*, pp. 376f.

6. Hitler, *Mein Kampf*, pp. 108f.

7. Cf. Rudolf Heberle, *Landbevölkerung und Nationalsozialismus. Eine soziologische Untersuchung der politischen Willensbildung in Schleswig-Holstein 1918–32* (Stuttgart, 1963); Gerhard Stoltenberg, *Politische Strömungen im schleswig-holsteinischen Landvolk* (Düsseldorf, 1962).

8. Cf. *NS-Jahrbuch 1929*, p. 144; *Völkischer Beobachter* (Reichsausgabe), December 22–23, 1932, and December 25–27, 1932.

9. The program, which appeared in all appropriate publishing organs of the party, is extant in pamphlet form in the Bundesarchiv (NS 26/962), and in printed form in Günther Franz, *Quellen zur Geschichte des Bauernstandes in der Neuzeit* (Darmstadt, 1963), p. 535.

10. See Darré's writings: *Das Bauerntum als Lebensquell der Nordischen Rasse* (Munich, 1929); *Erkenntnisse und Werden, Aufsätze aus der Zeit vor der Machtergreifung*, ed. Marie-Adelheid Princess Reuss zur Lippe (Goslar, 1940); *Neuadel aus Blut und Boden* (Munich, 1930).

10a. In the results of Reichstag elections from 1928 to 1933, comparison of six predominantly rural voting districts (East Prussia, Pomerania, Schleswig-Holstein, East Hannover, Hesse-Darmstadt, and the Palatinate) with six predominantly urban districts (Berlin, Westphalia-South, Düsseldorf-East, Chemnitz-Zwickau, Merseburg, and Hamburg) shows the following year-by-year changes in the proportion of the total vote received by the NSDAP:

PROPORTION OF TOTAL VOTE RECEIVED BY THE NSDAP

	1928	1930	1932(I)	1932(II)	1933
Predominantly Rural	2.8%	22.6%	47.1%	42.4%	52.4%
Predominantly Urban	2.4%	17.9%	34.5%	29.9%	39.6%

In 1928, the difference between the percentage of total vote received in the rural areas and in the urban areas is scarcely significant; in 1930 Hitler's party won a proportion of the votes in the rural districts higher by 4.7% than in the urban districts. The success of the NSDAP was greater in the rural than in the urban districts by 12.6% of the total vote in July 1932, and by 12.8% of the total vote in 1933; cf. *Statistisches Jahrbuch für das Deutsche Reich 1931*, pp. 546f; *1932*, pp. 542f.; *1933*, pp. 540f.; *Statistik des Deutschen Reiches*, 434 (Berlin, 1935), 76.

11. Secret directives by Kenstler dated June 1, 1929, and September 22, 1929 (Stadtarchiv, Goslar, Nachlass Darré, no. 437 [hereafter cited as St.A.Goslar, ND No. . . .]).

12. Kenstler in a letter to Darré of February 10, 1930 (St.A.Goslar, ND No. 94).

13. Darré in a letter to Kenstler dated March 2, 1930 (*ibid.*).

14. Darré in a letter to his wife Alma dated March 27, 1930, in Nachlass A. Bauer, Institut für Zeitgeschichte, Munich (hereafter cited as IfZ).

15. Darré in a letter to Lehmann dated July 19, 1930 (St.A.Goslar, ND No. 437).

16. Nuremberg Documents, Case XI, Prosecution Document Book 101, NG-448, Exh. 999 (IfZ); and Bundesarchiv, Koblenz (hereafter cited as BA-Koblenz), Nachlass Darré, AD 45.

17. Darré in a letter to Frau von Quast dated August 27, 1930 (St.A.Goslar, ND No. 85).

18. See note 16, above.

19. The concept "landwirtschaftlicher Fachberater" also appears in Darré's *Neuadel aus Blut und Boden*, p. 94.

20. Darré in a letter to Konopath dated August 27, 1930 (St.A.Goslar, ND No. 87).

21. BA-Koblenz, Nachlass Darré, AD 45; the directive is also found in *ibid.*, Sammlung Schumacher/214.

22. "Der nationalsozialistische landwirtschaftliche Fachberater" (BA-Koblenz, Sammlung Schumacher/214).

23. Darré in a directive to the aA dated November 27, 1930 (BA-Koblenz, NS 26/951).

23a. See note 22, above.

24. Cf. also Darré's comment in the directive to the aA of November 27, 1930 (BA-Koblenz, NS 26/951): "The less acquainted our opponents are with our aA and its structure, the harder it is for them to work against us."

25. *Abschnittsfachberater* (LAF) were appointed in September 1931 wherever a *Gau* was sufficiently large to be extremely heterogeneous, either in religious makeup, general outlook, or other respects (Darré's directive to the *Gaufachberater* (LGF), No. 82, September 24, 1931: St.A.Goslar, ND No. 142, sheet 134).

26. "These *Fachberater* remain organizationally subordinate to their political leader. For the agrarian policy carried on in their assigned areas, however, they are responsible not only to their political leader, but also to the agricultural *Fachberater* assigned to the next-highest political unit" (draft of a report by Darré on the aA and its level of development by the end of 1930, dated January 9, 1931, St.A.Goslar, ND No. 148; the final version of the report is in BA-Koblenz, Sammlung Schumacher/214).

27. Darré knew Arauner from their student days in Giessen (cf. Arauner's letter to Darré, dated March 9, 1926, St.A.Goslar, ND No. 81).

28. See note 26, above.

29. Cf. Hitler's acknowledgment of his services in a speech given at the first National Farmers' Convention in Weimar, *Völkischer Beobachter* (Reichsausgabe), February 11, 1931; cf. also Edgar von Schmidt-Pauli, *Die Männer um Hitler* (Berlin, 1932), p. 148: "The organization of this relatively young department (agriculture) is nothing short of exemplary. Its director, one of the most gifted personalities in the group surrounding Hitler."

30. The double accountability of the *Fachberater* caused these difficulties. It was hard for Darré to hold in check the influence which the political leaders of the NSDAP wished to exercise over their *Fachberater*. Overlapping of jurisdictions and competencies, political power struggles, and personal animosities between the aA and the Political Organization were the result. (Cf. Darré's and G. Strasser's directive to the *Gauleiter*, November 3, 1931, St.A.Goslar, ND No. 142; cf. also Darré's directive to the *Gaufachberater*, June 6, 1932, *ibid.*, No. 145; also Darré's special directive to the *Gaufachberater*, March 16, 1932, *ibid.*)

31. Darré in a letter to Hierl dated January 2, 1931 (St.A.Goslar, ND No. 148).

32. Cf. the report in the *Völkischer Beobachter* (Reichsausgabe), February 11, 1931.

33. See Darré's notes for the organizing of the first aA Convention in Weimar (St.A.Goslar, ND No. 148); cf. also Darré's directive to the *Gaufachberater*, December 13, 1930 (BA-Koblenz, NS 26/951).

34. Darré's directive to the *Gaufachberater*, No. 87, October 9, 1931 (St.A. Goslar, ND No. 142); cf. also H. Reischle, *Reichsbauernführer Darré* (Berlin, 1935), p. 49.

35. See, for example, Darré's directives to the aA dated November 6, December 11, and December 22, 1930 (BA-Koblenz, NS 26/951).

36. See Darré's directives dated January 18 and 19, 1932 (St.A.Goslar, ND No. 145).

37. Darré's directive to the *Gaufachberater*, No. 94, dated October 13, 1931 (*ibid.*, No. 142).

38. See, for example, the replacement of the *Gaufachberater* for Wurttemberg, announced by Darré in a directive on April 4, 1932 (St.A.Goslar, ND No. 145) and the dismissal of the *Gaufachberater* and *Landeskammerpräsident*, Freiherr von Buttlar, in East Prussia. The latter was relieved of all his offices for failing to give Darré adequate support in his suit against the former *Kammerpräsident*, Dr. Brandes (Darré's directive to the *Gaufachberater*, No. 51, November 14, 1932, *ibid.*; see in this regard also *NS-Landpost*, No. 50, December 8, 1932).

39. Darré's directive to the *Gaufachberater*, December 29, 1930 (BA-Koblenz, NS 26/951) and No. 82 of September 24, 1931 (St.A.Goslar, ND No. 142).

40. Darré's directive to the *Gaufachberater*, No. 32, August 6, 1932 (*ibid.*, No. 145).

41. Darré's directive to the aA, dated November 26, 1930 (BA-Koblenz, NS 26/951).

42. Darré's directive to the *Gaufachberater*, No. 65, July 23, 1931 (St.A. Goslar, ND No. 142).

43. Darré's directive to the *Gaufachberater*, No. 102, November 18, 1931 (*ibid.*).

44. See, for example, Darré's directive to the aA of December 13, 1930 (BA-Koblenz, NS 26/951).

45. See, for example: F. Hildebrandt, *Nationalsozialismus und Landarbeiterschaft*, *NS-Bibliothek*, Heft 17 (Munich, 1931); H. Schneider, *Unser täglich Brot. Lebensfragen der deutschen Landwirtschaft*, *ibid.*, Heft 19 (Munich, 1930); W. Willikens, *Nationalsozialistische Agrarpolitik* (Munich, 1931); H. Backe, *Deutscher Bauer erwache. Die Agrarkrise, ihre Ursachen und Folgerungen* (Munich, 1931); R. W. Darré, *Landvolk in Not. Wer hilft?—Adolf Hitler* (Munich, 1932).

46. Report on the activity of the Agricultural Department of the NSDAP in the *Gau* of Saxony for the period January 1, 1932 to January 1, 1933 (St.A. Goslar, ND No. 140).

47. Cf. the corresponding decree issued by Hitler for the reorganization of the NSDAP in the *Völkischer Beobachter*, December 14, 1932; cf. also Darré's directive to the *Gaufachberater*, No. 54, December 19, 1932 (St.A.Goslar, ND No. 145).

48. Schmahl-Seipel, *Entwicklung*, pp. 156f., gives quite a graphic portrayal of the events at an assembly of farmers.

49. Cf. the first supplemental page devoted to agriculture, "Im Kampf um Blut und Boden," *Völkischer Beobachter*, April 28, 1931.

50. Press report on a talk given by Darré on August 25, 1931, in Mecklenburg (Presse-Archiv of the RLB, East Berlin, 492 L/3, sheet 50).

51. Darré's directive to the aA, No. 46, October 14, 1932 (St.A.Goslar, ND No. 145).

52. Darré's directive to the *Gaufachberater*, July 22, 1931 (*ibid.*, No. 142).

53. Rudolf Hess in the *Völkischer Beobachter*, No. 60, July 31, 1921.

54. Cf. Darré's directive to his co-workers in the aA, dated December 1, 1932 (St.A.Goslar, ND No. 145) : "The National Socialist struggle for the support of the farmers can . . . only then be won, if it is made clear to the farmers that their survival in Germany is in the last analysis not an economic, but a philosophical question and that precisely therein lies the fundamental philosophical difference (*weltanschauliche*) between National Socialism and all other parties."

55. For example, an article in the CNBLP party press entitled "Politik mit zwei Gesichtern" pointed out that the National Socialists polemicized in the cities against an increase in food prices and attacked the government for promoting an agrarian policy, while in rural villages they demanded the most radical of measures to aid the farmers, measures which of course could be implemented only at the expense of the city-dwellers (*Löwenberger Anzeiger*, May 31, 1931, in Presse-Archiv of the RLB, No. 492 L/2, sheet 189).

56. The CNBLP was defamed by the NSDAP as "Jewish-liberal" and the "lackey of red depravity" (see *Völkischer Beobachter*, Reichsausgabe, December 6/7, 1931, and *NS-Landpost*, No. 14, December 6, 1931). In the agitational activity which ensued, no one shied away from personal attacks, slander, and even open threats: "Your functionaries are to be made aware once and for all," wrote Darré to the CNBLP, "that their previous behavior has guaranteed that in the likely event of a change of government, they will have scanty prospects of advancement in the Third Reich" (*Der Thüringische Landbund*, No. 95, November 28, 1931, in Presse-Archiv of the RLB, No. 492 L/3, sheet 107).

57. *Der Thüringische Landbund*, January 14, 1931 (*ibid.*, No. 492 L/2, sheet 125).

58. The explanation given by the RLB on February 2, 1931, is printed in Franz, *Quellen*, pp. 544f.; cf. also Karl Dietrich Bracher, *Auflösung der Weimarer Republik* (Villingen, 1960), p. 409; cf. also *Völkischer Beobachter* (Reichsausgabe), February 10, 1931, and *Frankfurter Zeitung*, No. 87, February 2, 1931.

59. On August 8, 1931, an interview of RLB Director von Sybel by Darré's co-worker, H. Dassler, was published in the Berlin Nazi tabloid, *Der Angriff*, under the headline: "Wir haben kein Vertrauen mehr zu Schiele und Brüning" (Presse-Archiv of the RLB, No. 492 L/3, sheet 38).

60. Darré's directive to the aA, September 23, 1931 (St.A.Goslar, ND No. 142). Wilmowsky, a brother-in-law of Gustav Krupp, had resigned as executive president of the RLB after differences between the *Reichsverband der deutschen Industrie* (National Association of German Industry) and the RLB over Schiele's policy on butter tariffs. He had taken over the office after Schiele's appointment as Agricultural Minister in March 1930. Wilmowsky's successor was Count Kalckreuth (cf. Topf, *Grüne Front*, pp. 128ff.).

61. See the letter written by RLB Director v. Sybel to Darré, October 20, 1931 (St.A.Goslar, ND No. 87); cf. also Darré's special directive, July 2, 1931 (*ibid.*, No. 142).

62. Cf. Hans Schlange-Schöningen, *Am Tage danach* (Hamburg, 1946), pp. 70ff.; Werner Conze, "Zum Sturz Brünings," *Vierteljahrshefte für Zeitgeschichte*, I (1953), 261–288; Bracher, *Auflösung*, pp. 481ff.; Heinrich Brüning, "Ein Brief," *Deutsche Rundschau*, LXX (1947), 7–22; arguing on the opposing side are: Henning von Borcke-Stargordt, *Der ostdeutsche Landbau zwischen*

Fortschritt, Krise und Politik (Würzburg, 1957); Heinrich Muth, "Zum Sturz Brünings. Der Agrarpolitische Hintergrund," *Geschichte in Wissenschaft und Unterricht,* XII (1965), 739ff.

63. See in this regard Wilhelm Peters, *Die landwirtschaftliche Berufsvertretung* (Berlin, 1932), p. 62.

64. The RLB had 1.7 million members, the *Vereinigung der deutschen Bauernvereine,* 560,000, and the *Deutsche Bauernschaft,* 60,000. In addition there were *Freie Bauernschaften* (40,000) and the Communist *Reichsbauernbund* (10,000). Cf. H. Neumann, *Der Landwirt auf dem Wege zum Erfolg* (Berlin, 1928), p. 89; Fritz Reichardt, *Andreas Hermes* (Neuwied, 1953), p. 112.

65. Especially in Schleswig-Holstein, Rhine Province, and Silesia, it was more evident than in Berlin that the farmers of the same region were divided into different interest groups which often worked against one another. Cf. Topf, *Grüne Front,* p. 45.

66. See Ferdinand Jacobs, *Von Schorlemer zur Grünen Front. Zur Abwertung des berufsständischen und politischen Denkens* (Düsseldorf, 1957), pp. 41ff. and 65f.; Hans Kretschmar, *Deutsche Agrarprogramme der Nachkriegszeit. Die agrarpolitischen Forderungen der landwirtschaftlichen Berufsverbände* (Berlin, 1933), pp. 64ff.; Reichardt, *Hermes,* pp. 119ff.; Bracher, *Auflösung,* pp. 314ff.; Topf, *Grüne Front,* p. 125.

67. Jacobs, *Von Schorlemer,* p. 66.

68. The successes of the Green Front included tariff increases and elimination of commercial treaties which had frozen some tariffs, mandatory use of domestic grain, setting price guidelines for rye, establishment of a corn monopoly, and, finally, elimination of parliamentary participation in the setting of tariff rates. See Reichardt, *Hermes,* pp. 120ff.

69. Cf. Kretschmar, *Agrarprogramme,* p. 84.

70. *Der Bauer im Kampf gegen den Landbund. Bauernarbeit in Nordwestdeutschland,* published by the Wirtschaftsverband bäuerlicher Veredelungsarbeit (Bremen, n.d. [1930]).

71. *Ibid.,* p. 38.

72. See, for example, the RLB's open admission that it sought "a reorganization of the present system from top to bottom." Quoted from directive, "Landwirtschaft und Nationalsozialismus," Dir. K.Tgb. No.Parl.2240, Lfd. No. 40 (August 6, 1930), in Presse-Archiv of the RLB, No. 492 L.

73. For these and other letters and petitions by agricultural organizations to the Office of the Chancellor: BA-Koblenz, R 43 I/1301.

74. In the Reichstag elections of 1928, the following parties put up their own candidates on a regional basis: the CNBLP, the RLB, the *Deutsch-Hannoversche Partei, Württembergische Bauern- und Weingärtnerbund,* and the *Sächsisches Landvolk.*

75. See Jan Bargenhusen, "Grüner Tisch und Grünes Feld," *Die Weltbühne,* XXVII (January 13, 1931), 46ff.; see also Stoltenberg, *Strömungen,* p. 167.

76. Peters, *Berufsvertretung.* The investigation was conducted under the auspices of a study commission composed of influential figures in agrarian affairs. Its goal was a restructuring of both official occupational organs (chambers of agriculture) and nonofficial associations. On the need for rural cooperatives, see

Max Sering, *Deutsche Agrarpolitik auf geschichtlicher und landeskundlicher Grundlage* (Leipzig, 1934), pp. 99ff.

77. Peters, *Berufsvertretung*, pp. 68f.

78. *Ibid.*, p. 69.

79. Quoted from Ernst von Salomon, *Der Fragebogen* (Hamburg, 1951), p. 271.

80. Darré, "Auf den Weg," editorial in *NS-Landpost*, No. 1, September 1931.

81. Darré in a speech in October 1932: "We have such an abundance of departments which confuse matters instead of clarifying them. . . . We must finance all kinds of institutes, three of them solely for research into business conditions . . ." (quoted from: *Wir haben's gewagt! Weg und Wollen der Führer in Deutschland und Italien*, ed. R. O. Stahn and F. Bojano [Stuttgart, 1934], pp. 56f.).

82. Topf, *Grüne Front*, p. 9.

83. Darré's directive No. 81, September 24, 1931 (St.A.Goslar, ND No. 142), in which excerpts from the memorandum were passed on to the *Gaufachberater*. For some measures adopted by the provincial branches of the RLB against its national headquarters (among other things, withholding locally collected dues), see Bargenhusen, "Grüner Tisch," p. 48.

84. On October 20, 1931, Sybel wrote to Darré that he must postpone, due to "certain considerations," the date on which he was to join the NSDAP officially. After July 1932, however, Sybel was an NSDAP delegate to the Reichstag (*NS-Jahrbuch 1933*, p. 187).

85. Nuremberg Documents, Case XI, Prosecution Document Book 101, NG-448, Exh. 999 (IfZ), pp. 23f.

86. Darré's directive to the aA, November 20, 1930 (BA-Koblenz, NS 26/951).

87. Darré's directive to the *Gaufachberater*, December 16, 1930 (*ibid.*).

88. *Ibid.* The aA was unsuccessful in intervening when a new RLB president was elected: in December 1930, Heinrich Lind of the CNBLP succeeded Karl Hepp, whose views he shared. (See also Darré's letter to the *Gaufachberater*, November 22, 1930, *ibid.*)

89. Schmahl-Seipel, *Entwicklung*, pp. 149f.

90. *Niedersachsen-Stürmer*, No. 46, November 14, 1930: "Is not the Rural League, if it understands its task correctly, obligated to liberate the united forces, mobilizing them into a powerful movement which draws everyone to it? It is not doing this. The German farmer in the East and the North has been aroused . . . but the individual organizations of the Rural League are still asleep. They are proud and do not want to subordinate themselves to Adolf Hitler" (Presse-Archiv of the RLB, No. 492 L/2, sheet 106).

91. Schmahl-Seipel, *Entwicklung*, p. 151.

92. *Ibid.*, p. 152.

93. In response to the request on March 1, 1930, of a deputy, Dr. Föhr (Landtags-Drucksache No. 85), a government spokesman read in the Baden Landtag a declaration making public large sections of directives written by Plesch, the *Gaufachberater* of Baden. These were letters which had been confiscated in connection with the Boxheim Documents affair. Quoted from a series of articles in the *Badische Bauernzeitung*, May 15, 1932, and following (Presse-

Archiv of the RLB, 45 N/2, sheets 121–127). See also *Verhandlungen des Badenischen Landtages,* 18. Session, April 26, 1932.

94. Cf. the corresponding reference in Darré's letter to the *Gaufachberater,* dated December 16, 1930 (BA-Koblenz, NS 26/951).

95. Even indications from the Thuringian branch of the RLB of its desperate struggle for existence, necessitated by its identification with the CNBLP, caused little disturbance in RLB circles: "The struggle [of the NSDAP against the Rural League] is not being waged against the League's alleged neutrality in party politics, but for precisely the opposite reason: the National Socialists want to eliminate political neutrality within the Rural League, so they can make it their own party organization" (*Der Thüringer Landbund,* January 1932, Presse-Archiv of the RLB, No. 45 N/2, sheet 87).

96. *Der Thüringer Landbund,* June 23, 1931 (*ibid.,* No. 492 L/2, sheet 198).

97. *NS-Landpost,* No. 6, October 11, 1931. A letter written by Darré and Hierl to the branches of the Rural League and agricultural chambers on July 30, 1931, had already been published in the *NS-Landpost,* No. 3, September 20, 1931. In it, the NSDAP had taken a stand for an ordering of the state according to occupational categories. To be sure, in December 1930, Darré had already explained to his confidants in the aA his conception of the "restructuring" mentioned there: "We need the apparatus of the Rural League as a working group to prepare for the farmers' (*Landwirte*) self-governing bodies on an occupational basis in the Third Reich. Thus we must get the Rural League firmly into the grasp of the NSDAP" (Darré's letter to the *Gaufachberater,* December 16, 1930, BA-Koblenz, NS 26/951).

98. Quoted from *Der Landbund Sachsen,* June 6, 1931 (Presse-Archiv of the RLB, No. 45 N/2, sheet 14).

99. For example, see the RLB directive, Dir.K.Tgb.Nr.Parl. 2240, Lfd. No. 40, dated August 6, 1930 (Presse-Archiv of the RLB, 492 L), in which National Socialist agitation was denounced as "destructive to the national energies of the German people." Such agitation had been directed against the RLB, the DNVP, and the Rural People's Party before the election of September 1930. "The NSDAP thus becomes unwillingly the most able handmaiden of Social Democracy. The best defense against this destructive activity is occupational solidarity." The directive also referred to the "Social Democrats' hankering for dictatorship."

100. For example, in May 1931 the Pomeranian *Gaufachberater,* W. B!oedorn, was chairman of the Cammin County Group of the Rural League and a member of the Federal Committee of the Pomeranian branch of the Rural League (Presse-Archiv of the RLB, No. 492 L/2, sheet 187; cf. also *ibid.,* sheet 171). As early as December 1930 Darré spoke before the agrarian agents of the Rural League branch in the Bitterfeld region, which had given him this opportunity to acquaint its membership with the NSDAP's amity towards the farmers (*Völkischer Beobachter,* No. 306/7, December 25, 26, and 27, 1930). On the immediate active response to Hit!er's summons in Schleswig-Ho!stein, see Heberle, *Landbevölkerung,* p. 164.

101. Special directive to the *Gaufachberater* ("Confidential!"), September 22, 1931 (St.A.Goslar, ND No. 142).

102. Darré's directive to the *Gaufachberater,* No. 58, July 1, 1931 (*ibid.*).

103. Darré's directive to the *Gaufachberater,* No. 61 ("Confidential!"), July 7, 1931 (*ibid.*).

104. Darré's directive to the *Gaufachberater*, No. 71, August 13, 1931 (*ibid.*).

105. Darré's directive to the *Gaufachberater*, No. 58, July 1, 1931 (St.A. Goslar, ND No. 142).

106. It was difficult for some *Fachberater* and especially for their political leaders to view the policy of simultaneous neutralization and infiltration of the Rural League as consistent and rational. Yet Darré was able to answer that this conception demanded action "no more and no less honest than that of our entire movement toward this state." Although the NSDAP rejected the "system," the party was obtaining for itself all available offices and ministerial posts (special directive by Darré ["Confidential!"] dated September 22, 1931, St.A. Goslar, ND No. 142).

107. Quoted from the *Badische Bauernzeitung*, June 12, 1932 (cf. note 93, above). In Munich on September 24, 1931, there was an "unofficial, non-binding talk" between representatives of the Franconian branch of the Rural League and the aA, in which the NSDAP gave Rural League representatives the following conditions for a coalition: depoliticization of the Rural League, public recognition of the NSDAP as a party which along with other corresponding parties would be recommended to the farmers by the Rural League (special directive by Darré to the *Gaufachberater*, dated September 28, 1931, St.A.Goslar, ND No. 142). Cf. also the arrangements made by Darré with the Saxon branch of the Rural League on December 9, 1930 (Darré's letter to the *Gaufachberater*, dated December 16, 1930, BA-Koblenz, NS 26/951).

108. Darré's directive to the *Gaufachberater*, No. 60, dated July 15, 1931 (St.A.Goslar, ND No. 142); cf. also the instructions which Darré gave the *Gaufachberater* in a special directive dated September 16, 1931 (*ibid.*).

109. Directive to the *Gaufachberater*, No. 69, dated August 7, 1931 (*ibid.*).

110. Special directive by Darré to the *Gaufachberater*, dated August 20, 1931 (*ibid.*).

111. Cf. a letter by Ernst Böttger, legal advisor to the Department of Agrarian Affairs, NSDAP *Reichsleitung*, to Schulz, October 26, 1931 (St.A.Goslar, ND No. 161).

112. Böttger noted the following in a memorandum written after a conference with Darré on December 5, 1931, in the Hotel Kaiserhof in Berlin: ". . . a considerable number of *Gauleiter* reported that the NSDAP was still poorly represented among farmers and that cooperation with the Rural League was urgently recommended" (St.A.Goslar, ND No. 161).

113. He was not only given advice by Dr. Winter, his research assistant (*Fachreferent*) on chamber affairs, but also obtained an opinion from his party comrade Böttger, who was an attorney employed by a Berlin court and a legal expert on administrative law; see Böttger's letters to Darré, September 21 and 22, 1931, and the latter's answer dated September 25, 1931 (St.A.Goslar, ND No. 161).

114. The NSDAP was very successful in the agricultural chamber elections in Saxony in the spring of 1931, obtaining 22 of 52 seats and the second presiding office (see *Völkischer Beobachter*, November 15/16, 1931). For this reason and because of his estimate, made with the help of his *Gaufachberater*, of popular sentiment in Prussia, Darré was counting on a clear-cut NSDAP success; see Darré's special directive to the *Gaufachberater*, dated August 20, 1931 (St.A.Goslar, ND No. 142).

115. Darré's directive to the *Gaufachberater*, No. 84, September 25, 1931 (*ibid.*).

116. See, for example, *NS-Landpost*, No. 12, November 22, 1931 ("Der grosse Skandal um die Rheinische Landwirtschaftskammer").

117. Special directive by Darré to the *Gaufachberater*, August 20, 1931 (St.A.Goslar, ND No. 142).

118. The editor of the National Socialist *Preussische Zeitung* in Königsberg told Darré on November 24, 1931, that in almost all departments of the agricultural chamber there were National Socialists on whose services he could draw (St.A.Goslar, ND No. 160). After April 10, 1931, the *NS-Landpost* regularly made new "revelations" intended to lower the prestige of the powerful members of the East Prussian agricultural chamber. A libel suit against Darré brought by Chamber President Dr. Brandes came too late to influence the election (cf. *NS-Landpost*, No. 10, November 8, 1931). See also Darré's special directive ("Confidential!"), November 20, 1931 (St.A.Goslar, ND No. 142).

119. In directive No. 84 of September 25, 1931, Darré wrote to his *Gaufachberater:* "The elections for the Prussian Chambers of Agriculture clarify even for me the problem of where the aA is accomplishing something and where it could be improved—in which *Gauen, Kreisen,* and *Bezirken*" (St.A.Goslar, ND No. 142).

120. The NSDAP's success was diminished in that according to the statutes of the chambers of agriculture only half the membership stood for reelection and in that only landowners (*Hofbesitzer*), not younger family members (*Jungbauern*), were enfranchised. Nevertheless, the aA achieved a clear breakthrough. For example, in Rhine Province, 10 of 40 newly-elected chamber members were National Socialists (*Landwirtschaftliche Zeitschrift für den Rheinprovinz*, 1931, p. 534), in East Prussia, 16 of 38 (*Berliner Börsenzeitung*, No. 592, December 22, 1931), in Oldenburg, 23 of 36 (*NS-Landpost*, No. 15, December 13, 1931), and in northern Hesse-Nassau, 13 of 30 (*ibid.*).

121. Copy of a letter written by Darré to Kriegsheim on November 6, 1931, which summarized the outcome of the discussion: Darré's directive to the *Gaufachberater*, No. 100, November 9, 1931 (St.A.Goslar, ND No. 142).

122. *Ibid.*

123. See also the memorandum by Böttger on a conference with Darré, held on December 5, 1932 (St.A.Goslar, ND No. 161). Up to then, Darré had decisively opposed such tendencies, which had become evident within the NSDAP at an early date (cf. Darré's directive to the *Gaufachberater*, November 20, 1930, BA-Koblenz, NS 26/951).

123a. See note 121, above.

124. See also Darré's special directive to the *Gaufachberater*, November 25, 1931 (St.A.Goslar, ND No. 142). In order not to offend members of the RLB delegates' assembly, Hierl, as second National Organization Leader, even halted the distribution of W. Seipel's brochure, *Landvolkpartei oder Hitler-Bewegung*, because of its sharp attacks on the Rural League; see Hierl's directive to the *Gauleiter, Bezirks- and Ortsgruppenleiter*, November 21, 1931 (St.A.Goslar, ND No. 160).

125. Darré, "Landbund und wir," *NS-Landpost*, No. 16, December 20, 1931.

126. Along with the elimination of the Rural League as a political force, the NSDAP also sought recognition and endorsement as a farmers' party. This is

evident from the text of an agreement concerning the relationship of NSDAP and Rural League in Hesse (-Darmstadt). There, the Rural League had suffered a painful defeat in the Landtag elections. The NSDAP won 26 mandates, while the Rural League lost 7. In April 1932 the following official agreement was reached: "The NSDAP acknowledges the Hessian branch of the Rural League as the occupational organization of agriculture. The Hessian branch of the Rural League renews its insistence on the principle of neutrality. It recognizes that the basic attitude of National Socialism toward the farmers, firmly founded in its agrarian program, allows energetic support of agriculture within the state" (*NS-Landpost*, No. 18, May 1, 1932). Naturally, the *Gaufachberater* Dr. Wagner and W. Seipel, who at that time joined the directorate of the Hessian branch of the Rural League, were members of the aA (cf. Schmahl-Seipel, *Entwicklung*, pp. 163ff.).

127. This was the case from January 1932 on, naturally in close cooperation with the new RLB President Willikens (see Darré's directives to the *Gaufachberater*, January 12 and March 29, 1932 [St.A.Goslar, ND No. 145]).

128. Darré's directive to the *Gaufachberater*, November 9, 1931 (*ibid.*, No. 142).

129. Darré's directive to the *Gaufachberater*, No. 110, December 19, 1931 (*ibid.*).

130. Darré's special directive, April 11, 1933 (St.A.Goslar, ND No. 140).

131. On February 29, 1932, Darré informed his *Gaufachberater* in directive No. 14 that the Thuringian, Saxon, and Anhalt branches of the Rural League had refused to publish the RLB's proclamation for the presidential election. He ordered the *Gaufachberater* to force publication of the proclamation (St.A.Goslar, ND No. 145).

132. The text of the RLB proclamation was published in *Völkischer Beobachter* (Reichsausgabe), February 19, 1932.

133. In a telegram sent by the RLB praesidium to Hitler, Kalckreuth wrote: "Congratulations and thanks for this powerful upsurge. The breakthrough of the National Socialist movement into the ranks of our opponents must be the starting point for resolute continuation of our struggle to the ultimate victory" (*NS-Landpost*, No. 12, March 20, 1932).

134. Darré's special directive to the *Gaufachberater*, March 17, 1932 (St.A. Goslar, ND No. 145).

135. Cf. *NS-Landpost*, No. 13, March 27, 1932; cf. also an entry made by Goebbels in his diary, March 15, 1932: "I telephoned Darré. The RLB has decided in our favor." See Goebbels, *Vom Kaiserhof zur Reichskanzlei* (Munich, 1934), p. 64.

136. *Landwirtschaftliches Beiblatt*, No. 6, *Völkischer Beobachter* (Reichsausgabe), May 22/23, 1932.

137. Darré's directive to the *Gaufachberater*, June 10, 1932 (St.A.Goslar, ND No. 145).

138. On Hindenburg's discussion with Hitler on August 13, 1932, see Bracher, *Auflösung*, pp. 616f.

139. In directive No. 33, September 7, 1932 (St.A.Goslar, ND No. 145), Darré called on all *Gaufachberater* to demand Braun's resignation in public resolutions. (See the text, *ibid.*, of Darré's telegram to the Minister of Agriculture, which was in the same vein.)

140. See Braun's speech before the plenary session of the Bavarian Council on Agriculture (*Landwirtschaftsrat*), September 26, 1932, *Völkischer Beobachter* (Reichsausgabe), September 29, 1932; cf. a recent treatment, Dieter Petzina, "Hauptprobleme der deutschen Wirtschaftspolitik 1932/33," *Vierteljahrshefte für Zeitgeschichte,* XV (1967), 31ff.

141. In a resolution of October 12, 1932, the RLB had endorsed the "principle of an authoritative national government independent of political parties." Papen's agrarian program had also been applauded. Delay on the part of the government in effecting the measures it had announced brought forth numerous negative statements in the rural press. See Presse-Archiv of the RLB, No. 76/38; also *Völkischer Beobachter* (Reichsausgabe), October 20 and 22, 1932.

142. See in this regard the documents of the Office of the Chancellor, BA-Koblenz, R 43 II/196.

143. See Bracher, *Auflösung,* pp. 678ff., on Strasser's resignation from all his party offices. Strasser had advocated toleration of the Schleicher cabinet by the NSDAP, but could not accept the prospect of participation in the government, with the resultant split in the NSDAP, as proposed to him by Schleicher.

144. *Der Angriff,* January 6, 1933. This issue included a compilation of protests to the government from eighteen contributors. See also the telegrams of protest in the *Völkischer Beobachter* (Süddeutsche Ausgabe), January 2 and 19, 1933.

145. Resolution of the leaders of the National Socialist *Landvolk* in East Prussia, printed in *Der Angriff,* January 2, 1933, in Presse-Archiv of the RLB, No. 76/38, sheet 102; see also H. Reischle, "Bilanz der neuen Agrarpolitik," *Völkischer Beobachter* (Süddeutsche Ausgabe), January 13, 14, 15, and 25, 1933.

146. In a letter to Schleicher, January 5, 1933, Braun accused his colleague Warmbold of failing to comply with arrangements which had been agreed upon and seeking to delay tariff ordinances in order to favor the export industry. He refused further responsibility for these "delaying tactics which have caused agriculture's position to deteriorate increasingly in recent months" (BA-Koblenz, R 43 II/192). See also Petzina, "Hauptprobleme," p. 32.

147. Franz Oppenheimer characterized the situation in German agriculture and the differences of opinion as to how it could be remedied: "At first glance, there are as many agrarian problems in Germany as there are interest groups in German agriculture." See Oppenheimer, "Grundprobleme der deutschen Landwirtschaft," in *Krisis, Ein politisches Manifest,* ed. Oscar Müller (Weimar, 1932), p. 161.

148. The Minister of Agriculture, in a letter to Chancellor Schleicher, January 5, 1933, referred to this attempt as his "principal task during my whole term of office in the cabinet" (BA-Koblenz, R 43 II/192).

149. See, for example, the memorandum and the original proposal of the *Notschutzbund deutscher Landwirte, Notgemeinschaft landwirtschaftlicher Pacht- und Eigenbetriebe* (Emergency League for the Protection of German Farmers, Emergency Working Group of Agricultural Tenant- and Owner-operated Enterprises), September 8, 1932 (*ibid.*).

150. Petitions, telegrams, and memoranda from the most varied occupational organizations are collected in the Documents of the Office of the Chancellor, BA-Koblenz, R 43 II/192 and R 43 II/196.

151. See, for example, the resolution of the Pomeranian Chamber of Agriculture, made known to the Chancellor in a letter on January 6, 1933 (*ibid.*, R 43 II/192).

152. See, for example, a telegram of the *Verband der Mitteldeutschen Industrie e.V.* (Association of Middle German Industry), January 13, 1933 (*ibid.*); cf. also the RLB directive (Dir.K.Tgb.Nr.Parl. 2240 Lfd. No. 40), August 6, 1930 (in Presse-Archiv of the RLB, No. 492 L): "The RLB has never regarded agrarian policy as the special field of special agricultural interest groups, but always as the affair of the whole nation."

153. The press of the left, obviously, was not satisfied with Schleicher's policy. "The Junkers get everything they demand!" (*Volksfront*, January 13, 1933; cf. also *Dortmunder Anzeiger*, January 9, 1933, in Presse-Archiv of the RLB, No. 76/38, sheets 121 and 143).

154. Heinz Haushofer, *Ideengeschichte der Agrarwirtschaft und Agrarpolitik* (Munich, 1958), p. 183.

155. Hans Schlange-Schöningen, *Acker und Arbeit* (Oldenburg, 1932), p. 39.

156. *Ibid.*, p. 38.

157. *Ibid.*, p. 56.

158. A letter by the Agriculture Committee of the DNVP to the Chancellor, December 13, 1932, includes the following allusion to the mutual opposition of Warmbold and Braun in the cabinet: "The latent conflicts between individual branches of the economy, unquestionably dangerous to the economy, cannot be resolved through conflict among the various ministries with jurisdiction over economic affairs; the statesman must intervene here with his leadership" (BA-Koblenz, R 43 II/196).

159. See Minister of Agriculture Braun's letter to Schleicher, written January 5, 1933, which reveals a mood of deep resignation: "If the arrangements agreed upon are not complied with from the other side [Minister of Economics Warmbold is referred to here] and agriculture is not put in a position to employ currently existing means in sufficient measure to provide protection against inundation of the market from abroad, then, Herr Chancellor, I will be in no position to bear further responsibility. In doing so, I would become an accomplice to a development which I foresee clearly and which will surely lead to disaster" (*ibid.*, R 43 II/192).

160. This statement, which originated in the Ministry of Agriculture around the turn of year 1932–1933, is found in Topf, *Grüne Front*, pp. 226f.

161. The *Landbund Anhalt*, press organ of the Sachsen-Anhalt branch of the Rural League, charged the Chancellor on January 7, 1933, with "leftist tendencies" and called for a "general offensive against Schleicher-Warmbold" (Presse-Archiv of the RLB, No. 76/38, sheet 113).

162. *Schulthess' Europäischer Geschichtskalender*, 1933, pp. 11f.

163. The events are discussed in detail in Bracher, *Auflösung*, pp. 697f.

164. After the break with Schleicher, the RLB and its provincial branches approached the President directly; see the telegram of the Pomeranian branch of the RLB, January 12, 1933, to Hindenburg: "We beseech you, Herr President, to protect the rural population against a floundering cabinet; above all, decree general immunity from bankruptcy proceedings." See also the letter written by the RLB to Hindenburg, January 12, 1933 (BA-Koblenz, R 43

II/192), and the resolution of the Hessian branch of the Rural League, sent to the President on January 18, 1933 (*ibid.*, R 43 II/196).

165. See Darré's open letter to the Chancellor of January 13, 1933, in *NS-Landpost*, No. 4, January 22, 1933. Concerning the events, on the whole still unclear, leading to Schleicher's break with the RLB, see also characterizations of the situation by National Socialist RLB President Willikens and National Socialist RLB Director Sybel in the *Völkischer Beobachter* (Süddeutsche Ausgabe), January 16, 1933.

166. Just as Hitler expected to obtain the office of Chancellor, Darré, as early as the time of Papen's fall, was definitely counting on being appointed Agricultural Minister for the Reich. "The Führer . . . had officially informed me that he intended this post for me . . ." (Personal special directive of Darré's to the *Gaufachberater*, January 20, 1933, St.A.Goslar, ND No. 140).

167. Surely the Green Front cannot be dismissed simply as a "destructive element" (Bracher). Doubtless the individual occupational organizations pursued their goals in agrarian policy separately, and here it was the RLB which allowed itself to be misused by Darré as an element in the destruction of the Weimar Republic. See in this regard H. Beyer, "Die Agrarkrise und das Ende der Weimarer Republik," *Zeitschrift für Agrargeschichte und Agrarsoziologie*, XIII (1965), 65f. It cannot be denied that the NSDAP achieved greater successes among rural than among urban voters between 1930 and 1933. Thus, the support given by certain leading officials in agricultural organizations to Darré and National Socialism cannot be dismissed as mere adherence to the principle of occupational self-administration (*ständische Selbstverwaltung*) (*ibid.*, pp. 67f.). In the RLB, the delusion prevailed that the aA could be brought into line; in the end, it had to be acknowledged that the opposite was the case.

4

HENRY A. TURNER, JR.

Big Business and the Rise of Hitler

In this selection one of the most controversial aspects of Nazism's march to power is reexamined in the light of new evidence. The selection was originally published in the American Historical Review, *LXXV (1969), 56–70. It is reprinted by permission of the author, who is Professor of History at Yale University.*

Dᴵᴰ ɢᴇʀᴍᴀɴ big business support Adolf Hitler's climb to power? A quarter of a century after the demise of the Third Reich, this remains one of the major unresolved questions about its inception. For Marxists, or at least those who adhere to the Moscow line, the answer to this question has never been a problem. From the outset, they have viewed Nazism as a manifestation of "monopoly capitalism" and the Nazis as tools of big business.[1] Among non-Marxists there has been no such unanimity. Some have in large measure agreed with the Marxist interpretation;[2] others have rejected it.[3] Most have adopted a cautious middle position, asserting that some capitalists aided the Nazis but avoiding any precise analysis of the extent or effectiveness of that aid.[4] This wide range of views is in part clearly the product of ideological differences. But another factor has been the scanty, sometimes ambiguous, and frequently dubious nature of the evidence on which all previous studies of the subject rest. Few aspects of the history of National Socialism have, in fact, been so inadequately researched. Now that new documentation is available, the time has come for another look at the problem.

None of the new evidence contradicts the widespread impression that German big businessmen were unenthusiastic about the Weimar Republic. Most were not, as is often assumed, unreconstructed monarchists; they displayed, on the whole, a surprising indifference to governmental forms. What offended them about the new state was its adoption of costly welfare measures, its introduction of compulsory arbitration in disputes between labor and management, and, most particularly, the influence it accorded to the prolabor Social Democratic party, which was most pronounced in the government of the largest federal state, Prussia. Despite abundant objective evidence that the republic, at least during its years of prosperity, provided generally favorable conditions for business enterprise, Germany's business leaders continued to eye it with misgiving. Their attitude had much in common with that of the army: they, too, refused to commit themselves to the new state, regarding it as a potentially transitory phenomenon, while viewing themselves as the guardians of something of more permanent value to the nation—in their case, *die Wirtschaft*, the industrial sector of the economy.[5]

In spite of its reserved attitude toward the new German state, big business was nevertheless politicized by the changes resulting from the Revolution of 1918. Whereas in the Empire its leaders had been able to influence governmental policy without wholesale commitment to partisan politics, in the republic they found it necessary to assume a more active political role.[6] In far greater numbers than in the Empire, they joined the ranks of the *bürgerlich,* or nonsocialist, parties and sought places in the Parliaments for themselves or their spokesmen.[7] For most big businessmen, politics was more a matter of interests than of ideology.[8] When they took the trouble to describe their political outlook, the words that reoccurred with greatest frequency were "national" and "liberal." The term "liberal" has always been problematical in German usage, but in business circles of this period it was more so than usual, as was revealed by one businessman who, writing to an acquaintance, explained: "As you well know, I have always been liberal, in the sense of Kant and Frederick the Great."[9]

Although big business entered the politics of the republic, it never found a political home there. From the beginning, its spokesmen were scattered among the four principal nonsocialist parties, the Democratic party, the Catholic Center party, the German People's party, and the German National People's party. This dispersal divided and thus weakened the business leaders politically. Within each party they had to compete with numerous other pressure groups whose interests rarely coincided with their own and who could usually deliver far more votes. Sometimes the spokesmen of big business succeeded in gaining the backing of their parties, but more often they were defeated or forced to settle for less than they regarded as acceptable.[10] Contrary to the belief of the Marxists, economic power did not translate readily into political power in the Weimar Republic. And nowhere was this recognized more acutely than in big business circles.

The political impotence of money was strikingly demonstrated by the fate of a project that enjoyed wide support from big business during the last years of the republic. Having grown impatient with the multiplicity of parties with which they had to deal, a number of influential businessmen proposed the formation of a single, united nonsocialist party, a *bürgerliche Einheitspartei*, as it was generally labeled.[11] The plan called for such an organization to absorb the squabbling older parties, sweep away their superfluous and anachronistic ideological differences, and erect an impregnable barrier to Marxism. It was confidently expected, moreover, that in such a united party the interests of *die Wirtschaft* would at last receive their due. Much enthusiasm developed for this plan in the ranks of big business during the period 1930–1932. But although considerable pressure was exerted on the politicians, including the withholding of financial contributions during election campaigns, nothing came of the project. Despite a barrage of importunities, threats, and punitive measures, the existing parties tenaciously defended their independence and the politicians their party posts. Again, the limits to the political utility of economic power had been revealed. The result was further disillusionment in big business circles, not only with the parties but with the democratic, parliamentary system as a whole—a disillusionment that deepened as a succession of unstable cabinets struggled unsuccessfully to cope with the Great Depression.

Crucial to the subject of this inquiry is the question of whether the unmistakably mounting discontent of big business led it to support Hitler and his movement during the last phases of the republic. The answer is, on the whole, no. The qualification is necessary because, as is well known, certain big businessmen, such as Fritz Thyssen, heir to one of the great steel enterprises of the Ruhr, did give money to the Nazis. If, however, one examines the political record of big business, it quickly becomes evident that these pro-Nazis are conspicuous precisely because they were exceptions. The failure to recognize this basic fact has led to great exaggeration of their importance, as has the reliance on untrustworthy sources, such as *I Paid Hitler,* a book published over the name of Thyssen, but not actually written by him.[12]

A number of legends about industrial support for the Nazis have been perpetuated by previous literature and, largely by virtue of repetition, have come to be accepted as fact. According to one of these legends, large sums of money flowed to the Nazis through the hands of Alfred Hugenberg, the reactionary press lord who became head of the Right-wing German National People's party in 1928.[13] This allegation probably derives from Hugenberg's role in the campaign against the Young plan in 1929. As one of the organizations supporting that campaign, the Nazi party did receive a share of the funds that Hugenberg helped to raise at the time.[14] There is not a trace of documentary evidence, however, that any of Hugenberg's resources were thereafter diverted to the Nazis.[15] Indeed, this seems highly unlikely: as the leader of a party that was itself beset by financial problems, Hugenberg had little motive to share any funds he received from big business, least of all with a party that was taking votes away from his own.[16] The amount of big business money at Hugenberg's disposal has, in any event, been grossly exaggerated. Contrary to the widespread belief that he was one of the foremost spokesmen of big business throughout the republican period, most of the industrial backers of his party had opposed his election as its chairman in 1928, rejecting him as too inflexible, too provocative, and too highhanded for their tastes.[17] In the summer of 1930 a large segment of his party's industrial wing took issue with his opposition to Heinrich Brüning's cabinet and seceded to join the new Conservative People's party.[18] Even among those who did not take that step, there was a strong movement to replace Hugenberg with a more moderate man.[19] As a result, Hugenberg, who had enjoyed wide support from big business during the first decade of the republic, was forced, during its last years, to rely increasingly upon the backing of agricultural interests.[20]

Another persistent legend concerns Emil Kirdorf, long universally regarded as a kind of industrial *alter Kämpfer.*[21] Kirdorf, an octogenarian survivor of the beginning phase of German heavy industry in the 1870's, was the first really noteworthy business figure to join the Nazi party, entering in 1927. But despite the tributes lavished upon him by Hitler and the party press during the Third Reich, he was far from a loyal Nazi. In 1928, only a little over a year after joining the party, Kirdorf resigned in anger, a fact that the Nazis long succeeded in concealing from historians.[22] Eventually, it is true, he rejoined the party, but only in 1934, when on personal orders from Hitler Kirdorf's records were rewritten to make his membership seem uninterrupted. But during the crucial years 1929–1933 Kirdorf was a supporter of the German National People's party, not the Nazi party. Nor is there any evidence that Kirdorf contributed appreciable sums to the Nazis during the struggle for power. Since he had retired from all active business posts even before joining the party for the first time in 1927, he had no access to corporate or associational funds.[23] Anything he gave had to come from his own pocket, and he was not known as a man who spent his money either gladly or lavishly. Kirdorf's reputation as a patron of National Socialism rests not on documented facts but on a myth created in large measure by the Nazis themselves following his reentry into the party, when they appropriated the aged industrialist as a symbol of respectability.

The reason for Kirdorf's resignation from the party is indicative of the attitude of most big businessmen toward National Socialism in the years before Hitler achieved power. Kirdorf did not withdraw because the Nazis were antidemocratic, aggressively chauvinistic, or anti-Semitic (even though he, like most business leaders, was himself not an anti-Semite). What drove him out of the party was the social and economic radicalism of the Left-wing Nazis. Like millions of other Germans of middle-class background, including big businessmen, Kirdorf was attracted to Nazism by its assertive nationalism and its implacable hostility toward Marxism, but, like most big businessmen, he was at the same time repelled by the fear that the National Socialists might eventually live up to their name by turning out to be socialists of some kind. Hitler, who began earnestly to court the business community in 1926, went to great pains to allay this fear. In 1927, at the request of Kirdorf, he wrote a pamphlet that was secretly printed and then distributed in business circles by the old industrialist.[24] In the pamphlet, as in his speech before the Düsseldorf *Industrie-Klub* in January 1932, Hitler sought to indicate that there was no need to fear socialism from his party. It is safe to assume that he said much the same thing in his numerous other meetings with representatives of big business.[25] His efforts, however, were repeatedly compromised, as in the case of Kirdorf, by the radical noises emanating from the Left Wing of the Nazi party.[26]

As a consequence, most of the political money of big business went, throughout the last years of the republic, to the conservative opponents of the Nazis.[27] In the presidential campaign of 1932 most of the business community backed Paul von Hindenburg against Hitler, despite the Nazi leader's blatant appeal for support in his *Industrie-Klub* speech.[28] In the two Reichstag elections of 1932, big business was overwhelmingly behind the bloc of parties that supported the cabinet of Franz von Papen, the first government since the Revolution of 1918 to arouse enthusiasm in business circles.[29] If money could have purchased political power, the republic would have been succeeded by Papen's *Neuer Staat,* not by Hitler's *Drittes Reich.* But the effort to transform marks into votes proved a crushing failure.

There were, to be sure, exceptions to this pattern. Certain big businessmen did give money to the Nazis, particularly after the 1930 Reichstag election showed them to be a major political factor. Some of these contributions can best be described, however, as political insurance premiums. This was clearly the case, for example, with Friedrich Flick, a parvenu intruder into the ranks of the Ruhr industrialists, who by the early 1930's had managed to secure a dominant position in the country's largest steel-producing firm, the United Steel Works (*Vereinigte Stahlwerke*). Flick's speculative transactions and his questionable dealings with the Brüning cabinet left him vulnerable to attacks from the press and apprehensive about the attitude of future cabinets toward his enterprises.[30] His solution was to spread his political money across the political spectrum, from the liberal and Catholic parties to the Nazi party. Flick may be a deplorable example of the politically amoral capitalist, but he was by no means an enthusiastic supporter of National Socialism prior to 1933. Nor is there any indication that he was especially generous toward the Nazis. According to the records he produced at his war crimes trial in Nuremberg, the Nazis received little more than token contributions in comparison to the sums that went to their opponents.[31]

The political activities of the I. G. Farben chemical trust were characterized by much the same pattern as those of Flick. From its formation in 1925, the company maintained contact with all the nonsocialist parties and made financial contributions to them. According to the postwar accounts of one official of the trust, the Nazis were added to the list in 1932. That same official estimated the total contributions for one of the Reichstag election campaigns of 1932 (it is not clear whether he was referring to the July or November elections) at approximately 200,000 to 300,000 marks. Of this, he reported, no more than 10 to 15 percent had gone to the Nazis.[32] I. G. Farben, like Flick, had special reason to be concerned about maintaining the good will of the political parties. In its case, this concern arose from heavy investments in elaborate processes designed to yield high-grade synthetic gasoline. Since the costs of production were initially high, the company could hope to break into the domestic market only if a protective tariff were imposed on oil imports. Such a tariff had been put into effect by the Brüning cabinet and maintained by the Papen regime, but in view of Germany's obviously chronic political instability, the tariff question remained a source of considerable anxiety to the leadership of the firm. When attacks on Farben appeared in the Nazi press in 1932, concern developed about the attitude of what was by then the country's strongest political party. Two minor officials were, accordingly, sent to Munich in the autumn of 1932 to sound out Hitler on the project.[33] Much has been made of this episode by some writers, who have inferred that it produced a deal that brought Farben behind the National Socialist movement at a crucial time.[34] From all available evidence, however, the firm's representatives came away with only vague assurances from Hitler that he would halt the attacks in the party press.[35] The Nazis apparently received at most the small share of the relatively modest political funds described above, although even this may, in view of the ambiguity of the evidence, have been granted earlier, at the time of the summer election campaign, and thus quite independently of the Munich meeting with Hitler. There is, in any case, no evidence that the chemical combine wanted a Nazi triumph or threw its financial support decisively to National Socialism. All indications are, in fact, that the leaders of Farben, acutely aware of their firm's dependence on exports, were apprehensive at the prospect of a take-over of the government by a party that preached economic autarky.[36]

As in the cases of Flick and I. G. Farben, most of the big business money that found its way to the Nazis was not given simply, or even primarily, with the aim of bringing them to power. Whereas Flick and Farben were seeking to buy political insurance against the eventuality of a Nazi capture of the government, others were attempting to alter the nature of the Nazi movement. This they hoped to accomplish by giving money to "sensible" or "moderate" Nazis, thereby strengthening that element and weakening the economically and socially radical tendencies that had always been the chief obstacles to cooperation between big business and National Socialism. There was, however, no agreement as to who the "sensible" Nazis were. Thyssen, one of the few who really wanted a Nazi triumph, was nevertheless concerned about radicalism in

the party. He sought to counteract it by subsidizing the man he regarded
as the bulwark of moderation, Hermann Göring, who used at least a
considerable portion of Thyssen's money to indulge his taste for lavish
living.[37] Hermann Bücher, head of the large electrical equipment concern, Allgemeine Elektrizitäts-Gesellschaft, tried to combat Nazi radicalism by giving financial aid to Joseph Goebbels's rival in Berlin, storm
troop leader Walter Stennes, in his short-lived revolt.[38] Surprisingly, the
directors of the principal organization of the coal industry, the *Bergbau-
Verein,* saw their "moderate" Nazi in Gregor Strasser—usually classified
as a leader of the Left Wing—and for a time channeled funds to him.[39]
Still others gave money to Walther Funk, the former editor of a conservative financial newspaper, who bore at least the title of economic
adviser to Hitler and who was regarded in some business quarters as a
"liberal" Nazi and a potential moderating influence.[40]

Not all attempts to alter the Nazis' economic and social attitudes involved financial contributions. Kirdorf, for example, maintained cordial
personal relations with Hitler even after resigning from the party in
1928, and sought to exert influence on the Führer by making clear his
objections to the Left-wing Nazis and to the radical planks in the party
program.[41] Much the same attempt was made by the *Keppler-Kreis,* the
group of businessmen assembled in the spring of 1932 at Hitler's request
by one of his advisers, Wilhelm Keppler. Later, during the Third Reich,
after this group was appropriated by Heinrich Himmler and transformed
into his *Freundeskreis,* it became a source of enormous contributions
for the SS.[42] But prior to the acquisition of power by the Nazis, it was
merely an advisory body, seeking, without success, to bring about a commitment of the party to conservative economic policies; it did not serve
as a channel for business contributions.[43]

The question of whether the Nazis were aided appreciably by the big
business money that did reach them from those who were seeking either
to buy protection or to alter the nature of the party cannot at present be
definitively answered: ignorance about Nazi finances is a major handi-
cap that deserves far more attention than it has received. But it is known,
from Goebbels's diary and other sources, that the Nazis were plagued by
acute money problems until the very moment of Hitler's appointment
as Chancellor.[44] It thus seems clear that the sums received were not
sufficient to solve the party's financial problems. The significant point,
in any case, is that the funds reaching the Nazis from big business were
but a small fraction of those that went to their opponents and rivals.
On balance, big business money went overwhelmingly against the Nazis.

In spite of all this, it is nevertheless true that most business leaders were favorably inclined toward the new cabinet installed on January 30, 1933, with Hitler as Chancellor. It has been alleged that this was only the expression of attitudes already discernible at least as early as November, when, following the poor showing of the Papen bloc at the polls, some businessmen had, at the instigation of the *Keppler-Kreis,* petitioned Hindenburg to appoint Hitler Chancellor. But the attitude of those who signed the petition was not typical of the outlook of big business in November 1932; nor did the list of signatories include any major business figures, aside from Thyssen, who had for some time made no secret of his support for the Nazis. Another signatory, Hjalmar Schacht, is often assigned to the ranks of big business, but as of 1932 he is more properly classified as a political adventurer.[45]

The change of outlook occurred for most businessmen in December 1932; its primary cause was Kurt von Schleicher. It is difficult to exaggerate their distrust and fear of the man who became Chancellor on December 3. They were hostile to him in part for his role in bringing down Papen, the one Chancellor they had admired and trusted. But even more important was Schleicher's apparent indifference to orthodox economic principles and traditional class alignments. Shortly after becoming Chancellor he caused the gravest apprehension in business circles by announcing that he was neither a capitalist nor a socialist. He also flirted openly with the trade unions, raising the specter of an alliance of the military and the working class against the propertied elements of society. As a result, Germany's big businessmen feared that Schleicher might turn out to be a socialist in military garb.[46] It was more from a desire to be rid of him than from enthusiasm for what was to replace him that they applauded the events of January 1933.

Contrary to what has often been asserted, big business played no part in the intrigues of that month. Much has been made of the role of Baron Kurt von Schroeder, the banker at whose home in Cologne Hitler and Papen met on January 4 to conspire against Schleicher. Schroeder was, however, not acting as an agent of big business. His importance lay in the fortuitous fact that he was acquainted with both Papen and Keppler, Hitler's adviser, and could thus serve as a convenient intermediary between two sides anxious to join forces.[47] Nor is there any evidence that the meeting at his house began a flow of business money to the Nazis, as has repeatedly been alleged.[48] Money was, in any event, not what mattered in January 1933. What counted was influence with Hindenburg, and big business had little or none of that. From the President's

Junker standpoint, even the most powerful bankers and industrialists were little better than shopkeepers.[49]

Most of the leaders of big business were, to the very end, under a basic misapprehension about the nature of the new cabinet taking shape in January 1933. Their information came mainly from Papen and his circle, and they were led to believe that what was coming was a revival of the Papen cabinet, with its base widened through the inclusion of the Nazis. Even when it was learned that Papen would be Vice-Chancellor under Hitler, big business continued to assume that he would be the real leader of the new government.[50] In the eyes of the business community, January 30, 1933, seemed at first to mark the fall of the hated Schleicher and the return of the trusted Papen, not the advent of a Nazi dictatorship.

By the time the leaders of big business were disabused of this illusion, they were ready to make their peace with Hitler. One factor in this turn of events was the ability of the new Chancellor, as the legally installed head of government, to appeal to their respect for constituted authority. But even more important, once he was in office Hitler demonstrated that he was, as he had always reassured them, not a socialist. He therefore had no difficulty in extracting large sums from big business, starting with the campaign for the Reichstag election of March 1933. These contributions unquestionably aided Hitler significantly. But they aided him in the consolidation of his power, not in its acquisition. He had achieved that without the support of most of big business, indeed in spite of its massive assistance to his opponents and rivals.

These observations are in no sense intended as an exoneration of German big business. Its political record in the period that ended with the establishment of the Third Reich is hardly praiseworthy. In numerous ways its leaders contributed indirectly to the rise of Nazism: through their failure to support the democratic republic; through their blind hostility to the Social Democrats and the labor unions; through their aid to reactionary forces, most conspicuously the Papen regime; and through the respectability they bestowed upon Hitler by receiving him into their midst on a number of occasions. Some contributed more directly, by giving money to the Nazi party, or at least to certain Nazis. None of this, however, should be allowed to obscure the central fact that the great majority of Germany's big businessmen had neither wanted a Nazi triumph nor contributed materially to it.

The last statement, it should be emphasized, does not necessarily apply to the German business community as a whole. There are, in fact, indications that Hitler received considerable support from small- and middle-sized business.[51] This is not surprising, for it was there that the real and potential entrepreneurial victims of the Great Depression were to be found. The giant businesses of the country knew from past experience that their importance to the national economy was so great that no government could afford to let them go bankrupt; in fact, the cabinets of the republic repeatedly came to the aid of ailing big business concerns rather than face the sharp increase in unemployment that their collapse would entail.[52] Smaller, less visible firms could expect no such protection from the abrasive mechanisms of cyclical contraction; for their owners and managers, economic extinction was a real possibility, with the consequence that they were often genuinely desperate men. But the fact nevertheless remains that these small- and middle-sized businessmen can by no stretch of the imagination be included in the ranks of German big business, or, to use Marxist terminology, "the monopoly capitalists." Therefore, unless one is willing to accept the simplistic *cui bono* approach, according to which the eventual economic beneficiaries of Hitler's acquisition of power must necessarily have supported him beforehand, or the sophistic distinction between subjective and objective roles in history that is so popular in Marxist circles, it must be concluded that during its rise to power National Socialism was, in socioeconomic terms, primarily a movement not of winners in the capitalist struggle for survival but of losers and those who feared becoming losers.

It can, of course, be argued that even if the big businessmen did not support Hitler, National Socialism was nevertheless a product of capitalism. Certainly the deprivation and anxiety occasioned by the downward turn of the capitalist economic cycle after 1929 heightened the susceptibility of many Germans to the panaceas offered by the Nazis. The country's capitalist economic system also fostered and exacerbated the class animosities that the Nazis exploited and promised to eliminate. It spawned as well the other long-term economic and social problems to which Nazism was in large measure a response, although a response that offered mainly quack remedies and flights from reality rather than real solutions. National Socialism was thus undeniably a child of the capitalist order. Still, care must be taken not to attach undue significance to that fact. Only a few capitalist societies have produced phenomena comparable to Nazism; on the other hand, the latter shares its capitalist parentage with every other political movement that has emerged from modern Europe, including liberal democracy and Communism.

NOTES

1. According to the thesis that was long accepted in Communist circles, National Socialism was built up and installed in power by a conspiracy of the "mo-

nopoly capitalists" (viewed as a virtually monolithic group) and the reactionary *Junker*, whose aim was to suppress the working class and to launch an imperialist war (see, e.g., Albert Norden, *Lehren deutscher Geschichte: Zur politischen Rolle des Finanzkapitals und der Junker* [East Berlin, 1947]). Recently, more complex and differentiated interpretations have begun to appear, apparently as a result of the relaxation of ideological controls following Stalin's death. These studies view the rise of Hitler as the product of "contradictions" within the capitalist system that pit rival groups of "monopoly capitalists" against each other in a struggle for power. According to these interpretations, which are not heavily dependent upon evidence and thus vary considerably in particulars, the political events that brought Hitler to office were mere surface expressions of behind-the-scenes power struggles in the less visible, but nevertheless decisive, economic sphere (see, e.g., Isakhar M. Faingar, *Die Entwicklung des deutschen Monopolkapitals* [East Berlin, 1959], a translation of a Soviet book first published in 1958; Eberhard Czichon, *Wer verhalf Hitler zur Macht? Zum Anteil der deutschen Industrie an der Zerstörung der Weimarer Republik* [Cologne, 1967], a book by an East German writer; Kurt Gossweiler, "Die Rolle des Monopolkapitals bei der Herbeiführung der Röhm-Affäre," diss., Humboldt University, 1963).

2. See George W. F. Hallgarten, *Hitler, Reichswehr und Industrie: Zur Geschichte der Jahre 1918–1933* (Frankfurt a.M., 1955); Arthur Schweitzer, *Big Business in the Third Reich* (Bloomington, Ind., 1964); Franz Neumann, *Behemoth: The Structure and Practice of National Socialism* (New York and London, 1942), the work of an independent scholar of Marxist background.

3. Some examples are August Heinrichsbauer, *Schwerindustrie und Politik* (Essen, 1948); Seymour Martin Lipset, *Political Man: The Social Bases of Politics* (New York, 1960); Louis P. Lochner, *Tycoons and Tyrant: German Industry from Hitler to Adenauer* (Chicago, 1954); Edward N. Peterson, *Hjalmar Schacht: For and against Hitler* (Boston, 1954).

4. See Alan Bullock, *Hitler: A Study in Tyranny* (London, 1952); Karl Dietrich Bracher, *Die Auflösung der Weimarer Republik: Eine Studie zum Problem des Machtverfalls in der Demokratie* (2d ed., Stuttgart, 1957); S. William Halperin, *Germany Tried Democracy: A Political History of the Reich from 1918 to 1933* (New York, 1946); Helmut Heiber, *Die Republik von Weimar* (Munich, 1966); and William L. Shirer, *The Rise and Fall of the Third Reich: A History of Nazi Germany* (New York, 1959).

5. This theme runs through the speeches of big businessmen during the entire republican period. Many of these can be found in the *Veröffentlichungen* of the national association of industry, the *Reichsverband der Deutschen Industrie* (Berlin, 1919–1932).

6. Two recent studies of the political role of big business in the Empire are Lamar Cecil, *Albert Ballin: Business and Politics in Imperial Germany, 1888–1918* (Princeton, N.J., 1967); and Hans Jaeger, *Unternehmer in der deutschen Politik (1890–1918)* (Bonn, 1967).

7. See Ingolf Liesebach, "Der Wandel der politischen Führungsschicht der deutschen Industrie von 1918 bis 1945" (diss., University of Basel, 1957).

8. On February 18, 1919, Albert Vögler, a prominent figure in the steel industry who had been elected to the National Assembly as a delegate of the German People's party, caused considerable consternation among his fellow deputies

by announcing in his maiden speech to the chamber: "I speak here as the representative of an industry . . ." (*Verhandlungen der verfassunggebenden deutschen Nationalversammlung,* CCCXXVI, 137). Thereafter, the parliamentary spokesmen of big business tended to be more discreet in their public statements.

9. Karl Zell, member of the *Vorstand* of *Kronprinz A.G.. für Metallindustrie,* to Witkugel, April 27, 1933, Papers of the German People's party (*Deutsche Volkspartei*), No. 151, *Deutsches Zentralarchiv,* Potsdam.

10. A striking example of this was the adoption in 1927 of national laws regulating the length of the industrial workday and establishing an unemployment insurance program despite the opposition of big business and despite the fact that the nonsocialist parties commanded a clear majority in the Reichstag and controlled the cabinet.

11. There is much material on the project in the Paul Reusch Papers, *Historisches Archiv, Gutehoffnungshütte,* Oberhausen; he was one of the most politically active of the Ruhr industrialists. Another source of information is the Fritz Klein Papers, which are in the possession of Klein's son, an East German historian, who kindly made them available to me. Klein was the editor of the Berlin newspaper *Deutsche Allgemeine Zeitung* during the last years of the republic, when it was controlled by a consortium of big businessmen. See H. A. Turner, Jr., "The *Ruhrlade,* Secret Cabinet of Heavy Industry in the Weimar Republic," *Central European History,* III (1970), 195–228; see also Friedrich Glum, *Zwischen Wissenschaft, Wirtschaft und Politik: Erlebtes und Erdachtes in vier Reichen* (Bonn, 1964), pp. 395–407.

12. The book was prepared by a ghost writer, Emery Reves, on the basis of interviews with Thyssen in France during the spring of 1940, after the latter had fled Germany and denounced Hitler. Some of the draft chapters (in French) were seen and approved by Thyssen, but work on the book was interrupted by the breakthrough of the German armies on the western front in June 1940. Thyssen remained in France and was turned over to the Nazis by the Vichy regime for return to Germany, where he was imprisoned throughout the war. Reves escaped from France and finished the book, publishing it in English translation in New York and London in the autumn of 1941 [my citations will be to the New York edition]. Among the chapters not seen by Thyssen prior to publication were those treating his financial relations with the Nazis. My examination of the stenographic records of the interviews with Thyssen and the original draft chapters (still in the possession of Reves) has established that the book contains numerous spurious and inaccurate statements, even in the chapters approved by Thyssen. See H. A. Turner, Jr., "Fritz Thyssen und 'I Paid Hitler,'" *Vierteljahrshefte für Zeitgeschichte,* XIX (1971), 225–244.

13. This view was first widely circulated by the journalist Konrad Heiden in *Adolf Hitler: Das Zeitalter der Verantwortungslosigkeit* (2 vols., Zürich, 1936–1937), I, 268–272. Since then it has been repeated in many other studies of Hitler's rise, including the most recent book by Karl Dietrich Bracher, *Die deutsche Diktatur: Entstehung, Struktur, Folgen des Nationalsozialismus* (Cologne, 1969), p. 176.

14. There is documentation on the finances of the plebiscite against the Young plan in two collections in the *Deutsches Zentralarchiv,* Potsdam: *Alldeutscher Verband,* No. 501; *Stahlhelm,* No. 25.

15. The only evidence ever cited to support the allegations about Hugenberg's

aid to Hitler is a passage in Thyssen, *I Paid Hitler*, pp. 102–103. But as Bullock has observed (*Hitler*, p. 157), that passage is unclear as to when the alleged financing of Hitler took place. Since the passage was not written by Thyssen or even seen by him prior to publication, there are, moreover, grounds for doubting its authenticity. See note 12, above.

16. See the papers of the German National People's party, *Deutsches Zentralarchiv*, Potsdam; see also Reusch Papers; Klein Papers.

17. There is evidence of this opposition in the papers of Hugenberg's predecessor as party chairman, Count Kuno von Westarp, now in the possession of his family in Gärtringen, West Germany; in the Reusch Papers; and in the files of the *Verein Deutscher Eisen- und Stahlindustrieller*, R 13 I/1064, 1065, *Bundesarchiv*, Koblenz; see also Manfred Dörr, "Die Deutschnationale Volkspartei 1925 bis 1928" (diss., University of Marburg, 1964), p. 448, n. 131.

18. On the revolt against Hugenberg in 1930, see the statement circulated in April by the organization of industrial representatives in the German National People's party, the text of which appears in the privately printed memoirs of Emil Kirdorf, *Erinnerungen, 1847–1930*, copy in the Emil Kirdorf Papers, now at the *Gelsenkirchener Bergwerks-A.G.*, Essen, pp. 226–233.

19. Especially active in this effort was Tilo von Wilmowsky, brother-in-law and close adviser of Gustav Krupp von Bohlen und Halbach as well as an influential figure in industrial circles in his own right. Among those considered as replacements for Hugenberg were Carl Gördeler and Hjalmar Schacht. Documentation can be found in the Gustav Krupp von Bohlen und Halbach Papers, *Krupp-Archiv*, Villa Hügel, Essen; and in the Reusch Papers.

20. By the time Hugenberg was appointed a minister by Hitler in 1933, with responsibility for both agricultural and economic affairs, he clearly functioned as a spokesman of the agricultural interests and thus as an opponent of industry, especially on the question of tariff policy which sharply divided the two at that time (Dieter Petzina, "Hauptprobleme der deutschen Wirtschaftspolitik 1932/33," *Vierteljahrshefte für Zeitgeschichte*, xv [1967], 45–55).

21. See Bracher, *Auflösung*, pp. 292, 334; Bullock, *Hitler*, p. 133; Czichon, *Wer verhalf Hitler*, *passim*; Konrad Heiden, *Der Fuehrer* (Boston, 1944), pp. 340–342, 356; Hallgarten, *Hitler, Reichswehr und Industrie, passim*; Lochner, *Tycoons and Tyrant*, pp. 97–98; Neumann, *Behemoth*, p. 360; Gerhard Schulz, in K. D. Bracher *et al.*, *Die nationalsozialistische Machtergreifung* (Cologne, 1960), p. 394.

22. I have dealt in greater detail with this and other aspects of the case of Kirdorf in "Emil Kirdorf and the Nazi Party," *Central European History*, I (1968), 324–344.

23. According to one legend still very much an article of faith in East German historical circles, Kirdorf in 1931 prevailed upon the bituminous coal cartel (*Rheinisch-Westfälisches Kohlensyndikat*) to impose a levy of five (in some versions fifty) pfennigs on each ton of coal sold, the proceeds to go to the Nazis (see Czichon, *Wer verhalf Hitler*, p. 19). No documentary evidence has ever been introduced to support this allegation. It was challenged from a number of quarters when it first appeared in the postwar German press in 1947. (A collection of this material is located in the papers of the de-Nazification trial of Fritz Thyssen, *Hauptakte*, pp. 283–286, *Hessisches Hauptstaatsarchiv*, Wiesbaden.) Overlooked by all who have repeated the allegation is the fact that Kirdorf's active

role in the coal cartel had come to an end in April 1925 (Walter Bacmeister, *Emil Kirdorf. Der Mann. Sein Werk* [2d ed., Essen (1936)], p. 100).

24. See Henry Ashby Turner, Jr., "Hitler's Secret Pamphlet for Industrialists, 1927," *Journal of Modern History*, XL (1968), 348–374.

25. Similar statements by Hitler appear in the recently discovered stenographic record of two conversations he had in the spring of 1931 with a business-oriented newspaper editor (Edouard Calic, *Ohne Maske: Hitler-Breiting Geheimgespräche 1931* [Frankfurt a.M., 1968], pp. 35–36).

26. Instances of this are too numerous to recount in full, but two more examples can be cited. In February 1926 Hitler delivered a lengthy speech before the Hamburg *Nationalklub von 1919* (see Werner Jochmann, *Im Kampf um die Macht: Hitlers Rede vor dem Hamburger Nationalklub von 1919* [Frankfurt a.M., 1960]). Three years later a Nazi spokesman in Hamburg reported that the speech was still remembered favorably in business circles but that there was general alienation from the Nazi party as a consequence of the radical stance of the local leadership and the party's *Revolverpresse* (Friedrich Bucher to Hitler, July 20, 1929, *Reichsleitung, Personalakte Hüttmann*, Berlin Document Center). During the early part of 1932, Hitler sought to cultivate allies in big business circles, addressing industrial groups and instigating, through his adviser Wilhelm Keppler, the formation of an advisory group of businessmen, the later *Freundeskreis*. The effects of these efforts were largely undone, however, by a campaign pamphlet for the summer Reichstag election, *Wirtschaftliches Sofortprogramm der N.S.D.A.P.* (Munich, 1932), which alarmed businessmen, by virtue of its anticapitalist slogans and its call for deficit spending and governmental controls aimed at ending unemployment. In September Hitler informed leading business circles through Schacht that distribution of the pamphlet had been stopped and that the remaining copies had been destroyed, but much damage had already been done by that time (Schacht to Reusch, September 12, 1932, No. 400101290/33, Reusch Papers).

27. In his conversation with the journalist Richard Breiting in May 1931, Hitler boasted that the Nazi party already enjoyed the financial backing of "Krupp, Schröder, and others from big industry" (Calic, *Ohne Maske*, p. 27). Only a few pages later, however, he told of his plans to win over big business, revealing that he regarded this as a task yet to be accomplished (*ibid.*, pp. 28–29, 35, 37–38). Further doubt is cast on the accuracy of Hitler's claim by the well-known coolness of Gustav Krupp von Bohlen und Halbach toward National Socialism prior to Hitler's appointment as Chancellor, an attitude recognized by authors of the most varied persuasions and confirmed by Krupp's private correspondence in the Krupp Papers (see Czichon, *Wer verhalf Hitler*, p. 53; Hallgarten, *Hitler, Reichswehr und Industrie*, p. 117; Lochner, *Tycoons and Tyrant*, p. 139). Baron Kurt von Schroeder (to whom the name "Schröder" apparently refers) may well have been aiding the Nazis by 1931, but he was an official of a medium-sized bank in a provincial city (Cologne), not a figure in "big industry" or even a confidant of the leading industrial circles. See note 47, below.

28. This is conceded even by Hallgarten (*Hitler, Reichswehr und Industrie*, p. 106). There is documentation on the fund-raising campaign in the papers of the industrialist who headed it, Carl Duisberg, cofounder of I. G. Farben and chairman of its board of overseers and its administrative council (*Autographen-Sammlung von Dr. Carl Duisberg, Werksarchiv, Farbenfabrik Bayer*, Leverkusen).

29. There is abundant documentation to this effect in the Klein Papers, Krupp Papers, and Reusch Papers, as well as in the informative diary of Hans Schäffer, State Secretary in the Ministry of Finance, now located in the archive of the *Institut für Zeitgeschichte*, Munich. See also Hans Radandt, " 'Freie Wahlen' und Monopolkapital," *Zeitschrift für Geschichtswissenschaft*, IX, No. 6 (1961), 1321–22. This East German publication provides details about a fund-raising meeting of industrialists in October 1932, but neglects to mention the use for which the funds were intended, thus leaving the impression they might have been destined for the Nazis. A report on the same meeting in the Reusch Papers makes clear, however, that the money raised would go to the Papen bloc, not to the Nazis (memo by Martin Blank, October 19, 1932, No. 4001012024/10, Reusch Papers).

30. This emerged clearly from the testimony and documentary evidence in the Flick trial at Nuremberg in 1947. (See the published excerpts in Nuremberg Military Tribunals, *Trials of War Criminals before the Nuernberg Military Tribunals under Control Council Law No. 10* [15 vols., Washington, D.C., 1949–1953], VI, *passim*.) Flick was particularly vulnerable as a result of the purchase of his United Steel Works stock by the Reich in May 1932 at a price far above the market value. Hallgarten has alleged, although with no supporting evidence, that this "Gelsenkirchen Deal" forged a link in the summer of 1932 between the steel industry and the Nazi party by virtue of the Nazis' having suppressed a projected parliamentary investigation of the transaction (Hallgarten, *Hitler, Reichswehr und Industrie*, p. 113). Hallgarten's allegation has, however, been effectively refuted by an East German scholar (Gerhard Volkland, "Hintergründe und politischen Auswirkungen der Gelsenkirchen-Affäre im Jahre 1932," *Zeitschrift für Geschichtswissenschaft*, XI, No. 2 [1963], 312–313).

31. For a summary, see *Trials of War Criminals*, VI, 382–383. The full documentation can be found in Record Group 238 (World War II War Crimes Records), Case 5, Dokumentenbuch Flick I, National Archives (hereafter cited as NA).

32. See the affidavits of Max Ilgner, Microcopy T-301 (Records of the Office of the U.S. Chief Counsel for War Crimes, Nuremberg, Military Tribunals, Relating to Nazi Industrialists), roll 13/NI-1293, *ibid.;* T-301/55/NI-7082, *ibid.*

33. See *Trials of War Criminals*, VII, 536–554. The two young emissaries were Heinrich Bütefisch, a technical expert, and Heinrich Gattineau, a public relations specialist who had studied with Professor Karl Haushofer at the University of Munich and was thus acquainted with Rudolf Hess, who arranged the meeting.

34. Czichon, *Wer verhalf Hitler*, p. 50; Albert Norden, *Die Nation und wir: Ausgewählte Aufsätze und Reden 1933–1964* (2 vols., East Berlin, 1965), I, 322; Schweitzer, *Big Business*, p. 102.

35. See *Trials of War Criminals*, VII, 536–554; see also the full testimony in Record Group 238, Case 6 (German transcript), XXIV, XXV, XXXIV, NA; interrogation of Bütefisch, 1947, T-301/71/NI-8637, *ibid.* The prosecution sought to establish a connection between the meeting of Bütefisch and Gattineau with Hitler and an agreement of the Reich government with Farben, consummated in December 1933, which provided price supports for the synthetic gasoline project. This interpretation was rejected by both Bütefisch and Gattineau. It was also refuted by affidavits from officials in the Ministry of Economics who had drawn up the agreement of 1933 and who denied that any political influence had been involved (Dokumentenbuch Bütefisch 4, Record Group 238, Case 6, *ibid.*).

36. At a meeting of Farben's "Working Committee" (*Arbeitsausschuss*) on April 15, 1932, the relationship between the firm's plans for agreements with foreign companies and the autarkist slogan, "Protection of the German Market" (*Schutz des deutschen Marktes*), was discussed. Director August von Knieriem emphasized that it was the company's policy to oppose both autarky and state controls of any kind, pointing out that Carl Bosch, one of the founders of the combine, had recently made a similar statement to the press (Nachtrag I zu den Dokumentenbüchern Gattineau [excerpt from the stenographic record of the meeting], Record Group 238, Case 6, NA).

37. Thyssen, *I Paid Hitler,* p. 100. This statement in the book is confirmed by the stenographic record of the interviews with Thyssen on which the book was based. See note 12, above.

38. This is revealed by Bücher's correspondence with Reusch in No. 400101290/5, Reusch Papers.

39. See the book written by the intermediary between Strasser and the *Bergbau-Verein* (properly *Verein für die bergbaulichen Interessen*), Heinrichs-bauer, *Schwerindustrie und Politik,* pp. 39–52. Czichon (*Wer verhalf Hitler,* p. 54) cites the as yet unpublished memoirs of Günther Gereke to the effect that the industrialist Otto Wolff also subsidized Strasser in 1932 at the request of Wolff's friend, General Kurt von Schleicher, who hoped thereby to make Strasser more independent of Hitler.

40. At Nuremberg in 1948 Flick described Funk as a "liberal thinking man" and a "man of liberal outlook" (see Record Group 238, Case 10 [German transcript], XV, 5584, NA). According to testimony of his former assistant, Otto Steinbrinck, Flick was among those who aided Funk (Case 5 [German transcript], XV, 4981, *ibid.*). Funk also received small subsidies from two young public relations agents of I. G. Farben, who acted independently of each other in providing funds for the maintenance of his Berlin office in 1932 (see affidavit of Ilgner, May 1, 1947, T-301/55/NI-7082, *ibid.*). Ilgner stated that he ceased payments when he discovered that Funk was also receiving money from Gattineau for the same purpose. According to Heinrichsbauer (*Schwerindustrie und Politik,* pp. 42, 44), the *Bergbau-Verein* also subsidized Funk.

41. Turner, "Kirdorf and the Nazi Party," pp. 335–336.

42. Klaus Drobisch, "Der Freundeskreis Himmler," *Zeitschrift für Geschichtswissenschaft,* VIII (1960), 304–328.

43. One of the founding members of the *Keppler-Kreis,* Baron Kurt von Schroeder, was repeatedly questioned about this after the war. On each occasion he denied that the group had made any financial contributions to the Nazi cause prior to the party's acquisition of power (see T-301/3/NI-246, NI-247, NA; also, Pre-Trial Interrogations, Schroeder, August 18, 1947, Record Group 238, *ibid.*). In an affidavit of December 5, 1945, Schroeder stated that fund raising began only in 1935 or 1936, when Himmler took over the group (Record Group 238, PS-3337, *ibid.*). This statement agrees with that of Steinbrinck, another early member, who dated the start of fund raising as 1935 (Pre-Trial Interrogations, Steinbrinck, January 25, 1947, Record Group 238, *ibid.*). See also the documentation on the beginnings of the *Keppler-Kreis* in the privately printed memoirs of Emil Helfferich, one of the founding members, *Ein Leben* (4 vols., Hamburg and Jever, 1948–1964), IV, 9–26.

44. Some writers have contended that Goebbels's diary, *Vom Kaiserhof zur Reichskanzlei: Eine historische Darstellung in Tagebuchblättern* (Munich,

1934), shows the finances of the Nazis to have improved markedly in January 1933, following the meeting of Hitler with Papen at the house of the banker Schroeder. Shirer (*Rise and Fall*, p. 179), for example, citing Goebbels's entry of January 16, writes: "he reported that the financial position of the party had 'fundamentally improved overnight.'" There is, however, no mention of finances in that entry; the overnight change in the Nazis' fortunes referred to by Goebbels was clearly the result of the party's successes the day before in the state elections of Lippe, not of capitalists' contributions. The same erroneous interpretation has been given to this diary entry by Bracher (*Auflösung*, p. 694, n. 33). Bracher cites as well a second entry, that of January 5, in which Goebbels remarked that the financial situation of the Berlin *Gau* had somewhat improved (*Vom Kaiserhof*, p. 235). It is hardly likely, however, that the Hitler-Papen meeting of January 4 could have, as Bracher infers, had such an immediate material effect on the treasury of the local Berlin organization only one day later. In any event, by January 6 Goebbels was again bemoaning the "bad financial situation of the organization" (*ibid.*, p. 236).

45. Schacht, a banker by background, had been out of private business for nine years, first as a government official and then, after his resignation as president of the Reichsbank in 1930, in retirement on his country estate. East German historians have made much of the discovery in their archives of twenty signed copies of the petition which reached President Hindenburg's office (see Albert Schreiner, "Die Eingabe deutscher Finanzmagnaten, Monopolisten und Junker an Hindenburg für die Berufung Hitlers zum Reichskanzler [November, 1932]," *Zeitschrift für Geschichtswissenschaft*, IV, No. 2 [1956], 366–369; also, Czichon, *Wer verhalf Hitler*, pp. 41–42). A comparison of the list of those who signed the petition with the list of those considered as potential signers by the organizers of the project reveals, however, that the great majority apparently refused to sign (see Record Group 238, PS-3901, NA; excerpt in International Military Tribunal, *Trial of the Major War Criminals before the International Military Tribunal, Nuremberg, 14 November 1945–1 October 1946* [42 vols., Nuremberg, 1947–1949], XXXIII, 531–533). It is also perhaps revealing that East German historians have made no mention of another document in the same archival file, also dating from November 1932: an election appeal issued by the *Deutscher Ausschuss 'Mit Hindenburg für Volk und Reich,'* calling for support in the November Reichstag election of the parties backing Papen's cabinet (and thus for opposition to the Nazis). In contrast to the twenty signed copies of the petition, this appeal bears 339 signatures, including those of some of the many prominent businessmen who did not sign the petition (*Büro des Reichspräsidenten*, No. 47, *Deutsches Zentralarchiv*, Potsdam).

46. There is ample evidence of this in a wide variety of sources. For examples, see the letter of the manager of the *Deutscher Industrie- und Handelstag*, Eduard Hamm, to Otto Most, December 10, 1932, in which Hamm wrote of rumors to the effect that the cabinet would be revamped on a parliamentary basis in a "certain soldier-worker direction," R11/10, *Bundesarchiv*, Koblenz; speech of Krupp to the *Hauptausschuss* of the *Reichsverband der Deutschen Industrie*, December 14, 1932, reported in a communication of the *Reichsverband* of December 15, No. 400101220/13, Reusch Papers; excerpts from the speech of the manager of the *Reichsverband*, Jakob Herle, January 2, 1933, Herle to Reusch, January 4, No. 400101220/14, *ibid.*; Reusch's letters to Hamm, December 22, 31, 1932,

No. 40010123/25, *ibid.;* Duisberg to Herle, January 9, 1933, *Reichsverband der Deutschen Industrie, Allgemeiner Schriftwechsel mit der Geschäftsführung, Werksarchiv, Farbenfabrik Bayer,* Leverkusen; Hugo Stinnes to Klein, January 18, 1933, Klein Papers. Some of the leading Ruhr industrialists had an additional reason for hostility toward Schleicher, for they suspected he had used to buy himself a newspaper (*Tägliche Rundschau,* Berlin) some of the money they had given him during the July election campaign in support of the parties backing Papen (see Kurt von Schleicher Papers, HO8-42/22, *Bundesarchiv,* Koblenz; Reusch to Fritz Springorum, October 12, 1932, No. 400101290/36, Reusch Papers).

47. The nature of Schroeder's role emerges clearly from the correspondence preceding the meeting (T-301/3/NI-200–16, NA). Schroeder's lack of standing in big business circles prior to 1933 is attested to by the almost complete absence of his name from the correspondence of major industrial figures cited elsewhere in this article. As is shown by a series of postwar interrogations, his industrial role began only during the Third Reich, largely as a result of his Nazi contacts (NI-226–49, *ibid.*).

48. Hallgarten (*Hitler, Reichswehr und Industrie,* p. 116) has alleged that immediately after the meeting a consortium of industrialists gave a million marks to the SS and paid the most pressing election debts of the Nazi party. As evidence, he cites an undocumented assertion by the journalist Konrad Heiden, plus a postwar affidavit by Schroeder. In the affidavit Schroeder mentioned payment of a million marks a year to the SS by the *Freundeskreis,* but stated that this began only in 1935 or 1936, specifying that no such payments to the Nazis were made prior to then by that group (this document, which Hallgarten cites by its exhibit number in the Flick trial, is better known as PS-3337; see note 43, above). Two further supporting references offered by Hallgarten lead to an English translation of an excerpt from the same affidavit by Schroeder and pages "1353 ff." of a volume containing only 1099 pages. Bracher has accepted Hallgarten's interpretation and offered as additional evidence a quotation from Thyssen, *I Paid Hitler,* which refers not, as Bracher indicates, to the effects of the Cologne meeting, but to the aftermath of Hitler's speech before the *Industrie-Klub* almost a year earlier (Bracher, *Auflösung,* p. 694, n. 33; see also note 44, above). If the Cologne meeting had opened the coffers of big business to the Nazis, there would hardly have been need for Hitler's appeal for funds to the leaders of industry on February 20, 1933 (see *Trials of War Criminals,* VII, 555–568).

49. In early October 1931 former Chancellor Wilhelm Cuno, head of the Hamburg-America shipping line, met secretly with President Hindenburg and suggested some of the country's most prominent big businessmen for inclusion in a projected economic council. It quickly became evident, Cuno told editor Klein of the *Deutsche Allgemeine Zeitung* later the same day, that Hindenburg had not recognized most of the names (diary entry, October 5, 1931, Klein Papers). The relative unimportance of money in the political constellation of January 1933 was recognized by Goebbels, who wrote in his diary on January 6: "In view of the satisfying progress of political developments, one hardly has the desire to bother any more about the bad financial situation of the organization. If we pull it off this time, then all that will not matter any longer" (Goebbels, *Vom Kaiserhof,* p. 236).

50. On January 26, 1933, in a letter to the chairman of the *Reichsverband der Deutschen Industrie,* Ludwig Kastl, managing director of that organization and usually well informed on political developments, reported that the talk in Berlin was of a Papen-Hitler-Schacht cabinet, with Papen as Chancellor (Kastl to Krupp, Dokumentenbuch von Bülow I, Record Group 238, Case 10, NA). As late as March, Reusch described the new government as "Herr von Papen's work of political unification" and promised further support of Papen (Reusch to Kurt von Lersner, March 4, 1933, No. 400101293/12, Reusch Papers). The expectation of a new Papen cabinet was widespread in late January (see Ewald von Kleist-Schmenzin, "Die letzte Möglichkeit: Zur Ernennung Hitlers zum Reichskanzler am 30. Januar 1933," *Politische Studien,* X [1959], 91).

51. Two recent studies show this to have been the case during the Nazi party's early years: Georg Franz-Willing, *Die Hitlerbewegung: Der Ursprung 1919–1922* (Hamburg, 1962), pp. 177–198; Werner Maser, *Die Frühgeschichte der NSDAP: Hitlers Weg bis 1924* (Frankfurt a.M., 1965), pp. 396–412. A study written at the time and based on the business press concluded that the same pattern had characterized the last years before 1933: Ernst Lange, "Die politische Ideologie der deutschen industriellen Unternehmerschaft," (diss., University of Greifswald, 1933), pp. 36, 80. This was also the view of Theodor Heuss, *Hitlers Weg: Eine historisch-politische Studie über den Nationalsozialismus* (Stuttgart, 1932), p. 122.

52. There is much documentation on this in the papers of the *Reichswirtschaftsministerium,* now located in the *Deutsches Zentralarchiv,* Potsdam.

5

HANS MOMMSEN

The Political Effects of the Reichstag Fire

[TRANSLATED BY JOYCE CRUMMEY]

On January 30, 1933, Adolf Hitler was appointed Chancellor of the German republic. He gained that office legally and constitutionally but not as a result of the democratically expressed choice of the German electorate. In fact, in the last national election prior to Hitler's appointment, held in November 1932, the NSDAP's vote dropped by two million, a loss that reduced its seats in the Reichstag from 230 to 196. Two out of every three voters had cast their ballots for other parties in this last fully free election prior to the imposition of the Nazi dictatorship. Nor was Hitler's installation as Chancellor the result of normal parliamentary coalition politics. He was named instead by means of a backroom intrigue, as a cabal of conspirators overcame the doubts of aged President Hindenburg and prevailed upon him to bestow the Chancellorship on Hitler.

Even though he was now Chancellor, Hitler had not yet attained his real goal: he was still not dictator of Germany. In order to obtain his appointment he had been obliged to agree to a coalition cabinet, in which conservative elements predominated. As a result, his authority was closely circumscribed. The task of acquiring full power thus still lay before him. This selection deals with Hitler's first major step in that direction, reassessing it in the light of a variety of new evidence. The author, Professor of History at the Ruhr-University of Bochum, has also published an important study of government employees in the Third

109

Reich: Beamtentum im Dritten Reich (*Stuttgart, 1966.*) *This selection first appeared as: "Der Reichstagsbrand und seine politischen Folgen," in* Vierteljahrshefte für Zeitgeschichte, XII (*1964*), *350–413. A portion of the original article which deals in detail with the responsibility for the outbreak of the fire has been omitted here. A few additions have also been made by the author on the basis of evidence discovered since the original publication. The selection is reprinted by permission of the author.*

THE TASK OF determining culpability for the burning of the Reichstag building on the evening of February 27, 1933, and of analyzing the political effects of that event, places the historian in a peculiar position. He must explain an occurrence which remained a puzzle even to contemporaries, with a few exceptions. Understandably enough, an abundance of rumor-like conjectures tends to arise in such a case; the historian must confront these with the sober question of what can be determined empirically. While remaining sensitive to the openness of historical situations, he will resort to hypotheses only when these are necessary to make evident the connections between the established facts. He must not pursue speculations, even contemporary ones, of the sort which cannot be verified or refuted on the basis of existing evidence.

The previous confusion about the Reichstag fire has been primarily the result of such contradictory speculations, which have not gained in veracity by being exploited for propaganda purposes—or simply believed—by both the Nazis and their opponents. It is not surprising that the fire in the Reichstag building, occurring as it did a few days before the March elections of 1933, in a situation of the most extreme tension and general nervousness, gave birth to conjectures and rumors. The murder of President Kennedy, after all, under incomparably more "normal" conditions, occasioned far-fetched suppositions. Clearly, the legends which immediately sprang up around the Reichstag fire allow only the most limited conclusions as to the actual course of events. The numerous versions attributing guilt to the Nazis owed their origin not only to Willi Münzenberg's successful Communist propaganda operation in Paris and to the justified belief that the Nazis were capable of a high degree of cynical brutality. They were also fueled by the failure of the trial before the Supreme Court to provide a clarification of the facts.

Whether contemporaries believed the Communists or the Nazis to be guilty, the background of the incendiarism remained a puzzle to them. This uncertainty was shared by those concerned with the case in an official capacity. The night of the fire, Rudolf Diels, head of the Prussian political police, thought it likely that the Dutchman Marinus van der Lubbe was the sole culprit; later he suspected Communist instigation; three weeks after the fire, he was considering the possibility of Nazi complicity. After 1945, he was questioned from all quarters, since he was regarded as a source of reliable information in view of his official role in 1933. Diels, however, was in no position to give even clues leading to a conclusive explanation and finally called for a systematic investigation himself, but in so doing expressed no optimism that the puzzle of the Reichstag fire could ever be solved.[1] Martin Sommerfeldt, who as Göring's press secretary compiled the initial reports during the night of the fire, doubted the official version edited by Göring. Yet his suspicion that Goebbels had planned the incendiarism rested on nothing more than vague rumors. After 1945, he too considered a clarification of the mysterious affair no longer possible.[2] Göring was evidently convinced on the night of the fire that the crime was Communist-conceived; subsequently he suppressed lingering doubts based on the possibility that van der Lubbe might after all have set the fire on his own, melodramatically claiming that he, Göring, had saved Germany from Communism.[3] Later, however, he was not sure of his story. At Nuremberg he left open the question as to whether or not an undisciplined Storm Troop (SA) commando unit might have set the fire without his knowledge.[4] Some have assumed that these self-contradictions were a sign of a guilty conscience, yet such behavior characterized most of those persons who merit consideration as direct or indirect witnesses. Almost all changed their original opinion, influenced either by the general psychosis produced by the event or by the later collapse of the Third Reich. After 1945 the custodian of the Reichstag building, Alexander Scranowitz, revised his earlier opinion that van der Lubbe must have had accomplices. The report drawn up after the event by the Berlin Fire Department was diametrically opposed to the testimony given under oath by the same officials before the Supreme Court.[5] To continue this list would only demonstrate that witnesses give questionable testimony about a subject on which passionate public debate is focussed; scarcely any of the surviving witnesses were able to remain unmoved by the stream of rumors or unburdened by the weight of clichés.

Surely more than mere political prejudice was involved in the historical profession's long acceptance of the theory of Nazi incendiarism and its reluctant and hesitant abandonment of that theory after Fritz Tobias had cast doubt upon it with his series of articles in the magazine

Der Spiegel.[6] A somewhat constricted methodological formulation of the problem had directed research on the initial phase of the Third Reich primarily toward manifestations of planned totalitarian manipulation. The Reichstag fire was regarded as a veritaole showpiece for the achievement of dictatorship through terror, a masterpiece of Nazi expertise in taking their opponents by surprise. The Emergency Decree for the Protection of People and State, to which the fire gave rise, was then obviously a well-calculated step in the gradual progress toward the totalitarian consolidation of power.[7] To be sure, Martin Broszat wrote after the publication of Tobias's *Spiegel* series that it was of little historical significance whether the Nazis were only virtuosos at swift improvisation or whether they set the fire themselves.[8] But he bypassed the real questions which necessarily follow once the idea of Nazi culpability is refuted: whether the Nazi leadership really exploited this event, which at least in its actual form was unexpected, with virtuosity; whether Hitler and his closest cohorts were really such splendid manipulators; whether they owed the success of the Reichstag fire and its consequences as an issue in the ensuing election campaign to political cunning or to blind luck. In investigating the complex problem presented by the Reichstag fire, it is not a matter of justifying the Nazi leadership in this or that point. What must be understood is that not everything the Nazis were able to exploit in order to consolidate their rule was the result of thoughtfully planned and purposeful behavior. In the Nazis' own statements—especially in Goebbels's propaganda—there is a consistent tendency to interpret as masterpieces of statesmanlike improvisation all the measures which were taken without previous deliberation, which were determined by confusion or surprise rather than planning and foresight. By the same token that it would be unacceptable to pass over the crafty scheming behind many Nazi tactical maneuvers, it would be quite wrong to ignore the fact that, in contrast to Bolshevism, Nazism had no carefully planned long-range strategy, but rather owed many of its successes to impatient, unpremeditated, snap decisions, made within a flexible framework of ultimate goals. Even the Nazis' self-incriminations with regard to the Reichstag fire are a result of this *post factum* propagandistic rationalization of their own actions. The "nervousness" (as Martin Broszat characterized it) with which Tobias's findings were received by the public, as well as the excessive skepticism displayed by experts, both resulted from his challenge—in connection with an incident that had come to have symbolic significance—to the widespread inclination to overestimate the manipulative skills of the Nazis in order to exculpate the German people.[9]

In accepting without question the results of the "criminal investigation" and the verdict of the Supreme Court (which was taken as proof of its opposite), historical research had in fact closed the door to a solution of the problem. There could be no escape from the direct and indirect influences of Münzenberg's masterful *Brown Book* forgeries, which were perpetuated, quite innocently it seems, in numerous memoirs. One significant by-product of Fritz Tobias's analysis is the exposure of the insidious influence of these Communist forgeries, which has continued down to the present.[10] The version of the Reichstag fire that is prevalent in historical writing was nourished chiefly by such sources. Richard Wolff's unfortunate investigation also failed because it was carried on without even the rudiments of a critical approach to the sources.[11] Fritz Tobias's indisputably great service to historical knowledge—breaking the "sound barrier" of Communist-influenced accounts —was as a rule overlooked by his opponents, who all too frequently reproached him with creating legends.[12] It is time to counter these severe attacks on Tobias's work with the elementary observation that, however controversial his interpretation may be, his investigation cannot be described as sensationalism, but instead deserves recognition as serious research. It is based on a carefully assembled, comprehensive body of material which cannot be disregarded.[13] If historians had been alert enough to note that even the prosecution at Nuremberg had refrained from entering the Reichstag fire in the list of Nazi crimes, then the outsider, Tobias, would not have been able to show them how insufficient their attention to the fundamentals of a critical use of evidence had been.

In contrast to the increasing acknowledgment of Tobias's findings in the West is the severe criticism they have encountered in the historical scholarship of the German Democratic Republic, which insofar as it seeks to pump life back into the old *Brown Book* thesis is a belated victim of Münzenberg's forgeries.[14] There is of course no need to refute expressly the grotesque East German reproach that Tobias, and Western historical research with him, aim at vindicating the Nazis and reviving the view that the Communists set the fire.[15] Otherwise, East German writers on the subject, with their natural wish to gloss over the failure of the Communist Party of Germany in those weeks so decisive for the consolidation of Nazi power, have become aligned with a group of Western authors, who, for reasons difficult to understand, ignore the available evidence and substitute conjecture for established knowledge.[16]

The refutation of the theory of multiple complicity and the acknowledgment that one individual could have set the Reichstag fire make it unnecessary to investigate in detail the question as to the spontaneity of Göring's and Hitler's reactions to the report of the fire. Their surprise was genuine. Goebbels thought that the news, which Hitler's press secretary, Ernst Hanfstaengl, gave him by telephone, was a bad joke.[17] Göring's immediate reaction seems to have been utter consternation; he went at once to the burning Reichstag building. His first thought was to save the Gobelin tapestries and the library.[18] He arrived at the Reichstag about 9:30 p.m., shortly after the Main Chamber had gone up in flames and the tenth-stage alarm for the Fire Department had been sounded. Göring's behavior does not lead to the conclusion that he welcomed the fire.[19] He gave the necessary instructions, spoke briefly with Fire Director Gempp, and asked to see Geheimrat Galle, Director of the Reichstag. Undersecretary Grauert, who accompanied Göring, began at once to investigate the incendiary act. He learned of the evidence against the Communist Reichstag deputies Ernst Torgler and Wilhelm Koenen, and remained thereafter convinced that the Communists were behind the fire.[20]

Göring later said that the word "incendiaries" had given him the spontaneous idea that the Communists were guilty.[21] However, it is more probable that Grauert's reports first gave rise to this impression. A bit later, Rudolf Diels arrived, learned of van der Lubbe's arrest, and attended the first interrogations.[22] Göring was probably informed at that time that only one of the incendiaries, a Dutch Communist, had been caught (that van der Lubbe was a Communist was assumed from the start). Göring can scarcely have disregarded the prevailing impression that the blaze was a case of large-scale incendiarism carried out by a whole group of accomplices. He ordered a search of the tunnel connecting the Reichstag and his official residence as President of the Reichstag, which his SS bodyguard Walter Weber and three policemen completed without results.[23]

Sommerfeldt reports having been awakened about 11 p.m. and taken immediately to the Reichstag building by car. But this must have occurred much earlier, about 10:15 p.m. For he met Göring before the latter "really got going," to quote Goebbels.[24] Göring is said by Sommerfeldt to have been quite composed, giving Sommerfeldt the impression that "even he was rather taken aback by this fire, without as yet assigning to it too much importance." Göring calmly directed Sommerfeldt to compile a report for the press.[25] It was probably a little after 10:00 p.m. when Göring ordered the first security measures, acting in his capacity as Minister of the Interior for Prussia. When Hitler arrived, Göring reported that he had mobilized the entire police force and placed all public buildings under their guard. *Wolffs Telegrafen-Büro* reported on the remaining security precautions in its second morning edition of February 28.[26]

Hitler, Goebbels, and their party probably did not arrive on the scene before 10:20 p.m. Sefton Delmer, an English journalist who was present, reports that Goebbels had first sent out Gauleiter Hanke to determine what was actually going on.[27] Göring met Hitler at the entrance to the lobby behind Portal II. Delmer confirms that Göring told Hitler that the fire was indubitably the Communists' doing, that one incendiary had been arrested, and that several Communist Reichstag deputies had been in the Reichstag building twenty minutes before the outbreak of the fire. Vice-Chancellor Franz von Papen had already arrived; Göring had greeted him with the statement: "This can only be an act of violence against the new government!"[28] Papen did not question this.

It must be borne in mind that Göring introduced the idea, based on the rumors conveyed to him, that the Reichstag fire involved a Communist "attempt at insurrection." This explains the extensive security measures which he undertook independently, measures immediately characterized by the British ambassador, Sir Horace Rumbold, as the emanations of "hysteria."[29] Delmer has commented, "I am convinced that he was serious and was not merely putting on a show."[30] After Göring's report on the situation to the other leaders of the government, the important officials made a tour of the building while the Fire Department tried to contain the terrible blaze in the Main Chamber. This tour served to illustrate the danger conjured up by Göring. Delmer, the only journalist who had succeeded in entering the building and in speaking with Hitler during the tour, reported, among other things, the following words: " 'God grant,' he said to me, 'that this is the work of the Communists. You are a witness to the birth of a great epoch in German history.' " A little later, Hitler declared to von Papen: "This is a God-given signal, Vice-Chancellor. If this fire is, as I believe, the work of the Communists, then we must crush that deadly plague with an iron fist." Delmer did not conclude from these words that Hitler was completely sure of himself, commenting that the Chancellor was "not yet entirely convinced on that evening that he was dealing with a Communist attack."[31] There is no doubt that Hitler very shortly thereafter adopted the latter view. Did he believe it or was he putting on an act?

In his memoirs, Rudolf Diels gives an account of Hitler's reaction. He met Hitler and his party on a balcony opening into the Main Chamber. Hitler, Diels writes, was extremely excited, and Göring came toward him to intone with portentous pathos, "This is the beginning of the Communist uprising; they are about to strike! Not a moment must be lost."[32] The dignitaries then gathered in the Reichstag President's Chamber. Diels writes that he attempted to report to Hitler on the results thus far of the interrogations of van der Lubbe. Hitler, he continues, was completely beside himself, demanding that every Communist official be shot wherever encountered. The Communist deputies, Hitler raged, were to be hanged that very night; no mercy was to be shown to Social Democrats or the *Reichsbanner* either. Under the circumstances, Diels's attempt to convince Hitler of the sole culpability of van der Lubbe was futile.

The report just summarized is indirectly confirmed by the notes on Diels's reaction which Schnitzler made indepedently.[33] "Diels described as 'wild' and 'excited' the first discussion among the Nazis in the burning Reichstag. The mood in which the initial political measures were ordered was one of impulsiveness rather than clear-headed consideration. After Hitler came to himself from a trance-like state, Diels said, he reviled the 'sub-human' Communists in a seemingly endless outburst of fury. Not even a glimmer of additional proof was needed to convince him that the Communists 'wanted to give the signal for their arrogantly proclaimed mass action through the shameful burning of a German monument.' Diels recounted that Hitler had ordered in all seriousness that every single Communist deputy in the Reichstag be hanged."[34] Was this inclination to monomaniac outbursts, so noticeable in Hitler, still rationally motivated here? Was this an instance of that self-induced excitement which allowed him to believe at any given moment in the truth of the words he was speaking? Surely the following excerpt from Goebbels's diary is dubious: "Now the decisive moment has come. The Führer has not taken leave of his calm for a moment; it is remarkable to see the same man who sat at our dinner table half an hour ago in carefree conversation now issuing his orders here."[35]

This consultation in the Reichstag President's Chamber lasted scarcely over half an hour. Those present, besides Göring, Hitler, and Goebbels, were Frick, the Minister of the Interior for the Reich, and Police President von Levetzow, whom Göring had summoned; probably Count Helldorf[36] was present, too, but Papen had left the building in order to brief the President.[37] The meeting was largely taken up with Hitler's tirades; there was no calm discussion, let alone cold-blooded calculation. Hitler seems to have concentrated mainly on demands for terroristic and coercive measures against the Communists. In all likelihood, he was thinking chiefly of the elections. A subsequent press communiqué contains the announcement that, "As reported, Adolf Hitler declared at the scene of the fire that the elections will take place under all circumstances on March 5. The Reich must now take those measures necessary to subdue and stamp out this most horrible danger not only to Germany but to all of Europe."[38]

Nevertheless it was not Hitler who gave orders, but rather Göring; the Führer's hate-filled declarations gave him a green light. His great moment had come! According to Diels's report, Göring overwhelmed him with an abundance of rather confused orders, among them "full-scale police alert, unsparing use of firearms, mass arrests of Communists and Social Democrats."[39] "In the discussion," Schnitzler recalls, "Diels took notes of individual points on loose slips of paper. Afterwards he was concerned whether he had included all the measures demanded in their frenzy by the men of the new government, who lacked any expert knowledge of the instruments of power and justice on which they pretended to be able to play."[40] Doubtless, Göring demanded not only a two-week suppression of the Social Democratic press in Prussia, but also the arrest of that party's officials. Evidence for this is provided by the inclusion of the Social Democrats in a parallel action under the command of Helldorf, who was either present at the meeting or was given his orders by Göring shortly thereafter. Schnitzler, probably in accord with Diels, had sent out to police radio stations an order for the arrest of all Communist deputies in the Reichstag, the state parliaments, and the city assemblies, and of all Communist Party officials, as well as an order for the confiscation of all Communist newspapers.

The critical observations which Diels and Schnitzler later made about this episode were directed at the manner in which political decisions of far-reaching consequence were made on the spur of the moment and without clear-headed consideration of their probable results. There was no reason for contrived and propagandistically motivated theatrics, since all these actions took place out of sight of the public. These were not cynically calculating power-politicians posturing for effect. It was therefore not a case of their clearly grasping the facts of the case and exploiting them in virtuoso fashion for their own purposes. Hitler and Göring were obviously in no position to establish the real causes of the fire, and even to say that they did not want to do so would be misleading. Their reactions sprang from a level beneath that of conscious reason, from one dominated by instinct and vanity. Using normal standards, there is no way to account for Hitler's outbursts of hatred and rage, culminating in the senseless demand that all Communist officials be hanged at once. Likewise, Göring's reactions were not histrionics; in normal circumstances, he was capable of giving clear and unambiguous orders. Given his intense rivalry with Goebbels, he was surely influenced by an ambition to distinguish himself as Prussian Minister of Police.

Under these circumstances, it is of some importance whether the commands to Diels were intended to deal with a real situation or were totally without basis. Göring's belief in a Communist uprising was not merely a product of his excitable imagination. It was nourished by reports to that effect from police headquarters. Detective-Inspector Heisig interrogated the chief suspect and certified that van der Lubbe had used the words "signal" and "beacon" and had referred to the coming of the time to "strike out" against a system inimical to the workers.[41] Under the circumstances, this was interpreted by Heisig and the observers present, who included Police President von Levetzow, as meaning that the Communists were attempting an uprising. In the hectic, unreal atmosphere the night of the fire, this was enough to convert suspicion into certainty. Only a few remained skeptical; it was not a matter of a general psychosis that had to be created artificially; the highly charged political situation was sufficient cause for it. There is no reason to doubt that the Nazi leaders for the moment took seriously the specter of a Communist uprising, especially since they expected one. On January 31 Goebbels had noted in his diary, "The Bolshevik attempt at revolution must first actually flare up. Then, at a suitable moment, we will strike."[42] He remarked concerning the consultation in the burning Reichstag building: "There can be no doubt that the Communists are making a last attempt to create disorder through fire and terror so as to seize power in the general panic."[43] The question of how great a danger the Communists actually were to the Nazis need not be asked at present. All evidence points to the arrest orders as being a spontaneous reaction to the idea of Communist revolt which was seized upon as a watchword by eager imaginations.

The inclusion of the SPD in these measures was also connected with the findings in the interrogation of van der Lubbe. His words had, after all, led to the suspicion, which the examining magistrate was forced to deny in a press communiqué on March 22, that not only the KPD but also the SPD was behind the presumed plot.[44] This, too, was understandable in view of the prevailing atmosphere of weird unreality in which the most senseless rumors were accorded credibility. National Socialist propaganda and a mentality which both consciously and unconsciously lumped Communists and Social Democrats together supported this grotesque assumption. Moreover, Paragraph 6 of the "Decree on Treason Against the German People and Seditious Agitation" of February 28, which was directed against political strikes, reveals that threats by the SPD and KPD regarding a general strike were taken quite seriously by the government.[45] It is hard to imagine what would have happened if Diels had followed the orders to arrest the Social Democrats, to disband the *Reichsbanner* by force, and so on. If there was any premeditated motive behind these directives, it could only have been aimed at exploiting a situation of general civil war in order to settle old political accounts. The consultation was concluded without further results in the Chamber of the Reichstag President at about 11 p.m. But there seems even then to have been some thought of proclaiming a state of emergency. According to a press communiqué, the cabinet was to "meet for a special conference that very night" in order to consider "the political consequences of the Reichstag fire."[46]

About 11:15 p.m. Hitler and Göring left the smouldering building and went to the Prussian Ministry of the Interior. There a conference took place which was designated—it seems erroneously—as a "cabinet meeting" in the aforementioned communiqué. Participants included Vice-Chancellor von Papen, Police President von Levetzow, Undersecretary Grauert, State Secretary von Bismarck, and Oberregierungsrat Diels. Frick, who had attended the previous meeting, was absent, perhaps simply because the others were charged with Prussian, rather than Reich, affairs. The composition of the assembled body indicates that the discussion was primarily concerned with security measures and arrests. In Göring's testimony before the Supreme Court, the conference is described thus: "There we discussed the entire situation again. It was immediately decided that I was at once to cancel my campaign appearances for the next few days. For it was clear that under the circumstances I could not leave Berlin." He was empowered, he continued, to make all necessary arrangements; furthermore, a cabinet meeting was scheduled for the next day.[47] As is evident in the aforementioned press communiqué concerning Hitler's words at the site of the fire, the uppermost consideration for him was that the elections be held "regardless of all else." It remains to be seen what occasioned this peculiar statement. According to Police Inspector Reinhold Heller's testimony, the precipitously launched wave of arrests was again officially sanctioned at the meeting in the Prussian Ministry of the Interior, and it is possible that the circle of persons to be arrested may also have been designated then.[48] The Reichstag Fire Decree, which has since aroused so much controversy, was by no means central to the discussion. Undersecretary

Grauert, probably thinking of the pressing necessity of legalizing the arrests, suggested issuing an "emergency decree against incendiary and terrorist acts." Grauert, who was firmly convinced that the Communists had started the Reichstag fire, thus gave the impetus for a decisive step in Hitler's march to unrestrained dictatorship.[49]

The draft of the emergency decree which Grauert submitted for consideration was definitely different from the one laid before the cabinet the next day. Initially, a decree valid only for Prussia was proposed, and Frick's reference to the Prussian Emergency Decree of July 20, 1932, may have been influenced by this memory. This is confirmed by Blomberg's statement at the Conference of Military Commanders on March 1: "It is a tribute to Hitler's presence of mind that the new emergency decree was extended to the whole Reich."[50] In the light of Blomberg's statement, Hitler must have accepted Grauert's suggestion but decided to discuss it the next day at the meeting of the Reich cabinet. This interpretation accords with Grauert's statement that the Prussian Ministry of the Interior played no further role in the matter.[51]

After the meeting in the Prussian Ministry of the Interior, Hitler went with Goebbels to the editorial offices of the *Völkischer Beobachter*. They stopped the linotype machines and had a new front page made up.[52] Since the South German Edition had already gone out, it did not contain a word about the Reichstag fire. Goebbels began a hectic press campaign. That very night he wrote an inflammatory editorial invoking the horror of a successful Communist campaign of terrorism, referring to the Communist Party's intention of seizing power amidst "general panic."[53] In the releases of the official Prussian Press Service, which *Wolffs Telegrafen Büro* published in its second edition for February 28, the Reichstag fire was characterized as a "signal for bloody revolt and for civil war," and it was asserted, in line with Göring's hunger for power, that "the first assault of the outlaw forces" had "for the moment been repulsed."[54] Actually, at the time the report was issued, the police action had barely begun.[55] Civil and criminal police, the report continued, had been given a full-scale alert, and 2,000 Nazi Storm Troopers had been called up as auxiliary police to protect the capital of the Reich. On March 1, the *Völkischer Beobachter* reported on a planned "St. Bartholomew's night" in Berlin and made disclosures about a Communist insurrectionary plot, which Göring had unearthed among outdated and erroneously interpreted Communist material dealing with a possible proletarian insurrection.

As Tobias has shown, Goebbels's direction of the press was, despite all his efforts, faulty, and not only with regard to reportage on the fire and its causes. In the general confusion, even the *Völkischer Beobachter* reported—only to deny it the next day—that the Communist deputy Torgler had given himself up voluntarily.[56] It is understandable that Göring should have referred on the night of the fire to Sommerfeldt's communiqué as "crap," as "a police report from Alexanderplatz" (the headquarters of the Berlin police) for which he had no use, since he was girding himself for a devastating counterattack against the Communists.[57] Sommerfeldt conjectured that Goebbels was behind Göring's change of mind, but the matter was much simpler than that; even if Göring had believed in the sole culpability of van der Lubbe, he could no longer abandon his political interpretation of the event without rendering himself—and the police measures—ridiculous.

That was the situation in the night of February 27–28. It presents a series of questions. It must first of all be borne in mind that the Nazi leaders acted in a state of surprise and agitation. Were they really convinced that the Reichstag fire represented a Communist act of terrorism? Hitler's initial uncertainty would not have prevented him from adopting Göring's view shortly thereafter. For the results of the investigation, including the false testimony concerning Torgler, confirmed this suspicion; moreover, there was a general inclination to attribute the fire to a political act. It can therefore be presumed that the Nazis were convinced that the fire was the work of the Communists. It is far more difficult to ascertain whether, and if so, to what degree, they believed in a Communist uprising or a planned chain of terrorist acts, and at what point they recognized this belief to be erroneous. The difficulty in answering this question is that there are almost no contemporaneous statements which the historian is not obliged to view as either possibly or necessarily motivated by tactical considerations. Moreover, the whole political style of Nazism consisted of consciously subordinating the quest for truth to partisan combat. Goebbels's expectation of an attempted Communist uprising corresponds to a variety of indirect indications to the effect that the KPD would not allow the Nazis to come to power without a fight.[58] From our present knowledge of the situation and policy of the German Communist Party in the weeks after the power seizure, we may conclude that the Nazis overestimated this opponent.[59] Hitler's belief that it was politically inexpedient to proscribe the KPD, as his German National coalition partners wanted him to, was certainly not based totally on the tactical consideration that the result might be a substantial increase in votes for the SPD.[60] The history of his own movement had taught him how little success such a ban would have.[61]

Nazism, after all, did confront an opponent whose defeat it had made an inflammatory campaign promise. Unquestionably, the rise of Nazism was substantially aided by the middle-class fear of Communism, which was not only promoted by the propaganda of all the rightist parties, but fueled as well by the actual condition of civil war between the German Communist Party and the National Socialist Party. Tactically, it was thus essential not to eliminate this opponent until the Nazis were firmly established in power. It is probable, however, that the Nazi leaders wondered with growing concern why the Communist Party submitted to the increasingly severe provocations of the SA rather than unleashing the counterattack—which would have freed Hitler from the fetters laid upon him by the German National People's Party cabinet members and the army. The unaccustomed nervousness which gripped Hitler on the night of the fire indicates that he saw the moment of the great confrontation coming, that he thought the Communist putsch imminent. That would explain the hasty reaction, for example, in immediately ordering security measures to protect public buildings, museums, palaces, bridges, railroads. These were measures aimed at forestalling the enemy.

To test this hypothesis, we must ask first of all whether, in light of the situation, there were grounds for the government to assume that the Communists were intent on violent insurrection. Certainly, memories of the Communist uprisings during the Weimar Republic were a factor. But in actuality things were more complicated than that. Characteristic of the vacillating tactics of the KPD in those weeks were the contradictory actions of the Central Committee, which indefinitely postponed the idea of an active struggle of the working class against Hitler but at the same time provided the lower units of the party with literature that called, directly or indirectly, for armed resistance.[62] Considerable quantities of such literature flowed into the news center of the Interior Ministry, along with a large number of confiscated weapons.[63] There is still no trace of the material found in the second search of the Karl-Liebknecht House, which Göring called the most substantial evidence justifying his measures.[64] These finds, along with the rumors in circulation, produced an intense nervous anticipation of Communist actions. On February 27 the Criminal Police Bureau of Berlin issued a radio communiqué to the effect that the KPD had laid plans for armed attacks on police patrols and nationalistic organizations, either on the day of the Reichstag elections or shortly before or after them. The communiqué recommended "suitable measures in advance, possibly protective custody for Communist Party officials."[65] This information could scarcely have corresponded to reality; but it must not be dismissed as a propagandistic move. It demonstrates instead the general overestimation of Communist activity and shows that it was in keeping with the prevailing mood to suspect the KPD of setting the fire.[66] The passivity of the leaders of the KPD despite numerous individual terrorist acts is confirmed by the extensive material gathered in connection with the Reichstag fire trial.

From the viewpoint of today's greater understanding of Communist revolutionary strategy, these pieces of evidence are pitifully inadequate proof of an alleged Communist resolve to revolt. But at that time, in the fog of general confusion, propaganda brochures such as Sommerfeldt's *Kommune* shone with the clear light of proof. Even the responsible criminal police, who had by no means yet been "brought into line" (*gleichgeschaltet*) by the Nazis, tended to overestimate Communist activity. A report dated March 14 gives the view that "the Communists not only advocate in their program preparation for armed revolt to overthrow the Constitution, but also intend to carry out in practice their programmatic demands and principles."[67] Police Inspector Heller, as an expert witness before the Supreme Court, assembled materials to prove that the Communists planned to overthrow the government, only to contest the assumption that they were ready for action.[68] Nevertheless Heller held to the view that the material he presented justified the theory of an attempt at insurrection.

It can be presumed with some certainty that Göring believed in the specter of a Communist uprising, at least on the night of the fire. Since he had become Prussian Minister of the Interior, he had dreamed of nothing but crushing such an attempt at revolution.[69] As he emphasized in the cabinet meeting of March 2, he did not expect it before the election. In addition, Göring made a number of remarks in his testimony before the Supreme Court which are completely credible by virtue of their cynical frankness and tactical clumsiness, and which were criticized sharply by Goebbels, probably just for that reason. The Reichstag fire had come as a surprise to him, said Göring; moreover, it in no way fitted into his plan of action. From the first moment, to be sure, he had been intent upon delivering a counterblow to the Communists. But the police apparatus which he had taken over still had shortcomings, lacking in particular the determination to display the necessary ruthlessness. Göring expressly admitted having given what was later termed the "order to shoot" (*Schiessbefehl*). He had, he testified, deliberately ruled out the possibility of carrying on the fight with the SA and SS alone: "I could not completely bypass the newly formed state, with its corps of officials—which I wanted to rebuild, reorganize, and fill with a new spirit—when it was called upon for the first time to serve as an organ for the preservation of the new state. That would have shaken at the outset the confidence of the government officials in the new leadership."[70] Undoubtedly, at the time of the Reichstag fire the reorganization of the Prussian police into a dependable instrument of Nazism was not yet complete. The SA Auxiliary Police, called into being by a decree of February 22, was still in the formative stages; it took no part worthy of mention in the wave of arrests in Berlin.[71] Moreover, personnel changes in the Berlin Police Department were only beginning.

The nonetheless considerable success of the improvised arrest action can be attributed chiefly to the fact that the political police organization was still intact, complete with the old officials, who dated from the time of the Social Democratic Interior Minister for Prussia, Carl Severing. The arrests were carried out on the basis of the lists prepared earlier by the democratic government in case the KPD were banned. Göring had had these lists augmented and brought up to date.[72] The official figure of 4,000 Communists arraigned during the weeks after the Reichstag fire cannot conceal the fact that the action was in great measure a shot in the dark which, being premature and improvised, caused the Communists to concentrate on building an illegal organization. The British Ambassador, Sir Horace Rumbold, reported on March 2: "Though Communist leaders have been arrested, I am told on reliable authority that their organization has gone to ground and is intact but that no instructions for armed resistance have been issued to the party members."[72a] Although the KPD was surprised by the action—the Central Committee was meeting at the very time of the Reichstag fire and could not be contacted even by the officials of the party[73]—numerous prominent Communists escaped arrest.

The action was thus by no means the brilliant success the Nazi press claimed. Göring indirectly admitted this, remarking at the trial before the Supreme Court that he felt the Reichstag fire had "completely upset" what was in itself a "beautifully constructed plan"; it had made him "uncomfortable, extremely uncomfortable"; he had been like a general who, wishing to carry out a great plan of battle, is forced by an impulsive action on his opponent's part suddenly to attack from a completely unforeseen direction, redispersing his troops and taking up a new combat position. He had expected the Communist counterthrust in the three to four weeks between the Reichstag fire and the convocation of the Reichstag, that is, "at the time when the Communists' deputies were being excluded from the parliament but when the Communist leaders were not as yet in prison." He wanted the attack to come from the other side and hoped to complete his deployment systematically. The elections were to serve as the buildup for the onslaught by providing information about Communist sympathizers. After the elections, Göring stated, the Communist deputies were "of course to be barred." They would, in his view, scarcely have submitted without a struggle, lest the leaders lose face among their followers. But in either case, resistance or passive compliance, the Communists could have been crushed easily, and the escape of parts of the KPD leadership, such as actually occurred after February 27, would have been avoided.[74]

This declaration, in the presence of the world press, reveals the cynical frankness with which the Nazis customarily disclosed the motives behind their own actions. For not only was it revealed that the KPD was to be incited to revolt but also that there were plans, in case the two-thirds majority for the Enabling Act could not be obtained by quasi-legal means, to achieve it by expelling the Communist deputies.[75] Göring explained that the Nazis had no interest in proscribing the KPD, which would only cause Communist voters to cast their ballots for the SPD or even the Center Party.[76] Göring admitted that the first search of the Karl-Liebknecht House had been primarily a propaganda maneuver and had yielded no significant results. Only concern for the mood of the general populace had brought him to initiate such an assault on the night of the fire.

Was this then an admission that Göring had decided out of concern for "general popular sentiment," and as a campaign tactic, to set in motion the wave of arrests and the use of force against the KPD during the night of the fire? The statement is on the same plane as Hitler's introductory remark, in the cabinet meeting of February 28, that the "psychologically correct moment" for a confrontation with Communism had now come. There are a number of arguments against such an oversimplification in interpreting these statements. At the time Göring spoke, the passivity of the KPD had rendered absurd the idea of a large-scale planned uprising. Precisely this fact gave such great plausibility to the accusations in the foreign press that Göring was the real incendiary. Like the criminal experts, Göring attempted to portray the Reichstag fire as a link in the chain of terrorist acts that were to lead to the uprising, since it was impossible to maintain the original assertion that the fire was to be the signal for an immediate rebellion. Göring held stubbornly to the general accusation, and represented the situation as one in which the KPD's plans had been forestalled by the measures taken the night of the fire. In response to Torgler's objections he asked, with rather unconvincing irony, why the Communists gave instructions for civil war if they did not mean to carry them out.[77] It was this same Göring who had thoughtlessly set in motion the whole vast panoply of the show-trial, much against the warnings of Diels.

We can conclude from all this that the National Socialist leaders expected Communist countermeasures, but only at a later date. The fragmentary sources permit only a partial answer to the question of how Hitler and his party evaluated the political situation the night of the fire and what political measures they envisioned. It is conceivable that Hitler worked himself into imagining, as described in Goebbels's diary, that the Communists intended to unleash a general panic. His first reactions, such as the demand that the Communists be hanged, were absurd. The paralysis of Communist agitation could be achieved effectively—and had in large measure already been achieved—through proscription of newspapers, meetings, and demonstrations. Of course, Hitler, with his ever-alert instinct for popular sentiment, must have immediately thought of exploiting the middle classes' fear of Communism as a campaign slogan. This may explain what Rumbold called the "panic-stricken" security measures[78] which were kept in force for two weeks—not merely until the elections. To include the SPD in the arrest action would have meant undercutting the effectiveness of this maneuver and, even more importantly, departing from Hitler's tactical line in the weeks before the adoption of the Enabling Act, which consisted of emphasizing the legality of the new government's methods.

This context gives special force to the statement that the elections "must take place under all circumstances" on March 5. The main topic of the conference in the Prussian Ministry of the Interior was the continuation of the election campaign. In the cabinet meeting the next morning, Hitler took up this theme again: "The assault on the Reichstag building must change neither the election date nor that for convening the Reichstag." At the same time he suggested the City Palace in Potsdam as a meeting place for the Reichstag.[79] From this it may be concluded that Hitler saw the fire as a clumsy attempt to prevent the convocation of the Reichstag. But it is not clear why Hitler, even before the session in the Prussian Ministry of the Interior, thought it necessary to take a stand against a change in the election date. Had von Papen expressed the opinion that it was expedient under the circumstances to postpone the elections? This is improbable, since in that case Hitler would not have troubled the cabinet further with the question. What did "under all circumstances" mean? It could only mean that the elections had to be held even in an emergency situation, perhaps even when a state of emergency had been proclaimed. These two reactions, the spontaneous assumption that a Communist putsch was beginning, and the refusal to postpone the elections, could not be the product of propagandistic manipulation.

If one takes into consideration the hysteria that seized members of the government in the burning Reichstag, it seems probable that Hitler saw in the "attack against the new government" an attempt to wrest from his grip the weapon of legality, to force the National Socialist Party into a civil war, and above all else to jeopardize the holding of elections. Significant in this connection are Hitler's opening remarks in the conference with the cabinet members held on the morning of February 28. "The Chancellor explained that a merciless struggle against the KPD was now urgent. The psychologically correct moment for the struggle had now come. It was pointless to wait any longer. The KPD was bent upon an all-out struggle. The fight against it must not be restricted by juridical considerations. Since the Reichstag fire, he no longer doubted that his government would now win 51 percent in the elections."[80] These words most obviously indicate a decision to fight the Communists sooner than expected. There is a double motivation: as always for Hitler, the propaganda value and the objective necessity of the struggle run parallel to one another, or rather, they blur into each other. To be sure, calm had been restored since the night of the fire, when suspicions of imminent Communist actions had been rife. There could be no thought that a Communist putsch was under way. On the other hand, it was not merely propagandistic exaggeration when Hitler maintained that the KPD was bent upon an all-out struggle. There was no way to foresee that the Communists would be subdued without the use of force. Hitler's statement that the struggle could not be restricted by juridical considerations was probably not so much a defense of SA Auxiliary Police actions as it was a justification for the arrest of the Communist Reichstag deputies, which violated the principle of parliamentary immunity.[81] The remark that he had no more doubts that the government would win a majority reflects the fact that on February 27 there was still no certainty as to whether the elections would bring the desired results; the same holds true for the numerous assertions that Nazi power would be maintained under any circumstances. In this context, these statements are best understood as arguments against postponing the elections due to a potential or actual state of civil war.

Significantly, the Chancellor assigned relatively little importance to the emergency decree, which was scheduled as the last item on the cabinet agenda, probably because he was only cursorily acquainted with it. In any case, he still referred to it throughout as a merely defensive measure, even pointing out that "special protection should be provided for all cultural treasures of the German people." Grauert's proposal had been very similar. Meanwhile, however, Frick had taken over and, probably in the early morning hours, had arranged for a proposal to be drafted which was fundamentally different from previous emergency plans. It is revealing that it did not occur to the authors of the new decree merely to amend the "Decree on Treason Against the German People and Seditious Agitation," which had been approved by the cabinet on the morning of February 27 and submitted the next day for the President's signature, even though that decree was partially applicable to the situation believed to have arisen from the Communist incendiary act.[82] This is indicative of the spontaneity with which the Reichstag Fire Decree originated and also seems to presuppose that the initiators of the other decree had no knowledge of any preliminary drafts of it.

The genesis of the Reichstag Fire Decree, which Helmut Krausnick has called the "constitution of the Third Reich,"[83] and which Karl Dietrich Bracher has indeed shown to be fundamental to the stabilization of the Nazi system of domination, is obscure.[84] Frick noted in the cabinet meeting "that he had originally intended to amend the February 4, 1933, Decree for the protection of the German People," as a consequence of the fire in the Reichstag building.[85] The February Decree represented the first effective obstruction of parties competing with the National Socialist Party in the election campaign. Frick may have considered tightening up and extending its criminal penalties, particularly Paragraph 22, in order to make possible unrestricted protective custody of Communist opponents.[86] A contributing factor may have been a feeling, in the rush of the moment, that a revision of the February Decree, complex by any standards, would be too complicated; at any rate, Frick announced that he had decided after all to base his draft on the Prussian decree of July 20, 1932.

The nature of the decree was thus fundamentally altered. The only remnant of the original version were the strict penalties of Paragraph 5 against high treason and a series of criminal acts attributed to the Communists. In part, the inclusion of these penalties was the result of Gürtner's wishes for revision, which incidentally shows that he was not present during the initial drafting of the decree.[87] Only conjecture is possible as to the genesis of the two decisive provisions of the decree, the suspension of civil rights and the authorization, in Paragraph 2, for the Reich to assume the powers of government in the federal states. Doubtless there is a direct connection between Paragraph 2 and Göring's remark in the cabinet meeting of the previous day that by March 6 at the latest —that is, by the day after the elections—he would ask for authorization to subordinate the Hamburg police to the Reich Minister of the Interior.[88] A bit later, Göring spoke of Hamburg as a "rallying point for Communists"; even earlier there had been heavy pressure on the city Senate to replace the chief of the Hamburg police with a Nazi.[89]

A large-scale counterblow against the Communists would have presupposed a simplification of the complicated mechanism on which cooperation of the police of the various federal states depended. The Weimar Republic had been substantially weakened in its struggle against the extremes of right and left because the Reich had no law-enforcement agency of its own, and because the Reich's Public Prosecutor could act only through the prosecutors of the individual states and their auxiliary bodies.[90] Invoking the Reichstag Fire Decree, Frick requested on March 1 that the state governments immediately forbid Communist pamphlets and meetings; formally, the decision on the extent of compliance with the measures demanded by Berlin was left to the interior ministers of the various federal states.[91] However, Paragraph 2 of the new decree went much further than this and was, as a result, immediately challenged by Papen. This paragraph had originated in Frick's ministry. In reply to complaints from Württemberg that the Reich had exceeded its powers, Frick had as early as February 20 and 21 threatened to appoint a Reich commissar, as authorized by Article 48, Paragraph 2, of the Constitution; in a public speech on February 24, he extended this threat to Bavaria and Hamburg.[92] By February 27 rumors of the imminent appointment of Reich commissars for the states were circulating.[93] Frick doubtless intended to accelerate the "coordination" (*Gleichschaltung*) of state governments through Paragraph 2 of the Reichstag Fire Decree. The changes effected by Popitz and Papen in the draft of the decree proved ineffective.[94] To be sure, Frick at first denied that he intended to impose his authority on the state governments, assuring the official representative of Württemberg on March 1 that the decree was directed primarily at the Hanseatic cities, since there was unwillingness to grant the powers set forth in Paragraph 1 to states under Marxist governments.[95] The original aim of the decree was thus properly described; however, it is obvious that Frick was motivated mainly by a desire to see the authority of his own ministry increased.

The Reichstag Decree combined provisions drawn from the emergency decrees of the Papen government and from the crisis of 1923. The idea of giving it such sweeping terms may have taken shape in the Reich Ministry of the Interior, where it may merely have been seen as the technically most effective means of legalizing a relentless suppression of the Communists. It is possible that the emergency plans of the Schleicher cabinet served as a model. It is also possible that the decree's far-reaching implications may simply not have been recognized.[96] The new situation created by Paragraph 1 was, however—as the *Frankfurter Zeitung* commented on March 1—almost tantamount to a military state of emergency.[97] This marked a considerable deviation from the political line adhered to since January 30. The Reichstag Fire Decree was in no sense a calculated preparatory step toward the Enabling Act, but rather an anticipation of it by means not unlike those of a coup d'état. That it formally remained within the framework of the President's emergency powers does not alter this fact. This can be demonstrated through stylistic comparison of previous decrees, such as that of February 4, with the Reichstag Fire Decree. That of February 4 retained *pro forma* legal guarantees such as the power of judges to investigate administrative measures, the right of appeal to superior authorities—although this right in practice had little value—and the precise delineation of circumstances under which the decree was to be invoked. The Reichstag Fire Decree, on the other hand, simply abrogated the principle of government by law. It was a general enabling law with a purely fictitious time limit.[98] The justification given in the preamble, "for defense against Communist acts of violence," in no way effectively curtailed the extent of its application. It was no accident that Frick cited as his precedent von Papen's coup d'état in Prussia in July 1932. The new measure was, however, fundamentally different from the Prussian decree, for it was not the President but the Reich government that was empowered to invoke Paragraph 2. It was because of this that Papen objected feebly at the cabinet meeting on the afternoon of February 28 that it would be better to empower the President to appoint Reich commissars for the states.[99]

Until now it has been held that the Reichstag Fire Decree was for the most part the product of election campaign tactics. But what need was there for the decree? It is true that it created a "better" legal basis for the proscription of publications, meetings, and speeches; for the dispersal of campaign rallies, for confiscation of pamphlets and propaganda material, for searches in party headquarters, and for the arrest of Socialist or Communist politicians. Yet the February ordinance had already provided a legal basis for the arrests made the night of the fire. A large number of opposition newspapers had already been banned on the basis of existing decrees with little concern for the boundaries of legal authorization. An analysis of the use of such bans up to the Reichstag fire reveals no really qualitative, but only a quantitative, change after February 28. As for states other than Prussia, the Reich Minister of the Interior had been able, even before the decree was issued, to effect a far-reaching suppression of the Catholic Center Party's press as well as suppression of the other moderate newspapers.[100]

These other options were pointed out in the enforcement decree issued March 3, 1933, by Göring as Prussian Minister of the Interior. It emphasized "that when measures become necessary against members or institutions of parties other than the Communists, anarchists, and Social Democrats, these measures may be authorized through the February 28 Decree for Protection of People and State only if they can be construed as combatting such Communist agitation." Otherwise, the Decree of February 4 should be invoked.[101] Göring received frequent detailed reports from the provincial officials as to how often and in what cases the Reichstag Fire Decree was actually invoked. As these reports and the ministry's abstracts of them reveal, the decree was virtually never employed against the nonsocialist parties. At first, measures against the KPD clearly predominated, the persecution of the SPD coming to the fore only in April.[102] It is probable that the limitations placed on the scope of the decree by Göring were intended to counter charges that the election campaign alone had provided the motivation for the decree's issuance.

If the emergency decree was created for campaign purposes, it was with an eye to further terrorizing the voters. The relative success of the NSDAP in the March elections has, however, concealed the fact that the measure was a two-edged sword. The pointed criticism made by the *Frankfurter Zeitung,* that never in Germany had an election campaign taken place in a state of emergency,[103] indicates that the Nazis risked the sympathy of some groups of voters through a clear violation of the constitutional order, a violation which could no longer be attributed to provocateurs or undisciplined party underlings. After the election, the government would easily have obtained by means of parliamentary authorization the powers prematurely seized with the emergency decree.

Since in general the Nazi leaders had trouble separating truth from fiction, the prospect of terror and rebellion evoked by Hitler on the night of the fire and the next day seems to have led to several blunders. After the conference in the Prussian Ministry of the Interior, the word went out that a state of emergency should be expected. All the evidence indicates that on the night of the fire there was consideration of such a measure, limited to Prussia, and based on President Ebert's emergency decree of September 26, 1923. Then press communiqués on the cabinet meeting of February 28 made known that the government had decided to refrain from declaring a military state of emergency.[104] And indeed, this idea had actually been brought up by that time. In a conference of military commandants on March 1, as described in General Liebmann's surviving notes, Blomberg discussed the Reichstag Fire Decree and the question of the relations between the army and the rightist political organizations. The following note is significant in this connection: "Noteworthy the elimination of the army (initially, military support provided for. But this would have meant a state of emergency). It is not to be assumed that the army will be called in."[105]

The difficulty of distinguishing clearly between Hitler's tactical maneuvers and his real evaluation of the situation also makes it more difficult to interpret the negotiations that must have taken place after the Reichstag fire with the leaders of the army. The conference of military commandants had been scheduled in advance and took place on the morning of March 1.[106] Its subject was the emergency decree and the relationship between the army and special auxiliary police units recruited from the SA in carrying out the intended measures against the KPD. The conference assumed there would probably be serious clashes between rightist organizations and the KPD on election night. Furthermore, the question of a "state of insurrection" was brought up.[107] A command issued by Liebmann on March 3 transmitted Blomberg's order to cancel all military leaves between 8 p.m. on election night and the morning of March 6. All army personnel stationed on military posts were to remain there, while those living elsewhere were to stay in their homes; furthermore, telephone lines were to be constantly manned; finally, commandants and garrison commanders had to make known their whereabouts at all times. However, no military personnel were to be seen in uniform on the street during the night.[108]

These orders can be interpreted in various ways. On one level, they are in line with Göring's statement in the cabinet meeting of the next day that the Communist leaders had originally wanted to strike during the evening and night of election day.[109] This would lead to the conjecture that the Nazi leadership really expected a Communist counterblow, and, since this did not occur at the moment of the Reichstag fire, they were led to assume that a later date had been set for the conflict. At the time the Reichstag Fire Decree was issued, they believed election night had been chosen; however, on March 2 Göring stated that the KPD had put off its action until March 15. From the record of the commandants' conference it is clear that the Nazi leaders felt it necessary to revise their conjectures as to the nature of the Communist counterattack. The terse remarks of Göring, Goebbels, and Hitler give the impression that they at first expected an uprising in the usual sense of an attempted revolution, for which there had been precedents during the Weimar Republic. A general strike and open military conflict would have produced a clearcut trial of strength, in which the government would have been able to rely on the army for support. Two factors, first, the feverish examination of available material on Communist activity—the material confiscated at the Karl-Liebknecht House on February 26 could scarcely have been evaluated before the fire—and, second, the complete absence of any revolutionary actions, despite the provocative arrests, indicated that these conjectures were groundless. Even so, it is conceivable that army involvement was initially considered and then dropped, since it would mean a military state of emergency, thus leading to postponement of the elections and a strengthening of the Nazis' coalition partners, the German National People's Party.

Certainly Hitler must have sought to avoid calling the army into a domestic political conflict. The correspondent of the *Frankfurter Zeitung* also mentioned that an involvement of the army was not intended.[110] The very mention of such an involvement is interesting. It may have been that the conservatives demanded it on the night of the fire, which would explain Hitler's obdurate insistence on holding the elections and his assurance of February 28 that the government would obtain an absolute majority. That military measures were in the wind is confirmed by Dertinger's statements, although these have limited value as sources. According to a report of Dertinger's, dated March 7, Blomberg had urged the President to proclaim a military state of emergency, because this would have the advantage of making it once more possible to maintain "order in the embattled capitals of individual states." On March 9, Dertinger reported that "In order to preserve the balance of forces in the cabinet, it had been suggested that the executive power for the entire Reich be turned over to a Reich commissar or that a military state of emergency be demanded."[111] This suggestion reflects the conservatives' utopian hopes for a last-minute reversal of Hitler's gradual consolidation of power. In any case, there are abundant indications that, in the wake of the Reichstag fire and the state of civil war conjured up by Goebbels and Göring, there had been demands for a military state of emergency.

Such a demand may well have brought Hitler to the realization that, come what may, he must avoid involving the army. This would explain both his manner of reacting, which was without question hasty, and the altered interpretation of the Communists' goals indicated in Blomberg's reference to the "new combat methods of the KPD." The Communists, he said, had realized that taking over "sizable centers of power" (probably meaning use of general strikes as a means of gaining control in the cities) did not suffice to overthrow the government and that they had therefore gone over to guerrilla warfare. Since the latter tactic could not be combatted with military means, he said, the army should remain neutral, although "benevolently" neutral, while the battle was carried on by the "people," that is, by the SA shock troops. To be sure, Blomberg explained, the Reichstag Fire Decree made it possible for the state to employ all its instruments of power against Communism—yet the militarily legal instrument of combat, the army, would be inadequate under the circumstances.[112]

In the conference of commandants, Blomberg had great difficulty in overcoming the distaste and skepticism of the generals toward the "national revolution" and the forces marshaled by the Nazis in preparation for civil war. He himself called the SA actions "revenge expeditions" but excused them as inevitable, like those in Italy. Contradictorily he demanded on the one hand benevolent support, "in order that the SA not be hindered in its struggle against the Communists" and on the other hand emphasized that "the soldier should remain aloof, refraining from getting involved in the 'acts of vengeance' carried out by the SA and the police." The ambivalent attitude of the army is clear in this speech, in which Blomberg went far to accommodate Nazi wishes. As Rumbold reported on March 2, there was fear in the Reich Ministry of Defense of a Nazi coup d'état on the night of the elections.[113] Perhaps Hitler decided on an offensive against the Communists not only to terrorize the parties of the Left but also to insure his power in case of a reversal in the elections.

The "Emergency Decree for Protection of People and State," approved on the afternoon of February 28 by the cabinet and submitted at once for Hindenburg's signature, substituted a civil state of emergency for the military state of emergency which conservatives had sought. It gave over to the cabinet all powers which in case of military dictatorship are normally reserved for the Supreme Commander, with the one exception that assignment of Reich commissars to the states was made subject to certain not very demanding conditions. This explains its form, which differs from comparable emergency decrees including the "Decree on Treason Against the German People and Seditious Agitation" issued the same day. There are a good many indications that the President's consent to immediate issuance may well have been obtained with the argument that it represented the lesser evil as compared with a military state of emergency. That same argument had been used to gain Hindenburg's support for the appointment of Hitler as Chancellor in place of Schleicher, who had asked for presidential approval of a possible resort to a military state of emergency.

The decree came into being *ad hoc*. It had an important psychological impact on the election campaign by virtue of its suspension of civil rights. Hitler deliberately ignored the call to annul the decree as soon as possible.[114] Yet it was only after the election that the Nazis exploited the provision of the decree that gave the Reich government power to impose its will on the federal states. There are many indications that Hitler expected stronger resistance than he actually met. Obviously he had believed, as he stood in the burning Reichstag, that he would have to force his way ruthlessly, employing all available legal and semi-legal measures to assure that the elections would be held and that the Nazis would win. That does not mean that Hitler was panic-stricken; it was not a matter, as Tobias maintains, of his acting out of fear.[115] Hitler was too much of a monomaniac for that; not fear but autosuggestive belief in his mission made of him—and not for the first time—a dictator intoxicated with power. But neither were the arrest action and all that followed it the result of clear and purposeful decisions. The emergency decree of February 28 was not brought into being by "skillful" manipulation, rather it was a desperate and hasty plunge. This is especially true of Göring, who became so lost in the fantasy of a Communist signal for political revolt that he made some major blunders from the propagandistic point of view.

Goebbels's reaction to the absence of Communist actions was characteristic of the Nazi analysis of the situation. "Nowhere is resistance being offered. The enemy camp *seems* so taken aback by our sudden and harsh measures that it no longer dares even to defend itself."[116] It is indeed no compliment to the perspicuity of the Nazi government that absolutely nothing occurred to justify the excitement felt on the night of the fire. No Communist conspirators' headquarters had been discovered. From the press anyone could learn that the police were dealing only in conjectures. In the cabinet meeting of February 28, Göring's guesswork as to why the Communists had set fire to the Reichstag led him to the typically harebrained conclusion that they had been moved to action by the confiscation of the secret material found in the Karl-Liebknecht House, which allegedly incriminated them heavily.[117] In a highly publicized radio speech, he stated on March 1 that the KPD was still trying to complete its preparations for a civil war. As evidence for the Communists' intentions of large-scale terrorism, he offered obsolete and hackneyed material. The alleged flight of Torgler and Koenen from the burning Reichstag, cited in a radio broadcast on February 27 as proof of Communist guilt, was interpreted by Göring as indicating "a conspiracy of some kind or other, the clarification of which is being vigorously sought by both the Public Prosecutor's Office and the police."[118] Not until March 2 did Göring possess more concrete evidence of an incriminating sort; even then, although genuine, it was not of a weighty nature.[119]

The numerous accusations against the Communists were based on material provided to the government—and of course exaggerated—by the political police. Only isolated statements, such as an alleged admission by van der Lubbe of his connection with the SPD or a report of Communist plans for widespread plundering in Berlin on the afternoon of February 28, were based on pure invention. The lack of incriminating evidence does not contradict the impression that Hitler and Göring were convinced of a Communist determination to revolt; on the contrary, it would have been inconceivable to have invented such an accusation and tactically exploited it without simultaneously setting about to acquire and, if necessary, fabricate incriminating evidence. Without such evidence, the Nazis had no weapons to use against the anti-Nazi reportage in the foreign press.[120] Eventually, the examining magistrate was commissioned to compile material against the Communists in order to counter the foreign press, which persisted in pointing accusingly at Göring.[121]

To understand why the Supreme Court trial against van der Lubbe, Torgler, and Dimitroff, along with his two compatriots, was initiated, one must be acquainted with the caricature of Communist activity drawn by persons in positions of responsibility, including Göring, in the first days of March. It was a combination of Communist brochures accepted without critical examination, questionable testimony of Communist renegades (many of them with police records), and exaggerated and misleading communiqués of the regional police departments; and it included notions about the technique of Communist conspiracy which were positively childish, even in view of the self-contradictory tactics of the KPD at that time.[122] Further evidence for indictment was being sought up until the last moment.[123] The trial had been initiated because of anti-Communist grudges and continued to be slanted by them throughout. It is hard to comprehend the political naïveté of the Superior Prosecutor's Office, the judges, the expert consultants, and in good part the press correspondents. Yet this naïveté goes a long way toward explaining why Nazi propaganda was successful, particularly with the middle class, and why the voters did not respond to the emergency decree of February 28 by voting against the NSDAP.

From the standpoint of foreign policy, on the other hand, the Reichstag fire affair was from the very beginning a propaganda debacle, bringing a painful loss in prestige which reduced Hitler to rage. Münzenberg's propagandistic artistry was all the more successful as repeated blunders of the government and the Supreme Court delivered effective material into his hands. As pointed out above, the prosecutor's brief quickly collapsed. Hitler had wished a quick trial, but instead the investigation dragged on until the end of June and the trial itself from September to December 23, 1933. Only when it was too late did Goebbels try, through manipulation of the Nazi press, to gloss over the unpleasant impressions made by the trial.[124] In the end, the *Völkischer Beobachter* protested helplessly against the acquittal of the Communist defendants, which in effect inculpated the Nazis. It is the fate of dictators to become victims of their own propaganda, eventually losing the ability to recognize the truth: Hitler in the case of the Reichstag fire is a case in point. Characteristically, he later insisted on strictly avoiding that painful subject.[125]

The acquittal of the accused Communists was no particular act of heroism by the court. In view of the fact that the public in other countries was attentively following every detail of the trial, the court could not have dared to convict if it wished to retain even a semblance of credibility. The Public Prosecutor's summation was pitiful; Torgler was included in the final accusation purely for show.[126] Large portions of the trial amounted to nothing more than efforts by the Nazis to defend themselves against the charges in the world-famous *Brown Book,* which had been prepared by the Communists and rushed into print in various countries. How unsuccessful those efforts were is obvious from the fact that even today the burden of proof rests on anyone who denies that the Nazis started the fire. The government's defensive position was so clear that the acquittal of Dimitroff, Popov, and Tanev could not be avoided.[127] The execution of van der Lubbe, which—even disregarding the obviously unjust retroactively increased severity of the penalty[128]—was at the very least problematical from the juridical standpoint,[129] and was carried out quietly and with no fanfare. Nothing came of Hitler's demand, in his declaration of March 23, for the public execution of the incendiaries.[139] Marinus van der Lubbe, who had protested in vain against the unjust nature of the new Germany, went to his death resolutely.

SUMMARY

Our investigation, which would have been impossible without the pioneering research of Fritz Tobias and which in large measure has confirmed his findings, has shown that an examination of the political side of the affair also rules out any Nazi complicity in van der Lubbe's incendiary act. Both the Nazi leadership and their German National coalition partners had no doubts that the Communists were guilty. Precisely because they were unable to arrive at a satisfactory explanation of the political motives which they felt compelled to attribute to the Communists in accusing them of arson,[131] they fell victim to hallucinations of a violent uprising that were in large measure the product of their own propaganda. Germany must be protected from "Marxist" domination. This was an effective propaganda tool and at the same time an integral component in their understanding of their own political role. The fascist cult of personality allowed no other interpretation of Hitler's political activity after the fire than that of self-assured, purposeful decisions made with complete mastery of the situation. Goebbels's diary entries in these weeks show how much the Nazis' habit of stylizing their deeds as "heroic" and "of worldwide historical import" had taken possession of their very thought processes. Whether Goebbels was hopefully referring to the fire as the last obstacle before the consolidation of Nazi power,[132] whether Göring was playing up his role as savior of the state against Communist onslaughts, or whether Hitler was casting himself in the role of Europe's champion against the "Asiatic plague" of Bolshevism,[133] all were to a large extent driven by their own wishful thinking.[134]

The actions of the Nazi leadership immediately after the Reichstag fire were characterized by an inseparable blend of, on the one hand, calculated determination to exploit developments for tactical gain and, on the other, chronic inability to grasp reality—an inability conditioned by their own grudges and preconceived goals. Their reactions were guided not simply by propaganda considerations, but resulted also from a false evaluation of the political situation. To augment their own power, they had manipulated the deep emotional currents of German political life, especially the middle classes' exaggerated fear of Communist and Marxist movements. But in the process they had themselves become caught up by those currents. Under normal political circumstances this lack of perspective would have led to setbacks—not however in the spring of 1933, when the atmosphere in Germany was dominated by overexcitement and irrational factors. Even the relative success of the Nazis in the elections of March 5, 1933—a success that fell short, to be sure, of their own expectations—cannot conceal the fact that in large measure their success was fostered not by carefully calculated manipulation but rather by precipitate and uncontrolled reactions.

On the night of the Reichstag fire Hitler abruptly entered a phase of totalitarian experiments. Up to that time he had adhered to what appeared from outside to be a moderate, quasi-legal course which was, however, accompanied by mounting terrorist activities on the part of the SA and SS. The Reichstag Fire Decree amounted to an anticipation through a coup d'état of the parliamentary Enabling Act to which he aspired. Rather than being planned in advance, it was triggered by the nervous impatience with which the Nazi leaders reacted to the imagined Communist counterblow. Hitler had no way of knowing that his first bid for unlimited power would succeed without a struggle. At the first sign of Communist resistance, he "went for broke"—like an unskilled gambler—and his luck held. To be sure, Fritz Tobias misleads the reader with his picture of a civilian chancellor transformed overnight into a dictator drunk with power.[135] Nevertheless it cannot be denied that the hysterical excitement of the fire contributed importantly to Hitler's abandonment of his last inhibitions and to his complete surrender to the dynamics of power.

In clarifying the origins of the Emergency Decree for the Protection of People and State and the policy pursued by the Nazi leadership between February 27 and March 5, we have attempted to work over a plethora of data. Some of it is contradictory; some of it has been disregarded until now, including the testimony of the Nazi leaders, testimony which can only be partially discounted in terms of its propagandistic bias. We have sought not to lose sight of the personal motives of individuals in the given situation. Owing to inadequate source materials, most especially the scarcity of official documents not intended for the public eye, some of the conclusions drawn here must remain hypothetical. Among these is the question as to whether the deployment of troops was for a time seriously considered, or whether this was merely a ruse intended to gain the army's acquiescence to terrorism. It is not at all clear to what extent Hitler influenced the shape of the emergency decree. Bureaucratic influences played a major role in its origins and it is quite possible that it was intended not as a calculated step toward unlimited dictatorship, but rather as the technically simplest legal basis for the suppression of an opponent whose power had been overestimated. This does not mean that Hitler might not have immediately grasped the decree's significance as a tool of totalitarian power. For the decree revealed that the new government, when faced with its first untoward incident—and it is probable that the Reichstag fire was viewed as a real crisis—regarded normal authoritarian measures as no longer adequate. The fire brought to the surface tendencies soon to become increasingly obvious: unplanned and conflicting activities by administrative departments, lack of coordination between party and state, and the decisive role of personal rivalries at the highest level. One example is the beginning, with the arrest action, of attempts by the SS and SA to establish private concentration camps. Perhaps the measures made possible through the Reichstag fire—the taut control of state and police apparatus which the emergency decree authorized—also contributed to Hitler's success in heading off the revolutionary putsch demanded by radical Nazis, who objected to the agreements entered into with the army in the wake of the Reichstag fire.

The Reichstag fire accelerated the establishment of unlimited Nazi rule. Dictatorship, however, is always the work not only of its supporters, but also of circumstances. Germany did not fall prey to cold-blooded manipulators whose planning was determined by *Realpolitik,* but to unscrupulously brutal, uncontrolled, and coarsely cynical condottieri, who displayed their motives more openly than anyone subsequently wished to admit. Mass psychosis had taken from German voters their political sobriety and their consciousness of justice; this was just as important in bringing Hitler to power as was the opportunistic support given the Nazis by the conservative Right. Among the many lessons of the Reichstag fire, by no means the least important is the enormous role played by political myths in the breakthrough of totalitarian forces.

NOTES

1. Cf. Rudolf Diels, *Lucifer ante portas* (Stuttgart, 1950), pp. 193ff.; Institut für Zeitgeschichte (hereafter cited as IfZ) Reichstag Fire Written Testimony A-7, Diels's Letter of June 6, 1955.

2. Sommerfeldt, *Ich war dabei* (Darmstadt, 1949), pp. 29ff.

3. Cf. Diels, *Lucifer,* pp. 202f.; confirmed by the testimony of Criminal Commissar Rudolf Braschwitz (Message to the Chief Public Prosecutor, State Court of Dortmund, dated August 17, 1961, Tobias Archive).

4. International Military Tribunal, *Der Prozess gegen die Hauptkriegsverbrecher vor dem Internationalen Militärgerichtshof* (42 vols., Nuremberg, 1947), IX, 481ff. (hereafter cited as IMT, *Prozess*).

5. Fritz Tobias, *Der Reichstagsbrand. Legende und Wirklichkeit* (Rastatt, 1962), p. 304. There is an American edition, in which, however, the documentary appendix is drastically abridged: *The Reichstag Fire* (New York, 1964).

6. Tobias's articles formed the basis for his book on the subject, cited in note 5, above. For examples of earlier treatments, see Hermann Mau and Helmuth Krausnick, *Deutsche Geschichte der jüngsten Vergangenheit* (Stuttgart, 1953); Karl Dietrich Erdmann, in Bruno Gebhardt, *Handbuch der deutschen Geschichte,* IV (Stuttgart, 1959); Karl Dietrich Bracher, in Bracher, Sauer, Schulz, *Die nationalsozialistische Machtergreifung* (Cologne, 1962).

7. Cf. Karl Dietrich Bracher, "Stufen der nationalsozialistischen Machtergreifung," *Vierteljahrshefte für Zeitgeschichte* (hereafter cited as *VZG*), IV (1956), 36ff.; also Bracher in Bracher, Sauer, Schulz, *Machtergreifung,* pp. 75 and 81.

8. Martin Broszat, "Zum Streit um den Reichstagsbrand," *VZG,* VII (1960), 277.

9. *Ibid.* Bracher in Bracher, Sauer, Schulz, *Machtergreifung,* p. 81, n. 25. Rudolf Pechel in *Deutsche Rundschau,* 1960.

10. I fail to understand why Bracher still adheres to his version of the Gempp case (Bracher, Sauer, Schulz, *Machtergreifung,* p. 81), although it has been proved conclusively that Gempp never contradicted the official line; cf. his testimony before the Supreme Court, 16th day, in stenographic record of the proceedings against van der Lubbe *et al.* (hereafter cited as Stenogramm). Also, *Völkischer Beobachter,* March 3 and October 15/16, 1933, reprinted in Tobias, *Reichstagsbrand,* pp. 667ff.

11. Richard Wolff, "Der Reichstagsbrand 1933," in *Aus Politik und Zeitgeschichte* (Supplement to *Parlament*), January 18, 1956. Wolff's analysis, which historians accepted for some time, is a perfect example of tendentious bias in an otherwise sincere effort.

12. Heinrich Fraenkel, "Zu viel und zu wenig. Kritische Bemerkungen zu 'Der Reichstagsbrand' von F. Tobias," *Der Monat,* XIV (1962), 19ff.; Hans Bernd Gisevius in *Die Zeit,* XV (1962), Nos. 10ff.; Harry Wilde, "Legende um den Reichstagsbrand," *Politische Studien,* XIII (1962), 295. More recently, K. O. Freiherr v. Aretin: "Zeitgeschichtliche Aufkärung von Legendenbildungen um Ereignisse von 1933," *Frankfurter Hefte,* XIX (1964), 600–602, with the typical confusion as to causes and political effects of the Reichstag fire.

13. I am indebted to Mr. Tobias for numerous items from his archive, and an abundance of suggestions; he showed a willingness to render all possible aid. His manner of presentation leaves him vulnerable to the criticism that his method

142   NAZISM AND THE THIRD REICH

lacks precision. In particular, Hans Schneider has been responsible for such criticism (cf. Wolfgang Schwarz's article in the Munich *Süddeutsche Zeitung,* December 21–22, 1963). Although I acknowledge that Tobias has made a number of altogether insignificant mistakes of citation and translation, Schneider's view that Tobias's intent was "objective falsification of the facts" remains incomprehensible and totally unacceptable to me. It remains to be seen whether Schneider will publish his manuscript countering Tobias's arguments. Schneider has shown me his work, and I am indebted also to him for valuable suggestions.

14. Ernstgert Kalbe, *Freiheit für Dimitroff. Der internationale Kampf gegen die provokatorische Reichstagsbrandstiftung und den Leipziger Prozess* (East Berlin, 1963); K.-H. Biernath, *Der Reichstag brennt. Hintergründe und Auswirkungen der faschistischen Reichstagsbrandprovokation* (East Berlin, 1960); Alfred Kurella, *Dimitroff contra Göring* (East Berlin, 1964); O. Winzer, *Zwölf Jahre Kampf gegen Faschismus und Krieg. Ein Beitrag zur Geschichte der Kommunistischen Partei Deutschlands 1933–45* (East Berlin, 1955). Completely uncritically, Kalbe uses the London countertrial as a source (p. 45), regards Wolff's work as dependable (p. 51), likewise uses the Fire Brigade Report as a basis (p. 55), thinks the Oberfohren Memorandum was genuine (p. 43), and, after having laid claim to having clarified the problem of the Reichstag fire "except for a few factual remnants(!)," concludes: "At present it can no longer be determined with complete certainty (!) which of the Fascist leaders had the idea of burning the Reichstag" (p. 51, n. 51).

15. *Ibid.,* p. 34.

16. Besides Heinrich Fraenkel, Harry Schulze-Wilde, and v. Aretin, Hans Bernd Gisevius, in his *Bis zum bitteren Ende* (Hamburg, 1947) perpetuates the version accusing the Nazis. His account may have been influenced indirectly by the Communist *Brown Book* (cf. Erich Wollenberg in *Echo der Woche,* August 12, 1949, p. 9).

17. Ernst Hanfstaengl, *Unheard Witness* (Philadelphia, 1957), pp. 210f.; confirmed by Goebbels, *Vom Kaiserhof zur Reichskanzlei* (Munich, 1934), pp. 269f.; cf. Fraenkel, "Zu viel und zu wenig," p. 14, who insists on Hanfstaengl's version.

18. Göring's reaction was subsequently described by F. W. Jacoby, his adjutant at the time (recorded February 16, 1961, Tobias Archive): "On the day of the Reichstag fire, I gave the news to Göring as the sole adjutant then serving him. I was at that time and still am today convinced that his surprise was genuine." Similarly, State Secretary Grauert's testimony of October 3, 1957 (Tobias Archive): Grauert said he had been making a report to Göring when an official (Grauert recalled it was Daluege, but it was Jacoby) rushed in with the word that the Reichstag was burning. "Göring's reaction was so obvious and convincing that Grauert doubted as little then as later Göring's honest consternation." Cf. Tobias, *Reichstagsbrand,* p. 108.

19. Sommerfeldt, *Ich war dabei,* p. 25; Gempp's testimony as given by Tobias, *Reichstagsbrand,* p. 668. See also note 25, below.

20. Grauert's testimony, confirmed by Göring's testimony before the Supreme Court, 31st day, Stenogramm, pp. 104f.

21. *Ibid.,* p. 94: "When I heard the word 'arson' (while stopping by the sentry) . . . , a swift curtain dropped and I saw the whole drama before my eyes. The moment the word 'arson' was uttered, I knew: the Communist Party is guilty of setting fire to the Reichstag."

22. Diels, *Lucifer*, p. 192, erroneously referring to an interrogation in the Reichstag building (it actually took place in the guardhouse at the Brandenburg Gate), but in characteristic fashion repeating Lateit's impression of van der Lubbe as insane (cf. Tobias, *Reichstagsbrand*, pp. 66f.).

23. *Ibid.*, p. 111. Weber expressly confirmed his original testimony in 1960 for Tobias.

24. Goebbels, *Kaiserhof*, p. 170.

25. Sommerfeldt, *Ich war dabei*, p. 25.

26. Tobias, *Reichstagsbrand*, Appendix 14, p. 633.

27. Delmer, *Die Deutschen und ich* (Hamburg, 1962), p. 188, translation of his *An Autobiography* (2 vols., London, 1961–1962).

28. Franz von Papen, *Der Wahrheit eine Gasse* (Munich, 1952), p. 303.

29. *Documents on British Foreign Policy* (hereafter cited as *DBFP*), Second Series, Vol. IV, No. 246; Rumbold succeeded in entering the barricaded Reichstag the night of the fire.

30. Delmer, *Die Deutschen*, pp. 191f.; cf. letter to *Der Spiegel*, No. 52, 1959 (previous publication in the *Daily Express*, July 21, 1939).

31. Delmer, *Die Deutschen*, p. 190.

32. Diels, *Lucifer*, p. 193.

33. Diels's decisive report on the events in the burning Reichstag is corroborated by Sommerfeldt's statements, by the testimony of other witnesses, and above all, by the account of the same events published anonymously in a Swiss magazine by the man who accompanied him at the fire, Assessor Heinrich Schnitzler: "Der Reichstagsbrand in anderer Sicht," *Neue Politik. Organ für Freiheit und Recht*, X (1949), No. 2. This article is cited here on the basis of a photocopy in the IfZ, Munich, Zeugenschriftum, A-7).

34. Schnitzler, "Reichstagsbrand," sheet 2.

35. Goebbels, *Kaiserhof*, p. 270.

36. Diels, *Lucifer*, p. 194; Schnitzler, "Reichstagsbrand," sheet 2; Helldorf denied before the Supreme Court that he had been with Göring during the night, while Göring was probably telling the truth when he said he had summoned Helldorf (31st day, Stenogramm, p. 105). One of the two witnesses committed perjury.

37. Delmer, *Die Deutschen*, p. 192.

38. *Völkischer Beobachter*, March 1, 1933: "Das Fanal des Bolschewismus."

39. Diels, *Lucifer*, pp. 194f. Reading Diels's account of these events makes it quite impossible to dismiss Hitler's speech as "play-acting," even when bearing in mind Henderson's observation that a capacity for self-deception was part of Hitler's technique; see Alan Bullock, *Hitler: A Study in Tyranny* (London, 1952), p. 343.

40. Schnitzler, "Reichstagsbrand," sheet 11.

41. Testimony at Supreme Court trial, 2nd day. Stenogramm, pp. 71ff.

42. Goebbels, *Kaiserhof*, p. 254.

43. *Ibid.*, p. 270.

44. *Wolffs Telegrafen-Büro*, February 28, 1933, Second Early Morning Edition, quoted in Tobias, *Reichstagsbrand*, Appendix 14, p. 633.

45. *Reichsgesetzblatt*, I (1933), 86. Cf. Tobias, *Reichstagsbrand*, p. 133.

46. Cf. *Braunschweigische Landeszeitung*, February 28, 1933, wire report.

47. 31st day, Stenogramm, p. 106.

48. 46th day, Stenogramm, pp. 60ff. As the arrest order for Torgler (Tobias

Archive) shows, the arrest orders were mimeographed in the early hours of February 28. They were based on Paragraph 22 of the February 4th Emergency Decree.

49. Grauert's testimony, October 3, 1957 (Tobias Archive). He himself had not participated in formulating the draft.

50. IfZ Zeugenschriftum, ED I—Liebmann, sheet 44—General Liebmann's manuscript notes.

51. There are no other indications of initiative on Hitler's part. The documents of the *Reichskanzlei* (Bundesarchiv, Koblenz) contain nothing; those of the Ministry of the Interior are missing; thus for the present only hypotheses as to the evolution of the Reichstag Fire Decree are possible. Papen, who must have known by what processes the decree was formulated, obviously confused it with the Decree on Treason Against the German People of February 28: *Der Wahrheit eine Gasse*, p. 304.

52. Goebbels, *Kaiserhof*, pp. 270f.; Henry Picker, *Hitlers Tischgespräche im Führerhauptquartier, 1941–42*, ed. P. E. Schramm (Stuttgart, 1963), p. 325; the report by Wilfried von Oven, *Mit Goebbels bis zum Ende* (Buenos Aires, 1949), lacks credibility.

53. Josef Goebbels, *Wetterleuchten* (Berlin, 1943), pp. 373ff.; cf. Diels, *Lucifer*, p. 195.

54. In Tobias, *Reichstagsbrand*, Appendix 14, p. 633.

55. *Ibid.*, pp. 262ff.

56. *Völkischer Beobachter*, March 1 and 2, 1933.

57. Sommerfeldt, *Ich war dabei*, p. 26.

58. For instance, Delmer, *Die Deutschen*, p. 190.

59. Cf. Siegfried Bahne, "Die Kommunistische Partei Deutschlands," in *Das Ende der Parteien*, ed. Erich Matthias and Rudolf Morsey (Düsseldorf, 1960), pp. 685ff., 710ff. However, there is no material providing a dependable basis for assessing Communist activity after the Nazi takeover.

60. Cf. Bracher's version in Bracher, Sauer, Schulz, *Machtergreifung*, pp. 158f.

61. Even in the cabinet meeting of March 24, 1933, Hitler doubted the usefulness of a ban on the Communist Party unless "there was a possibility of deporting the Communists." Hitler saw no point in interning Communists in concentration camps. See Tobias, *Reichstagsbrand*, p. 628.

62. Cf. the relevant material in the trial before the Supreme Court, Stenogramm, 45th and 46th days; also Maria Reese's unpublished memoirs, Bundesarchiv, kleinere Erwerbungen.

63. For example, on January 24, 1933, the News Center of the Reich Ministry of the Interior transmitted to news-gathering centers of the federal states an instructional booklet of the Communist paramilitary organization (*Rotfrontkämpferbund*), entitled "Der bewaffnete Aufstand in Reval," copy in Bundesarchiv, Koblenz, R 58/1, 672. This material is interpreted tendentiously by Martin H. Sommerfeldt, *Kommune* (Berlin, 1934).

64. Diels, *Lucifer*, pp. 189f. The material provided the theme of Adolf Ehrt's propagandistic *Bewaffneter Aufstand* (Berlin and Leipzig, 1933).

65. Stadtarchiv, Oldenburg, Aktenband Geheim und "Persönliches" vom 1.1.–29.3.1933.

66. The above interpretation of the Nazi attitude toward the Reichstag fire was confirmed after its writing when the author learned of a message from Rudolf Diels (Prussian Ministry of the Interior, Az: I 2b 4270 VIII) to

Daluege, with a copy to Helldorf, which was sent on February 28. The message (now located in the Berlin Document Center, Daluege Papers) was drawn up the day before the fire but was dispatched (probably as a routine matter) on February 28. It bears the warning: "Secret! To be delivered personally!" The text reads: "I have been informed that the Communists intend in the immediate future to paralyze the lighting system and transportation (railroad, etc.), as well as all vital production by means of violent acts and sabotage. There is said to be sufficient explosive material available for acts of sabotage. I have not yet learned the precise day and hour for which the actions are planned. A general order will make possible simultaneous execution everywhere. The necessary countermeasures have been taken.—Further, I wish to report that the Communists intend to identify all prominent leaders of the nationalist parties and diagram the layout of their homes. Moreover, the national direction of the *Rotfrontkämpferbund* [Communist paramilitary organization] is reported to have instructed its members to make immediate use of firearms in case of any conflict with members of rightist organizations."

This message, although its content corresponds to Göring's argument in the cabinet meeting of March 2 (cf. note 119, below), corresponds to similar instructions issued by the Prussian Interior Ministry to the regional police agencies, which were delivered on the morning of February 27; it explains the immediate connection of the fire with the expected general Communist putsch.

67. Sent out through the News Center of the Reich Ministry of Interior on April 19, 1933: Bundesarchiv, R58/1-718.

68. 46th day, Stenogramm, p. 61.

69. Cf. Diels, *Lucifer,* pp. 170ff.

70. 31st day, Stenogramm, pp. 34–40, 43ff., 52.

71. Cf. Gerhard Schulz, in Bracher, Sauer, Schulz, *Machtergreifung,* pp. 430f., 438ff.; Sauer, *ibid.,* pp. 866ff.; also Schnitzler, "Reichstagsbrand," sheet 3.

72. 31st day, Stenogramm, pp. 81f.; IMT, *Prozess,* IX, 481f.; in this connection Diels, *Lucifer,* pp. 194f., and Grauert's testimony, October 3, 1957 (Tobias Archive).

72a. *DBFP,* 2nd Series, IV (No. 253), 438.

73. Cf. Bahne, "Kommunistische Partei," p. 692.

74. 31st day, Stenogramm, pp. 86ff.

75. Cf. Bracher, Sauer, Schulz, *Machtergreifung,* pp. 158ff.

76. 31st day, Stenogramm, p. 84.

77. 31st day, Stenogramm, pp. 72ff.

78. *DBFP,* 2nd Series, IV (No. 246), 431; cf. Tobias, *Reichstagsbrand,* p. 133.

79. Reprinted in Tobias, *ibid.,* Appendix 11, p. 623; there are in addition numerous press reports to the effect that the elections would take place "in any case." Cf. *Generalanzeiger* (Wuppertal), February 28, 1933; *Braunschweiger Neueste Nachrichten,* March 2, 1933; *Nationalzeitung* (Berlin), February 28, 1933, etc.

80. *Ibid.*

81. It remained unclear in any case whether Communist deputies were supposed to be included in the arrest action (cf. 47th day, Stenogramm, p. 94).

82. Drawn up February 28, proclaimed as law March 1, 1933 (*Reichsgesetzblatt,* I [1933], 84ff.); reference (Bracher, Sauer, Schulz, *Machtergreifung,* p. 87) to the "Reichstag Fire Decrees" is thus somewhat misleading.

83. Helmut Krausnick, "Stationen der Gleichschaltung," in *Der Weg in die Diktatur 1918 bis 1933* (Munich, 1962), p. 183.

84. Bracher, Sauer, Schulz, *Machtergreifung,* pp. 83ff.; cf. the recent interpretation of the decree's genesis by Heinrich Bennecke, "Die Notverordnung vom 28. Februar 1933," *Politische Studien,* XIX (1968), 37ff. Bennecke stresses the importance of the so-called *Planspiel Ott* of November 1932 as forerunner of the Reichstag Fire Decree.

85. Morning session of the Reich cabinet, February 28, 1933 (text in Tobias, *Reichstagsbrand,* Appendix 8, p. 619).

86. *Reichsgesetzblatt,* I (1933), 35ff.

87. Tobias, *Reichstagsbrand,* p. 617.

88. Session of the Reich cabinet, February 27 (*ibid.,* p. 617).

89. Cf. Schulz in Bracher, Sauer, Schulz, *Machtergreifung,* p. 434.

90. See, for example, Gotthard Jasper, *Der Schutz der Republik. Studien zur staatlichen Sicherung der Demokratie in der Weimarer Republik 1922–1930* (Tübingen, 1963), p. 162, with reference to the ban on the Communist paramilitary organization, *Rotfrontkämpferbund;* Hans Buchheim, "Die organisatorische Entwicklung der Politischen Polizei in Deutschland in den Jahren 1933 und 1934," in *Gutachten des Instituts für Zeitgeschichte* (Munich, 1959), pp. 197ff.

91. Cf. Police Telegraphic Radio Service of Braunschweig (Documents of the Braunschweig Ministry of State; copy in Tobias Archive).

92. See Waldemar Besson, *Württemberg und die deutsche Staatskrise 1928–1933* (Stuttgart, 1959), pp. 336f.; Karl Schwend, *Bayern zwischen Monarchie und Diktatur* (Munich, 1954), p. 510.

93. Besson, *Württemberg,* p. 338.

94. In question was authority for execution of the decree, which was to lie not with the Reich Ministry of the Interior, but with the Reich government as a whole, and, secondly, a material limitation through insertion of the word "as far as." Cf. Schulz in Bracher, Sauer, Schulz, *Machtergreifung,* p. 432, n. 225.

95. Besson, *Württemberg,* p. 338.

96. Unfortunately, it has never been determined who was made responsible for the composing of the draft of the decree. The possibilities include Dr. Werner Hoche, *Ministerialrat* in the Reich Ministry of the Interior, the author of the Emergency Decree of February 4. Cf. *Juristische Wochenschrift,* VIII (1933), 506; also Dr. Hans Heinrich Lammers, and Dr. Kaisenberg.

97. *Frankfurter Zeitung,* March 1, 1933, 1st Edition, from a wire report dated February 28.

98. Bracher, Sauer, Schulz, *Machtergreifung,* p. 86; on pp. 54f. it is correctly emphasized that even previously the police authorities had been allowed a freedom of judgment which was subject to no effective limitations.

99. Reich cabinet session, afternoon of February 28 (Tobias, *Reichstagsbrand,* p. 619).

100. *Völkischer Beobachter,* February 28, 1933.

101. Tobias, *Reichstagsbrand,* Appendix 10, p. 622.

102. Deutsches Zentralarchiv, Potsdam, Repository 77 (Microfilm IfZ, Ma 198/2).

103. *Frankfurter Zeitung,* March 1, 1933, 1st Edition, Editorial.

104. For example, *Deutsche Allgemeine Zeitung,* February 28, 1933; *Niedersächsische Tageszeitung,* March 1, 1933; *Nationalzeitung,* February 28, 1933.

105. IfZ, Zeugenschriftum, ED I—Liebmann, sheet 40.

106. Liebmann letter dated August 28, 1955 (*ibid.*, sheets 361f.) in which the commanders' conference formerly thought to have preceded the Reichstag fire is dated March 1, as is confirmed by the prominence in Liebmann's diary entries of the theme "emergency decree."

107. Liebmann's entries on questions opened up by Blomberg's speech (*ibid.*, sheet 43).

108. *Ibid.*, sheets 46f.

109. Tobias, *Reichstagsbrand*, p. 623.

110. The army "was not to be associated with this internal affair" (wire report dated February 28 in the 1st Edition, March 1, 1933); cf. in this connection Sauer's presentation in Bracher, Sauer, Schulz, *Machtergreifung*, pp. 720ff.

111. Bundesarchiv, Brammer Collection, Zeitgeschichtliche Sammlung, 101/26, sheets 167, 175; cf. the dispatch of March 11, sheet 181, which contains another reference to Papen and Blomberg's demand for a military state of emergency, but according to which the Reich President had chosen to compromise with Hitler.

112. Liebmann Notes, IfZ, Zeugenschriftum, ED I—Liebmann, sheets 40ff. The tactical arguments indicate Hitler's influence, although words of his to this effect are not documented elsewhere and although no reference thereto was made in the cabinet session of February 28; on Blomberg's attitude, cf. H. Krausnick, "Vorgeschichte und Beginn des militärischen Widerstandes gegen Hitler," in *Vollmacht des Gewissens* (Munich, 1956), pp. 210ff. To be sure, the extant version of the commanders' conference shows that by March 1 Blomberg no longer held that the army was above politics: "*One* party on the march. Then the phrase 'above politics' becomes meaningless and only one way lies open: unqualified support."

113. *DBFP*, 2nd Series, IV (No. 253), 438. Göring denied this in his radio speech, referring to falsified SA and Stahlhelm orders (cf. Tobias, *Reichstagsbrand*, p. 640).

114. *DBFP*, 2nd Series, IV (No. 255, March 3, 1933), 439; according to this version, Neurath intervened, expressing to Rumbold the hope that the decree would be annulled immediately after the elections. "In his opinion it was not possible to maintain such a state of exception for any length of time."

115. Tobias, *Reichstagsbrand*, pp. 113, 115f.

116. Goebbels, *Kaiserhof*, p. 271.

117. Reich cabinet morning sessions, February 28 (Tobias, *Reichstagsbrand*, p. 618).

118. *Ibid.*, Appendix 17, pp. 641f.

119. Reich cabinet session, March 2, 1933, *ibid.*, p. 623. Cf. Schulz in Bracher, Sauer, Schulz, *Machtergreifung*, p. 527: "No further proof is needed that the material with which Göring duped the cabinet ministers the day after the Reichstag fire existed solely in his imagination." This assertion does not bear up under closer examination. Göring's arguments in the cabinet sessions were based on findings provided to him by the political police. Later, too, Göring made use of the extremely dubious conjectures of the preliminary investigation, which were not very useful even as material for agitators. The questioning of the criminal police before the Supreme Court (45th, 46th, and 47th days) sheds light on the development of evidence to sustain the indictment against the KPD. This evidence was held to be dependable even by such a distinguished expert as Heller.—For example, the accusation worded "poisoning of food served in

government buildings" (cf. Criminal Commissar Will's testimony, 47th day, pp. 24f.) originated in Düsseldorf. There, arrests were made in order to apprehend a supposed "Communist poisoners' ring." Experts calculated that the poison confiscated would have been sufficient to kill 18,000 persons. The dispatch was reported upward in this form, although proceedings had not even begun. Thus Gürtner came to introduce into the emergency decree an increased penalty for poisoning. The assertion that Lubbe maintained a close connection with Moscow (Cabinet Session of March 2; also *Wolffs Telegrafen-Büro*, February 28) goes back to Lubbe's statement that in 1932 he had wanted to travel to the Soviet Union. It is characteristic of the uncritical mentality of all the participants that the German Embassy in Moscow was eventually charged with tracking down the alleged instigators of the Communist insurrection in Germany. The Embassy telegraphed its reply on September 14, 1933: "It would be desirable if the informants would make more precise statements to the Chief Public Prosecutor, in order to provide at least indirectly statements that can be followed up" (telegrams to ORA, AA Legal Department: Correspondence and Newspaper Clippings on the Reichstag Fire Trial, Microfilm, IfZ Ma-194, I, sheet 125).

120. Cf. the telegrams to diplomatic missions abroad sent on February 28 and March 3, 1933, as reprinted in Tobias, *Reichstagsbrand*, Appendix 15, pp. 636f.

121. Mentioned by Schulz in Bracher, Sauer, Schulz, *Machtergreifung*, p. 527. The government's utter helplessness in the face of Münzenberg's offensive is evident; cf. also Bundesarchiv, R 58/718: Memorandum on Communist agitatory activity in winter 1932–1933 concerning preparations for a violent overthrow of the constitution by the KPD for March 14, 1933.

122. There has never been a thorough investigation. For the undependable assessment of KPD tactics by the political police, see the Confidential Report of April 7, 1933, in *Nachrichtensammelstelle* (Bundesarchiv, R 58/626).

123. See Rudolf Hess's message of September 16, 1933, to the Supreme SA Command, including the request to circulate available evidence of Communist revolutionary intent and determine whether "the membership of the SA includes former Communists, who are able and willing under certain circumstances to testify that the methods foreseen by the KPD for such actions included arson, etc." (Bundesarchiv, Schumacher Collection: Röhm, Röhmputsch u. Reichstagsbrand, sheet 402).

124. Brammer Collection, Bundesarchiv, Zeitgeschichtliche Sammlung, 101/26, Instructions Nos. 55, 62, 77, Communiqué No. 107.

125. A. François-Poncet, *Als Botschafter in Berlin 1931–1938* (2nd ed. Mainz, 1949), p. 94; cf., however, Picker, *Hitlers Tischgespräche*, p. 325.

126. See, for example, the report of the *Münchner Neueste Nachrichten,* December 14, 1933.

127. See Diels, *Lucifer,* pp. 269f.

128. Cf. in this connection Schulz in Bracher, Sauer, Schulz, *Machtergreifung,* p. 523 (judgment on pp. 94ff.); cf. also Schlegelberger's expert testimony, Bundesarchiv, RK 43/II/294.

129. Tobias (*Reichstagsbrand,* p. 470) rightly points out that the principle *in dubio pro reo* was crassly violated by the verdict, based as it was on the assumption that Lubbe had acted "in conscious and voluntary association with unknown accomplices." The court might have recognized Seuffert's plea that Lubbe's deed be qualified "as a preparatory action to high treason," thus avoiding the death

penalty (cf. 55th day, Stenogramm, pp. 133ff. and Handakten Sack, Bundes-archiv, I, 269ff.).

130. Tobias, *Reichstagsbrand*, p. 628. The strong criticism of the Leipzig verdict by the National Socialist press and the attitude of the Reich Ministry of Justice are presented by Schulz in Bracher, Sauer, Schulz, *Machtergreifung*, p. 563, and Hubert Schorn, *Der Richter im Dritten Reich* (Frankfurt, 1959), pp. 67ff.

131. A characteristic attitude, it seems, is that of Martin Bormann in his letter to Elfriede Conti of March 2, 1933: "One would almost prefer not to believe the Communists capable of the folly of burning the Reichstag building a few days before the elections; purely from the standpoint of party politics, nothing better could have happened to us" (Schumacher Collection; see note 123, above).

132. Goebbels, *Kaiserhof*, p. 271.

133. This phrase is reported by Delmer, *Die Deutschen*, p. 195.

134. Cf. Rudolf Vierhaus's analysis entitled "Faschistisches Führertum. Ein Beitrag zur Phänomenologie des europäischen Faschismus," *Historische Zeit-schrift*, CLXXXIX (1964), 631: "On the other hand, the cult of the Führer concealed almost completely the measure in which the Führer were victims of their own wishful thinking. . . ."

135. Tobias, *Reichstagsbrand*, p. 593. Even though some criticism of this over-drawn interpretation is justified, one should not overlook the validity of his central argument to the effect that the Nazis' behavior can only be grasped if one takes into account "the inability to perceive reality which is incurably a part of an authoritarian dictatorship (*Führerstaat*)."

6

ROBERT KOEHL

Feudal Aspects of National Socialism

The government established by the Nazis was a puzzling creation, un-
like any other modern regime. No constitution was ever enacted for the
Third Reich. Instead, Hitler merely ruled dictatorially with the sweep-
ing powers he had obtained by means of the Reichstag Fire Decree and
the Enabling Act he extorted from the Reichstag elected in March
1933, when the Nazis again failed to gain a majority, despite widespread
intimidation of their opponents. But instead of producing a streamlined
autocratic system, Hitler left most of the old structure standing and
added to it a proliferation of new state and party agencies, allowing
lines of authority to become confused and areas of competency to over-
lap. Scholars have long struggled to explain the reasons for such a seem-
ingly inefficient arrangement and to account for its ability to function.
The author of this selection, a Professor of History at the University of
Wisconsin, employs a comparative approach in an effort to arrive at an
understanding of the basic nature of the institutional structure of the
Third Reich. The author has also published an important book dealing
with the wartime policies of a key government agency in the Third
Reich, RKFDV: German Resettlement and Population Policy, 1939–
1945 *(Cambridge, Mass., 1957). This selection first appeared in the*
American Political Science Review, LIV *(1960), 921–933. It is re-*
printed here by permission of the author and publisher.

A<small>TTEMPTS</small> T<small>O</small> establish a "morphology of civilizations" seem to continue in spite of dire warnings from scholars. Indeed, while rejecting Toynbee and Sorokin with one hand, many a scholar has beckoned with the other to adventurous young men to leave the barren tracts of specialization and reenter the broad panoramic fields of *Weltgeschichte*. Current interest in "comparative feudal institutions" illustrates the case in point.

I

The notion that "feudalism" is a "form of society," especially a "stage in development," can be traced back to Marxist historiography, and from there back to eighteenth century French thinkers. But instead of becoming thoroughly discredited, the notion has recently led to new thinking on the subject which may turn out to be fruitful. In *Feudalism in History,* for example, Rushton Coulborn has combined eight separate papers on feudalism in various parts of the world by different historians, with his own critical and synthetic studies.[1] Though he fails to find even one "fully developed" feudal society according to his own definition— a not unexpected result—his study contains an amazing amount of suggestive analysis.

His suggestions are particularly valuable in the construction of "working models" or "ideal types" as research tools. Even when we remain safely within our own "fields," if we are to go beyond highly specialized fact-gathering and at the same time avoid "presentist subjectivism," we will need such tools.

Feudalism, above all, is a power-relationship. Its essential ingredients are vassalship and the fief. Vassalship is based on personal dependence and loyalty, while the fief represents a *conditional* proprietary right, often to landed property. The fief is the basis of personal power; it is presumably held subject to limits defined in terms of service to superiors. Feudalism is always marked by "a dispersal of political authority amongst a hierarchy of persons who exercise in their own interest powers normally attributed to the state, which are often, in fact, derived from its break-up." Vassals tend to be "a specialized military class occupying the higher levels in the social scale." "The performance of political functions depends on personal agreements between a limited number of individuals. . . . Since political power is personal rather than institutional, there is relatively little separation of functions."[2]

Coulborn has suggested that feudalism is "a mode of revival of a society whose polity has gone into extreme disintegration." "Political reformers seek to restore the disintegrating state by calling to its aid the personal vassalage relations which have come to permeate its upper ranks." "The culture of a jaded civilized society is reinforced in its elemental nucleus, the relationship of man to man, by an ethic drawn from a primitive source."[3]

It is quite remarkable how much of this applies to the internal politics of National Socialism. Moreover, Nazi thinkers quite consciously tried to model the New Order along feudal lines.

II

Superficially, National Socialism and Italian Fascism were alike. Both managed to combine a revolutionary ethos with the promise of imperial restoration. Behind the talk of a "New Order" lurked the ghost of an empire long dead. But Mussolini's imagery was based upon a centralized, legalistic Roman Empire. Hitler's propaganda spoke of a second thousand-year Reich. Not the short-lived Bismarckian creation, but the fabled medieval empire of Ottonians and Hohenstaufens gleamed in the back of Hitler's mind. Indeed, to Nazi theorists, the Roman tradition as well as all modern state bureaucracy was anathema. Franz Neumann has pointed out why: National Socialism recognized that even harsh laws protect the subject and the underling administrator.[4] Ultimately, totalitarianism must be lawless. Mussolini's must inevitably be incomplete, a pale reverberation of eighteenth-century enlightened despotism.

Mussolini, to be sure, sought to escape from the limitations of the rationalistic state. The appeal which this dictator at first had for Lincoln Steffens had little to do with the Roman Empire. Here was a fellow like Steffens himself, who had parted company with all doctrinaire thinking, with intellectualized reforms. Mussolini recognized that obedience and loyalty could be had for the asking if the right man asked. The very same processes of "corruption" which Steffens found to be necessary in democracy were the devices Mussolini substituted for legality and parliamentary government. Unlike Lenin, he did not get rid of the competing economic and religious sources of power in Italy. He corrupted them, and sought to make the state so powerful that it could always swing the balance in any dispute. Toward the end of his stay in Italy Steffens became doubtful. He looked to Germany and to Stinnes's idea of *doing away with the state* as a cleaner, more efficient solution to the problem of conflicting interests, loyalties and powers.[5]

Offhand, one would scarcely expect Nazi thinking to go along with so un-German a suggestion. But when Stinnes's reasons have been probed, they turn out to be the same as the Nazi objection to rationalistic legal systems. Underneath talk of "administrative duplication" and in the guise of a search for efficiency, both the industrial monopolist and the terror-and-propaganda monopolists desired to do away with all protective frameworks in which their victims and their rivals could hide. The Nazis, however, did not see eye to eye with Stinnes & Co. when it came to a substitute for the state.

Stinnes's substitute seems to have been a kind of politburo of industrialists, one of the many versions of right-wing corporativism so popular in Germany just before and after the First World War. Technocratic "experts" who had proved themselves in the world of high finance and production-management were to be combined with class-and-occupational representation to counterbalance the effects of universal and equal suffrage and the idea of Workers' Councils. While, as we shall see, echoes of this substitute were to appear in National Socialist propaganda, Nazi theory increasingly turned to feudal and medieval models for political relationships.

Nazi predilection for Teutonic imagery is well known. There is an essential connection between this love of the archaic and the primitive and Nazi glorification of the medieval Reich-idea. They found in *Gefolgschaft* and *Treue* the basis for a Germanic Reich as opposed to a Roman legalistic structure or a Byzantine theocratic *Machtstaat*. Oversimplifying the scholarly theories of the Germanic origin of feudalism, they asserted that it was the "sound judgment of the Nordic ethos" which rejected the subjugation of creative talents either to dead laws or to autocratic personal authority. An honorable self-subordination by mutual contract was the genius of the Germanic Reich-idea. Loyalty (*Treue*) and honor (*Ehre*) were made the ultimate values in life for all upholders of the contract, whether lords or vassals.[6]

The *comitatus* (*Gefolgschaft*) for the Nazis was the natural political unit, the model for all political relationships. Indeed, the *Führerprinzip* was a kind of twentieth-century *Gefolgsordnung*. National Socialists denied allegations that the "leadership principle" was equivalent to unrestrained and arbitrary tyranny on the Byzantine model. The power of a leader was said to be proportional to the confidence and loyalty of his voluntary followers. Far from extolling naked force, the *Führerprinzip* was "the rediscovery of the basis of political power: loyalty." And behind that loyalty lay the "full and honest acceptance of responsibility" by the strong. Thus the National Socialist ideology made much of "Germanic" feudalism and condemned the modern state both for its autocratic and its bureaucratic elements.[7]

The problem of German history for many a Nazi thinker was the location of the point where German history "went wrong." There had been a golden age of promise marked not only by Ottonian and Hohenstaufen imperial power, but by Hanseatic and proto-Prussian expansionism. For approximately five hundred years (A.D. 750–1250) Germanic society bloomed, but at the close of the age the fruit was blighted and misshapen. As a consequence National Socialists could not unreservedly idealize the medieval Reich. The aspects they emphasized point up inherent tendencies in Nazism which might be termed feudal. Even some of the disagreements of interpretation reflect different aspects of the same Nazi ideology.

The Frankish monarchy was a necessary stage, said the Nazis, in the transsubstantiation of the classical-Roman heritage into a "Germanic organism." However, in the hands of Charlemagne, the state threatened to overpower the creative impulses of "natural" political units such as the stem-duchies. Hitler disagreed with Rosenberg and Himmler in blaming Charlemagne: *Sachsenschlächter* was an unfair epithet. Society was always threatened from two great and equal dangers; one of them was barren autocracy, and the other was the endless internal bickering of numerous small "equals" without a leader. Charlemagne had to push forward the unification of the German *Stämme* by force because they would not or could not combine voluntarily. On the other hand, Himmler and Rosenberg saw in the Carolingian *restauratio imperii* the first fatal move toward an alien *Weltanschauung*.[8]

Himmler in his admiration for Henry the Fowler, and Rosenberg with his romantic conception of Henry the Lion, illustrate differing Nazi ideals which, nonetheless, glorify the feudal nexus. According to Himmler, Henry the Saxon embodied the simple Germanic political virtues. He was personally a brave soldier, a hard fighter and a tough-minded realist. On the other hand, he practised a policy of live-and-let-live with the other stem dukes whom he had led against the centralizing Conrad I. Instead of empty bickering with his countrymen, he focused on the alien enemy, the Magyars. Above all, he looked east, not south. Rosenberg argued that Henry the Lion had to play the part of a contumacious vassal against the "alien universalism" of Barbarossa. "Germandom" needed to advance beyond stem-duchy to "Prussiandom" and Henry would have been the man to do it. The nobility which joined with

Barbarossa against him was "good material" which could have been converted into a "loyal Junkerdom." Instead Barbarossa heightened the divisive tendencies in the Reich.[9]

Yet Hitler himself never tired of extolling the "Reich-idea." The notion of a German hegemony in central Europe, over Burgundy, Italy, the Low Countries, Denmark and western Slavdom filled him with a sense of grandeur.[10] On the other hand he repudiated Germanization and uniformity for these imperial areas. Indeed, his conception of "the good old days" included the same ideals which Himmler and Rosenberg stressed. There had been no bureaucracy. A divisive nationalism had not yet come into being. Central Europe had been sufficiently unified by the respect for Germanic traits and the use of the German tongue so as to permit a large-scale political decentralization by means of viceroys and *Reichsstatthalter*. Everything really important could be dealt with by meetings of leading men and smaller details referred to the local nobility with the security that they would handle matters in the shortest possible order. The great emperors had always retained just enough domains to hold the balance of punitive striking power in the Reich.

The National Socialist doctrines of "Blood and Soil" are similarly reminiscent of feudal property relationships. R. W. Darré, the Nazi agrarian, called private property rights "Roman." The Germanic idea of property, said he, was the right of usufruct and inheritance in return for service rendered to the community. Darré waxed eloquent on the subject of a past and a future "Germanic aristocracy of the soil." Without denying the fighting prowess of the medieval German nobility, Darré derived it and aristocratic conceptions of honor and loyalty from its free-peasant foundations rather than the battlefield. The rough honesty and simplicity of the Teutonic spirit were preserved on the land. A "true communalism" allegedly developed in this class of noble farmers which was based on mutuality; it was purchased neither by the servility of the west-Frankish serf nor the destruction of individuality by the Slavic village community. In fact, "it was the Germanic genius to combine noble breeding with land-management responsible to the community." This limited freedom in the use of land was the price paid by the Germans; when modern Germans refused to pay it—because of the "reforms" of the French Revolution—German property relationships became chaotic, said Darré.[11]

Thus, the first task of National Socialism according to Darré was to free the German peasant from "the chaos of a market economy." The famous *Erbhofgesetz* re-created the principle of entail for peasant farms. While it was never possible to apply this law across the board, qualified farmers were "freed" from indebtedness, past and future, at the same time receiving their "hereditary estate" as a fief from the Reich. Similarly, just as such farmers became dependent on government loans for farm improvements, so all farmers were required to take part in a co-operative marketing network to "free them from the chaos of the market." This *Reichsnährstand* was much more than a compulsory marketing organization, however. As its name implied, it was intended by Darré to be a corporative estate of food producers. Darré meant it to be an autonomous, self-governing unit of a future pluralistic German society. Through its power, vis-à-vis the individual peasant, and vis-à-vis German society, he hoped it would pave the way for a "New aristocracy of Blood and Soil."[12]

It is somewhat surprising to encounter the "left-wing" Strassers in the assembly of feudal-minded Nazis. Actually, however, they and Darré were closely akin. Darré dreamed of a re-created *Ständestaat*, a medieval estate-system, in which the agrarian estate would be paramount. The Strassers conceived of a new social order too, which they called "state feudalism." It was the "industrial estate," however, which they sought to place at the top of the heap. They wanted to "nationalize" German industry, then parcel it out as fiefs to the managers and tycoons who had built it. Each industry was to be run like a medieval guild, with a regular provision for advancement to managerial status for the gifted, and strict internal controls on competition and production. They wished to do away with Prussia and with the Reichstag, substituting an economic-regional federalism and a chamber of corporations.[13]

The last item in our catalogue of Nazi medievalism, while not precisely feudal, is composed of many related elements. National Socialist historians, as well as Rosenberg and Himmler, gave a high place to the Teutonic Order. For them all, the essence of the Order was its elitism. It, too, was an elaboration of the war-band, the self-constituted league of fighting aristocrats. However, only the dedicated were able to sustain the pitiless self-subordination to the higher purposes of the order. It was in the Teutonic Order that the Hegelian synthesis of Germanic pride and Christian humility was fused to create Prussiandom. The *Ordensritter* was a knight *sans peur et sans reproche,* not for himself, not for Holy Church, but for an Idea. That this Idea was not fully revealed to him, though it had something to do with the future and with Europe as a whole, was an advantage, not a drawback. Quite consciously

Rosenberg called upon the NSDAP to make itself the German Order of the twentieth century in the service of the "unknown god." Similarly Himmler devised his *Schutzstaffel* or Elite Guard (SS) in the conscious effort to form a new pioneer-nobility for a future German east. He tried to instill in them a natural piety and a worshipful attitude toward the creative forces of nature, as a substitute for Holy Church. On their belt buckles he inscribed *Meine Ehre heisst Treue* (My honor is loyalty).[14]

III

In spite of its pretentiousness, National Socialist talk of man-to-man loyalty and of the leader-and-his-following really expressed their deepest convictions. This is revealed in both the formal systems they created to run Germany and in the informal structure of their internal politics. It is sometimes said that National Socialism lacked a real ideology. Insofar as a rational and systematic philosophy is meant, this is true. Yet no elaborate semantics are necessary to find consistency in the Nazi *Weltanschauung*.

Above all, they believed in a modern version of elective kingship. The Führer replaced a figurehead president and a prime minister responsible to a parliamentary assembly. He was elected for life by acclamation, but was in reality chosen and maintained in power by his paladins. They chose him for his personal qualities. In the form in which political battles are fought in the twentieth century, his prowess was supposed to outshine that of the fighters grouped around him.[15]

The Nazis tried to do away with the Germans' instinctive loyalty to abstract law and order, to "the state" and to tradition. They instituted an oath of personal loyalty to the Führer Adolf Hitler and sanctioned an almost ludicrous series of subinfeudations via oaths extorted by "little Führers." In legislation, in jurisprudence, police practice, and administrative policy they tried to substitute men for laws, personal judgment and responsibility for the rule-book and anonymity. They did away with the power of the old constitutional organs like the cabinet and the Reichstag and erected a system of *Reichsleiter* and *Gauleiter* whose positions depended, of course, on the Führer's good will and loyalty *to them,* but also on their ability to get things done and to command the loyalty and respect of their underlings and of the German people entrusted to their care.[16]

It was the aim of the Nazis to develop both the institutions and the political atmosphere conducive to furthering the exercise of power. Rejecting the modern bureaucratic state with its elaborate channels, they wished to simplify the exercise of power, to pin down the responsibility for decisions, and to encourage independence and aggressive problem-solving. Not strangely, the military analogy seemed to offer a substitute for the bureaucratic state. At least the soldier could always be brought to account by his superior. But here, too, lay a danger that "artificial hierarchies" and "paper structures" would get in the way of on-the-spot action.[17] The solution? *Führerprinzip!* But the doctrine that a leader must be allowed full freedom to solve a problem meant in effect a neo-feudal system.

According to this *Weltanschauung,* the nation's leader had total power, received from the *Volk,* and revocable by it, though not through legalistic processes so much as through withdrawal of confidence expressed in his failure to carry them with him in his exploits.[18] This total power he parceled out among proven followers. The long battle for control over the streets and the parliament, followed by the battle for the total support of the German people after 1933, afforded a maximum testing ground for these sub-leaders. It never ended. A *Reichsleiter* or a *Gauleiter* was continuously being weighed in the balance and not a few were found wanting between 1933 and 1945, not to mention the years 1923–1933.[19] As a consequence the Nazi political scene was filled with ever-changing groups and clusters of protagonists. Their relationship to each other was only semi-hierarchical. The student of Nazi administration has difficulty even with the formal structures because of their fluid character.

One of the most amazing similarities to the feudal system in Nazi administration is the nominal subordinate who acquired power to give his superior orders through appointment by a still higher superior as his "personal agent." Of course the universal example of this is the party member in the line organization, such as the Foreign Office. However, it is more striking when we realize that full-fledged *Altkämpfer* (party veterans) like Darré, Ley, Rosenberg and Hans Frank found themselves in a position similar to Foreign Office career diplomats, forced to take orders from subordinates like Herbert Backe, Fritz Sauckel, Erich Koch, and F. W. Krüger.[20] The effect of this Nazi habit was an ever-modified network of personal loyalties. At any given moment a German with an ax to grind (and the modern student) had to ask, not "what is the chain of command," but who has the actual "connections"—the nominal boss, or someone else?

Equally characteristic was the practice among National Socialist bigwigs of appointing each other as "deputies." Thus a man like Himmler was a Supreme Reich Authority as *Reichsführer SS,* though technically subordinate to the Ministry of the Interior, and also the deputy of Hermann Göring for the management of confiscated Polish agricultural properties. Himmler, in turn, as Reich Commissar for the Strengthening of Germandom, named as his deputies the Minister of Agriculture (Darré), the Minister of Labor (Ley), the Reich Health Leader (Conti), the chief of the Foreign Section of the NSDAP (Bohle), and the *Reichsstatthalter* of the annexed Polish territories.[21] A delicate hierarchy can be discovered: men like Göring and Goebbels spurned nomination as anyone's deputy save Hitler's. They were *Reichsunmittelbar* (direct vassals). Himmler and Ribbentrop were powers in their own right, but they could not do without the added authority of responsibilities assigned by their colleagues. Lesser lights collected deputyships the way Göring collected medals: mere symbols of status. Darré, Frank and many of the *Gauleiter* fall in this third group. Finally we come to those Nazi officials glad to have one great connection (often with Hitler) or lacking even that: men such as Otto Dietrich, the Press Chief; Arthur Seyss-Inquart, handyman and trouble-shooter; and Baldur von Schirach, the Youth Leader.[22]

A third aspect of National Socialist political life which may be likened to the feudal nexus was the "private war" with its rule of neutrality, peace treaties, and its schemes of mediation and arbitration by higher authority and by peers. Göring, Goebbels, Hess, Himmler, Ribbentrop and Rosenberg were the principals in such encounters, though often the combatants were lesser figures chosen by one or another. Needless to say, such wars were the result of the criss-crossing ambitions of rival empire-builders. They were productive of juntas and coalitions depicted in the diaries and memoirs of the Nazi era. Some feuds were very old, such as that between Albert Forster and Heinrich Himmler; others blew up and passed like that between Goebbels and Göring in 1942.[23] Some developed slowly, gradually involving many leading Nazis on both sides, and finally requiring a Solomon's judgment by Hitler. This type most usually involved economic power, because control over economic resources was the most essential basis for independence.[24]

At an early stage of such a quarrel, the principals exchanged notes, containing veiled ultimatums but also suggesting solutions such as the creation of "joint administration," the acceptance of liaison-men in each others' offices, and the ubiquitous "deputyships." An effort was made to conceal the quarrel from the Führer. Next we find letters, telephone calls and "chance meetings" with potential supporters. These in turn, if they wished to remain neutral, sent friendly letters to both contestants, or occasionally referred the matter to Lammers at the chancellery, not for Hitler's eyes, but for high-level arbitration short of the top. If they chose sides, they often sent the offending appeal to the opposite side, with a supporting cover letter. Meetings were arranged among the supporters, and a united front constructed. This might include an appeal to the Führer, supported by all and sundry, or united sanctions against the offender. The battle was joined usually in terms of failure to carry out measures of cooperation with the rival agency, or moves in direct opposition. Naturally, the effects were felt first by the German people, but they gradually penetrated through the party, state, or Gestapo grapevine, and a settlement was arranged "for the good of Germany."

A kind of jury trial resulted. The rivals each spoke in their own defense before the Führer, Lammers, Hess or Bormann, and some of the neutral bigwigs. Spokesmen were also heard from the opposing camps. Questioning began; from the neutrals, suggestions were made. The Führer speaks. He assigns the blame, and directs the character of the solution in broad lines. The contestants shake hands and agree to meet with each others' experts shortly. At the following negotiations a *modus vivendi* agreement [*sic*] was achieved. Sometimes this resulted in some institutional changes; often it led to the creation of some new joint agency, or in "personal union" of the rival agencies through a single executive officer. Both of these solutions increased the complexity of the network of loyalties. The new agency was inserted into the old channels with special authority—often given it directly by the Führer—to go over the heads of the line people in the rival parent organizations. The executive with two hats was supposed to cut through red tape, but he also had two evenly matched bosses to worry about.[25]

The consequence of these practices for the Nazi empire approximated feudal monarchy. Numerous eyewitnesses have reported that Hitler held his power not as an absolute monarch but through his ability to operate a delicate system of checks and balances.[26] He was a unifying factor for the disparate and competing elements of National Socialism, possessed of a considerable power of his own over the masses and over many leading Nazis which has been termed "charismatic." These characteristics are precisely those of the successful feudal monarch like St. Louis. Without precisely encouraging strife among his cohorts, Hitler was capable of remarkable neutrality—an ability to remain above the battle. Thus he could intervene when he had discovered where lay the advantage to his own power and to the Reich as he saw it. He also had the habit of so "impartially" deciding an issue that aggressor and victim were treated equally, with the result that there was an advantage to activist policy.[27] Since he could not be everywhere, especially in the continuous crisis of wartime, Hitler had to encourage self-reliance and independence, both in his paladins and in the regional chieftains, the *Gauleiter*.

In the last years of the Nazi era there is the most striking evolution along feudal lines. The *Gauleiter* became so fully identified with the interests of their bailiwicks that we find them behaving more like ancient stem dukes in their refusal to recognize the authority of the central government than like *missi dominici*. Hitler had to inveigh against the idea of hereditary Gauleitership, though he did not dare transfer recalcitrant *Gauleiter* where they had personally won the *Gau* for National Socialism.[28] As for the paladins, Göring, Goebbels, Himmler, and the newcomers, Speer and Bormann, had constructed virtually impregnable appanages. The more dependent Hitler became upon their empires for German victory, the more easily they looted the power of rivals like Rosenberg and Ribbentrop, Sauckel and Keitel. They made their systems independent of the central authorities and even of the Führer's support by absorbing some vehicle of power, usually economic, though Goebbels also used the mass media and Himmler the secret police.[29]

IV

An explanation of the feudal analogies to be found in National Socialism must inevitably draw upon the great amount of work already done on the institutional and ideological origins of the whole Nazi movement. These origins fall into five or six by no means mutually exclusive categories. One of the most popular sources of explanation, and with good reason, has been the nationalist tradition with its idealization of the state and the *Volk*. Less well known until recently are the contributions of German romanticism, both those of right-wing intellectuals and the more popular versions of the educated middle class. Equally significant are the devastating yet strangely self-compensating influences of the First World War with its trench brotherhood and "self-realization." Then there is the era of the Weimar experiences, culminating in the fiasco of both liberal democracy and modern capitalism. Finally we have the German social system and its foundations in the economic order, in which the middle class failed to develop to maturity as defined by classical liberalism, due to the survival and predominance of a "feudal" aristocracy. Closely allied with this familiar explanation is the Marxist or semi-Marxist observation that Nazism was a kind of mask which modern capitalism was forced to wear in order to survive.

German idolization of the nation-state contributed to National Socialism the habit of fanatical loyalty to commands and to things German. German nationalism was not alone in being feverish and fanatical, before the First World War, but the newness and hothouse character of its object, the Bismarckian Reich, was all there was to be enthusiastic about. Unlike the English and French traditions with their ancient ingredients and recent glories, the German tradition was a poor resource for nationalism. Luther and the Old Fritz were the best they had. The Holy Roman Empire was something to be forgotten. On the other hand the prospects of colonialism among "inferior" peoples stimulated the Germans to refurbish their own colonial tradition in the Slavic East. The Pan-Germans and the East Marches League had the same outlook, the same appeal, the same speakers. If they debated the comparative merits of overseas and continental empires, they agreed that Germans were a *Herrenvolk*. They became ecstatic at the thought of Germans out on the eastern frontier or in darkest Africa, fighting the good fight for civilization in spite of a stupid central government at home. "They had to take matters into their own hands out there." Efforts at treating "inferiors" on the same basis as Germans, according to the same laws, infuriated the *Grossdeutschen*.[30] Everyone knew a Czech had to be shown his place, not to mention the Poles. Out of disillusionment with a too fanatically idealized *Kleindeutschland,* and the conviction of German superiority to *Helotenvölker,* sprang Hitler and his paladins.

The Germans were thoroughly permeated by the currents of romanticism which swept Europe in the nineteenth century. Underneath a thin crust of materialism and practicality developed in the good years of the Bismarckian era, there were two romantic streams which merged in the Nazi era. One stream was the *petit bourgeois* romanticism of sentimentality and utopian dreams; the other was the aristocratic and intellectual romanticism of the far right. The idealization of the feudal past was the contribution of this aristocratic tendency, while the idealization of Germandom as an elite was the contribution of the popular sentimentality of bank clerks and greengrocers. Both shared the Great Man Theory of history without the mitigating suspicions of the French or the commonsense of the British. The *petit bourgeois* stream of romantic feeling opposed the prevailing dogmas of laissez-faire and liberal constitutionalism. Its devotees had no wish to see Czechs and

Poles (or Jews) profit from economic freedom or uniform civil rights. The organicism of the Lagardes and the Spenglers led to utter opposition on the part of "enlightened intellects" to rationalistic and "mechanistic" solutions to problems of political, social and economic organization. An aristocratic elitism became the hallmark of leading German writers like Stefan George, Hugo von Hofmannsthal, and even Thomas Mann.[31] All that was necessary for these undercurrents to break out and flow together was the frustration of the immediate success of the German political and economic edifice in the First World War. Wartime fanaticism bred xenophobia, racism, and utopian revolutionism, as well as the mysticism of charisma and the primitive magic of "blood and soil."

Probably no factor in the formation of National Socialism is more vividly embodied in Nazi language and institutions than the impact of the First World War. Their uniforms, their rank-consciousness and their idealization of the simple soldier (i.e., Adolf Hitler) do not seem, offhand, to have any affinity for feudalism. Yet the five years of combat experience, sometimes augmented by postwar paramilitary service in some free corps, infused future Nazis with the notions of loyalty, responsibility, and the *Gefolgschaft*-ideal. Actual frontline veterans developed personal loyalties to able junior officers, battle-proven captains and majors, who had the courage to make decisions. Such veterans acquired the deepest distrust—even hatred—for the official hierarchy, civilian and military, which was too big to understand what it was doing, too blindly uniform and illogically logical.

They developed into what the National Socialists called *Kampfnaturen,* men who saw life itself as eternal conflict, who divided the world into "we and they," those for us and those against us. Such men had been hurt too badly to classify friends and enemies naïvely, that is, solely by the color of the uniform. Indeed, except for the few close comrades of the *Kampfverband,* all outsiders were enemies—to be divided into the external and internal enemies. Out of their practical experience with the testing of leaders, these veterans evolved their own ideal of a natural elite, which served further to establish feudal patterns of organization in the paramilitary formations of the postwar era, the matrix of the NSDAP: "Listen to me, youngster. . . . Get this through your head once and for all. There is no peace and there are no laws. You come with me and I'll show you . . . a power higher than all your laws!"[32]

The war revived in German civilians the romantic conception of the knight, of soldierly self-realization through self-sacrifice and of "Prussianism." The latter ideal was avidly picked up by the rear guard of the aristocratic-intellectual wing of romantics and set over against the "inadequacies" of bourgeois parliamentary leadership. The Ludendorff-Hindenburg dictatorship from 1916 on, as well as the fantastic dreams of empire in eastern Europe aroused by an ever-enlarging zone of military occupation from 1915 to 1918, lessened the tenuous hold on political realities of the German bourgeoisie. In consequence, the collapse of the Second Reich both militarily and politically came as a terrible surprise to romantic civilians, but, to aristocratic thinkers and hard-bitten infantry lieutenants alike, as a grimly foreseen result of following false gods. The *Dolchstosslegende* represented the blending of these different reactions in a devastating rejection of the self-satisfaction of 1914. The "free corps" movement was only the most obvious embodiment of the German confusion: the need to act, to fight back, both against the external enemy (e.g., the Poles) and the more frightful and hated internal enemy (e.g., the Bolsheviks). In it all the feudal tendencies of the war years could be realized.[33]

One of the anomalies of the Weimar era was the apparent comeback, after the difficult postwar years, of German liberalism and commonsense. It was not until the 1930's that the real weaknesses of the Republic showed up. Perhaps the Germans were rendered even more prone to antirationalist, anti-Western solutions by the failure of their more or less sincere efforts in the period 1919–1929. At any rate, the continued existence of a vocal minority for whose *Weltanschauung* the war had dotted the *i*'s and crossed the *t*'s was assured by the initial failure of the German revolution of 1918 to soften the hearts of the Allies at Paris. Furthermore, the success of German moderates of all classes and political creeds in the construction of a liberal capitalism and a democratic central state did not prevent Germany's former enemies from being suspicious or worse in the troubled negotiations of the early thirties. The depression put the finishing touches on a case the future Nazis had been building up since before 1914.[34]

It was their underlying belief that the whole of Germany's recent past had been based on false assumptions. The effort to construct a modern nation-state on liberal lines in the image of France had been pursued since 1807. The notion that the disunity of Germans had been overcome prevailed after 1871. Both of these errors had been compounded in 1919. The Weimar state was a rationalistic nightmare, they asserted, and a Frankenstein to boot. Since the contradictions among Germany's social classes, regions, and special interests had *not* been surmounted, the administrative and police powers of Berlin had been hugely augmented without clear-cut lines of responsibility. Parliamentary government allowed for the most devastating powers with the least personal responsibility. No single party had an adequate popular base to win a majority with which to act.[35]

From its outset the Weimar state and indeed the Weimar society depended upon shaky coalitions. This inevitable condition became the Achilles' heel of the "System." Bolsheviks and Nazis, Nationalists and racists discovered that in temporary alliance they could tear down the edifice they so much despised. Thus it was not only by antithesis that the Weimar era contributed to the feudalistic thinking of the Nazi era, but directly, through the growing pains of men like Adolf Hitler and parties like the NSDAP.[36]

The often expressed desire to "escape the destructive effects of liberal economics" in German social thought found an echo in the views of both extremes of the German middle class well before the First World War. The German bourgeoisie had been very tentative during the nineteenth century with regard to *Manchesterismus*. *Kleinbürger* retained a nostalgic feeling for self-regulating guild-life; the tycoons of Wilhelmine Germany regarded the "cooperative spirit" of the cartel as both natural and necessary. Meanwhile the typical exponent of laissez-faire and free trade, the well-to-do or middle bourgeois, had been wheedled and threatened into believing that *for Germany* the Bismarckian economic and political solution was better. As a result, this pillar of society became a defender of inequality of treatment, rather than the traditional defender of liberty and equality. It is with all three versions of this German middle class in mind that scholars like Franz Neumann and Edmond Vermeil have characterized it as a "feudal bourgeoisie," and termed the German social order before the war as a *mariage de convenance* between Junkerdom and the industrial barons.[37]

It would scarcely be a surprise to discover that the intellectuals attached to such a combination would romanticize the medieval aristocracy and develop an elaborate feudal imagery of loyalty, blood and soil, decentralized responsibility and contractualism. Lacking the bedrock assumptions of equality derived from the political successes of the French and English lower middle class, the German *petit bourgeois* was easily made the dupe of a romantic revolutionism which offered to overthrow for him precisely those rationalistic safeguards which were his only protection from the strong and the ruthless.

It has sometimes been alleged, even by non-Marxists, that National Socialism was the offspring of the unholy union of predatory capitalists and reactionary landlords with the romantics of the right in service as midwives.[38] If this were true, there might well be feudal traits in the offspring. There is also the milder judgment, that German Big Business sought unsuccessfully to use the Nazis, who had other origins and motives, to keep the allegiance of the disgruntled middle class from gravitating to Moscow.[39] Here we encounter one of the most fascinating and difficult aspects of history and politics: the ambiguity of motivation. At one level there is most certainly the effort to disguise the ever-increasing power of the industrial and banking elite by the appeals of false socialism and the cheap bread and circuses of fascism. Here we will find the middle classes purposely taken in with a pretense at decentralization, medieval analogies, *petit bourgeois* romanticism and a new aristocracy of blood and soil. At this level we will find the "reality" quite different. The Nazis are brought in as partners, or force their way in on the ground floor, to the great economic empires of Germany. These interlocking power systems did not fall victim to the revolutionists' axes because they were scarcely understood, scarcely visible. They continued to grow during the Nazi era, concealed by the elaborate romantic propaganda of the Nazis, many of whom were themselves dupes of their own making, a few of whom were cold cynics like Göring, Goebbels, and Speer, who knew perfectly well that economic strength followed its own laws.[40]

In a way then, Nazi "feudalism" was merely play-acting. Rosenberg acknowledges this in his prison memoirs when he states that the Third Reich was a theatrocracy, a notion he borrows from Jacob Burckhardt.[41] Some Nazis "lived their parts" better than others. The German middle class, from which the rank and file of supporters came, had turned to a fantasy world and a make-believe language, which they called the "higher truth" just because they found the level of rationalization in real economic and political life too cruel. "Cold rationality" and "the colorless network of self-interest" were the reality, even after an intellectual flight from the scene occurred in the form of National Socialism. Both *petit bourgeois* preoccupation with blood and soil and aristocratic-intellectual preoccupation with "leadership" disguised the mounting *rational* impersonality of economic forces of which even the cartel chiefs were merely agents.[42]

And yet there was a deeper level of motivation. Unconsciously German industrialists and Nazis alike seemed to be trying to adapt themselves to factors of disintegration within German society.[43] Not merely as a form of protest against the rationalization of the economy and society, nor as a mere flight into fairy-tales, *but as a sincere but primitive effort to hold together a crumbling social order,* Nazi neo-feudalism is worthy of attention. It is particularly in this sense that Coulborn's formulations apply.

V

Like most revolutionaries, the Nazis sought to restore a "natural order." Their predilection for Wagnerian opera reveals their conception of the universe of natural forces. It is a pluralistic universe. Instead of one divine lawgiver, there are many rival wills—with man's fate the product of their struggle. Dimly perceived in the nineteenth century by romantics like Wagner, the notion that man is a small weak object, buffeted about by the crosscurrents of huge competing powers, not only reproduces the social conditions of the early middle ages, but also the character of modern western society. Germany represents merely a pronounced case of this "pluralism." The "natural order" the Nazis imagined was derived from the social reality of the twentieth century, abstracted and romanticized, and then reified again as neo-feudalism.

Nineteenth century liberalism, and to a lesser extent the society which invented it, was also pluralist. Where it was most successful, in France and England, an elaborate and intricate combination of cooperation and competition between the social atoms (men and firms) resulted in a unity more perfect than that achieved by the New Central Monarchies of the sixteenth and seventeenth centuries. Germany did not achieve this atomistic pluralism, much less the delicate and fragile unity of nineteenth century liberal Britain. Instead Germany came upon the scene as a world power just when modern capitalism had developed into a small number of competing monopolistic units, and when popular government and modern technology had created deadly imperial rivalries. Within Germany, on the other hand, the old security-giving social structures of village and guild were dissolved by the power of the state, the modern business corporation, and pressure groups. Unable to draw upon a clear and precise traditional definition of the state, some Germans defined it as merely the sum total of all the rival interest groups in the society, with the consequence that proportional representation of these interest groups became the fetish of the twentieth-century German democrat. Other Germans, less democratically inclined, sought in charisma and symbolism to discover a new cement which would make the state, the cartel and the pressure group *one,* instead of rival solvents of the old relationships.

In the idealized personal loyalty of feudalism, applicable to the firm, the battlefield, the party, and the government agency, the Nazis found a kind of anodyne to the devastating sense of chaos and isolation which the twentieth century brought especially to the Germans. They, in effect, were converting the rivalry and struggle, the temporary agreement, and the network of "connections" of modern society into a way of life. They sought to make, of what appeared to be necessity, a virtue. In a strange blend of hard-headed realism and romanticism, they attempted to accept the pluralism of the world of politics, of economics and of men in general, and to construct from the pieces a *Mythos* or world-view which would sustain them instead of destroy them.[44] But they were never able really to accept a plural universe, and their *Mythos* was only a patchwork.

In fact, this "wreckage of dead classes"[45] which constituted the Nazi elite could only team up with surviving elements of a decomposing political and economic system. Their "constructive" contributions to German survival represented a cannibalization of the remaining social system for the benefit of the contracting parties. Thus we have the Nazis and the cartels, the Nazis and the bureaucrats, the Nazis and the army. The feudal analogy is very pronounced at this point: barbarians are hired to defend the body politic; they also gravitate to rival elements in that disorganized system and become rivals of each other in the process; ultimately they dissolve the old network of relationships entirely. With luck, they may carve out for themselves new power-constellations, more or less stable. Or they may function only as destroyers.[46]

National Socialism is to be understood, then, as an effort of a disorganized society to repair itself, or rather, as an effort *of certain of its members,* whose own experience and character were the product of the very disorganization they sought to repair. To be sure they conceived of themselves as especially chosen by fate or history for this role; a disintegrating society *does* call forth such types: cutters of Gordian knots, empire-builders, scorners of theory. But only rarely were National Socialists able to escape from their own romanticism and wishful thinking. As a result their constructions were not truly empirical; their *Mythos* was too bound up with their own immediate past. Yet it is sobering to recall that it was only a thorough military defeat by a powerful coalition of three great societies, the United States, the British Commonwealth, and the Soviet Union, that drove these improvisers from the stage.

A question universally asked is whether the conditions which made their appearance possible have been radically altered. Much of the current optimism with regard to Germany is based upon explanations of National Socialism which do not stress the neo-feudal or pseudopluralist aspects of Nazism. The optimism is, of course, primarily based on the successes of the German Federal Republic, its economic strength, its relative homogeneity, its political maturity and flexibility. The total collapse of specifically Nazi figures and Nazi legends (i.e., Hitler) is reassuring, but it may indicate the inadequacy of the specific National Socialist response to German social disorganization, rather than a guarantee that another crisis cannot develop in the relationships of the state, the parties, the corporations, and other pressure groups. The German people may well have been inoculated against the superficial aspects of neo-feudalism: medievalism, *Gefolgschaft,* Teutonic Orders, and *Gauleiter.* The question remains whether they have been welded together sufficiently in the fiery furnace of national disaster and in the short period since 1945 to counteract the legacy of their past and the divisive forces of modern industrial society.

NOTES

1. Rushton Coulborn, ed., *Feudalism in History* (Princeton, N.J., 1956). See also *From Max Weber, Essays in Sociology,* ed. H. Gerth and C. W. Mills (New York, 1946), p. 300. Cf. C. Sjoberg, "Folk and 'Feudal' Societies," *American Journal of Sociology,* LVII (1952), 231–239.

2. F. L. Ganshof, *Feudalism* (London, 1952), p. xv. Joseph R. Strayer and R. Coulborn, "The Idea of Feudalism," in Coulborn, *Feudalism,* p. 5.

3. Coulborn, *Feudalism,* pp. 364–395, esp. pp. 364, 392.

4. Franz Neumann, *Behemoth: The Structure and Practice of National Socialism 1933–1944* (London and New York, 1944), pp. 77–80.

5. *The Autobiography of Lincoln Steffens,* II (New York, 1931), 812–829.

6. "Der Staat ist nun nicht die Verwirklichung der deutschen Volksordnung schlechthin, sondern er ist aus der Gefolgsordnung heraus gewachsen." ("The state is not the direct embodiment of the national structure, but rather grew out of the feudal order.") Carl Johanny and Oscar Redelberger, *Rechtspflege und Verwaltung: I. Allgemeiner Teil, Heft 2: Volk. Partei. Reich* (2d ed., Berlin, 1943), 3–4.

7. Fritz Nova, *The National Socialist Fuehrerprinzip and its Background in German Thought* (Philadelphia, 1943), pp. 1–14, 71–72, 90–94. According to National Socialist critiques of modern western society, a man's chance to act responsibly, indeed a man's *right* to be responsible, had been taken from him in the leveling and anonymous processes of mass democracy. Furthermore, the attempt to create uniform, rationalistic rules of procedure in political affairs had served to conceal the role of decision-making, and thus rendered decision-makers irresponsible.

8. *Hitler's Secret Conversations 1941–1944* (New York, 1953), pp. 236, 308–310, 343.

FEUDAL ASPECTS OF NATIONAL SOCIALISM 171

9. *Rede des Reichsführers SS im Dom zu Quedlinburg am 2. Juli 1936* (Berlin, 1936); cf. Robert Koehl, "Heinrich the Great," *History Today,* 7 (1957), 147–153. *The Memoirs of Alfred Rosenberg,* ed. S. Lang and E. von Schenck (New York, 1949), pp. 272–273.

10. Cf. *Hitler's Secret Conversations,* pp. 325–329; *Mein Kampf* (New York, 1940), pp. 596–606, 935–943.

11. R. Walther Darré, *Neuadel aus Blut und Boden* (Munich, 1935), pp. 43–47, 62, 67–76.

12. Hermann Reischle and Wilhelm Saure, *Der Reichsnährstand: Aufbau, Aufgaben und Bedeutung* (Berlin, 1934), pp. 15–30, 38–44, 133–152.

13. Otto Strasser, *Hitler and I* (Boston, 1940), pp. 81–82, 111–114; Douglas Reed, *Nemesis? The Story of Otto Strasser and the Black Front* (Boston, 1940), pp. 244–247, 256–263. Similar views are even attributed to Hitler, especially in his early days, by E. Vermeil, "German Nationalist Ideology in the Nineteenth and Twentieth Centuries," *The Third Reich* (New York, 1955), pp. 277, 324, 326. Alan Bullock makes the same attribution, but his source seems to be Strasser himself: *Hitler: A Study in Tyranny* (New York, 1952), pp. 121, 141.

14. Karl O. Paetel, "Die SS, Ein Beitrag zur Soziologie des Nationalsozialismus," *Vierteljahrshefte für Zeitgeschichte,* II (1954), 1–33; Hans Buchheim, "Die SS in der Verfassung des Dritten Reiches," *ibid.,* III (1955), 128–155. Cf. Gerald Reitlinger, *SS: Alibi of a Nation* (London, 1956). In keeping with the development of an elite the Nazis gave up one of the oldest ideals of Prussian education: uniform public education. They tried to substitute for it the special school for the future elite in which not only the aristocratic virtues were encouraged but in which the sense of difference from the *hoi polloi* was reinforced.

15. "When our opponents say 'It is easy for you, you are a dictator'—we answer them, 'No, gentlemen, you are wrong; there is no single dictator, but ten thousand, each in his own place' " (Adolf Hitler in a speech, April 8, 1933, cited in Nova, *Fuehrerprinzip,* p. 4).

16. For an oath demanded by Seyss-Inquart, see *Hitlers Tischgespräche* (Bonn, 1951), p. 243. The oath of personal loyalty to Hitler of February 1934 was exacted precisely because Hitler did not have patriarchal authority; such an oath was also a visible repudiation of *Rechtstaat* loyalty to the office (Vermeil, *Third Reich,* p. 304).

17. Hitler speaks of "die Fehler des ewigen Reglementierens" as specifically a German exaggeration of modern bureaucracy. Both in the relations of Berlin with the provinces and of Germans with foreign races the maximum of freedom was to be observed. Not totalitarianism, but its opposite, feudal decentralization, was the goal: *Hitlers Tischgespräche,* pp. 110–111, 116–118. Cf. Max Weber's contrast of feudal and patriarchal dominion, *Wirtschaft und Gesellschaft,* II (Tübingen, 1956), 751.

18. Cf. the slogan "Gebt mir vier Jahre!" (Give me four years!) used in the years 1933–1936 to win public confidence. See also Nova, *Fuehrerprinzip,* pp. 31–33; Vermeil, *Third Reich,* pp. 301–302.

19. For example, "Osaf" Pfeffer-Salomon: K. Heiden, *Der Fuehrer* (Boston, 1944), pp. 350, 742; *Gauleiter* Josef Wagner of Silesia: testimony of SS General Bach-Zelewski, U.S. Military Tribunal case 8, transcript, p. 383; *Gauleiter* Streicher of Franconia (reluctantly!): *Secret Conversations,* pp. 126–127.

20. E.g., the case of Martin Luther in the Foreign Office: Erich Kordt, *Wahn und Wirklichkeit* (Stuttgart, 1948), p. 373, n. 1. On Darré: affidavits of Aufsess and von Hannecken, U.S. Military Tribunal case 11, Darré defense book I; on Ley: Neumann, *Behemoth*, pp. 619–621; on Rosenberg: *Memoirs*, pp. 282–289; on Hans Frank: NO 2202, case 8, prosecution document book V-A.

21. E. K. Bramstedt, *Dictatorship and Political Police* (London, 1945), p. 98; NO 2676, case 8, prosecution document book XIV-A; NO 3078, case 8, pros. doc. bk. II-B.

22. Darré and Frank both attempted to play off Himmler and Göring against each other in this fashion: NG 1759, case 11, pros. doc. bk. 104; 2233 PS, *Trials of War Criminals,* IV, 889–891. Dietrich was attached dependently to Goebbels, Seyss-Inquart to Göring, and von Schirach to Hess.

23. Guenther Reimann, *The Myth of the Total State* (New York, 1941), pp. 198–213. On Forster and Himmler, see the testimony of Richard Hildebrandt, case 8, transcript, pp. 3887–3889. On the Goebbels-Göring feud, see *The Goebbels Diaries, 1942–1943,* ed. Louis P. Lochner (New York, 1948), pp. 260, 262, 264, 267–269, 276–277.

24. F. Neumann suggests that the ever-increasing "Party Sector" of the German economy "follows the familiar pattern of American gangsters" (i.e., "robber barons") who become honorable (and even more powerful) by entering into "legitimate business": *Behemoth,* pp. 298–305. But economic resources were not the only weapons in the private war. The struggle over the private army, that essentially feudal instrument, gave rise to the ambush of June 1934 in which Göring and Himmler and ultimately, Hitler, brought down the SA, in the interests of the Reichswehr, and eventually, the SS. Cf. G. Reitlinger, *The SS: Alibi of a Nation* (London, 1956), pp. 54–71. The Secret Service was also the subject of a vicious fight to the finish: Walter Schellenberg, *The Schellenberg Memoirs* (London, 1956), pp. 227–240, 277–285, 398–412.

25. See for example the Schacht-Göring episode described by Earl R. Beck, *Verdict on Schacht. A Study in the Problem of Political "Guilt,"* Florida State University Studies, No. 20 (Tallahassee, 1955), pp. 96–99, 60, 89–91. Cf. Frederick S. Burin, "Bureaucracy and National Socialism: A Reconsideration of Weberian Theory," *Reader in Bureaucracy,* ed. R. K. Merton *et al.,* (Glencoe, Ill., 1952), pp. 33–47. For a surprisingly favorable view of the "personal union" device, see K. Brandt, *Germany's Agricultural and Food Policies in World War II, II. The Management of Food and Agriculture in the German-occupied and other Areas of Fortress Europe* (Stanford, 1953), xxiii–xxiv.

26. Hans B. Gisevius, *Bis zum bitteren Ende* (Hamburg, 1947), I, 121–123, 138–139, 155ff. Otto Strasser, *Die deutsche Bartholomäusnacht* (6th ed., Zürich, 1935), pp. 17–33, 47ff., 73–81. Cf. Walter Görlitz and Herbert Quint, *Adolf Hitler* (Stuttgart, 1952), pp. 629–631.

27. Rosenberg, *Memoirs,* p. 231.

28. *Tischgespräche,* pp. 250, 252, 254. Cf. Neumann, *Behemoth,* p. 535; Vermeil, *Third Reich,* p. 299.

29. A characteristic stage in the development of feudal offices is the assignment of tasks by the leader to table-companions and household employees. Precisely this stage was reached in 1945 Hitler Germany, especially in the Führer-Bunker. Furthermore, whether guilty or innocent, Göring and Himmler were accused in April 1945 by Hitler of that fatal feudal disease: *frondieren.* Each absented himself from the court, in a suspiciously distant corner of the kingdom

30. Cf. Ernst Hasse, *Das deutsche Reich als Nationalstaat,* Deutsche Politik, Heft 1 (Munich, 1905), 61–62.

31. See Peter Viereck, *Dream and Responsibility: Four Test Cases of the Tension between Poetry and Society* (Washington, D.C., 1953), pp. 23–25; Harry Slochower, *Three Ways of Modern Man* (New York, 1937), pp. 57–69; cf. Hugo von Hofmannsthal, "Die Rede Gabriele d'Annunzios," *Gesammelte Werke, Prosa,* I (Frankfurt am Main, 1950), 335–348. "Der Schutzherr bestimmt den Feind, kraft des ewigen Zusammenhangs von Schutz und Gehorsams," Carl Schmitt, *Der Begriff des Politischen* (Hamburg, 1933), p. 35.

32. From Edwin Dwinger's autobiographical *Auf halbem Wege* as quoted in Robert G. L. Waite, *Vanguard of Nazism. The Free Corps Movement in Postwar Germany 1918–1923* (Cambridge, Mass., 1952), pp. 269–270.

33. Parallel tendencies after World War II are strikingly revealed in an article in the SS-veterans' monthly, *Wikingruf* (September, 1956). "Suum cuique: Ein Bekenntnis zum Preussentum," by G. Bardey, emphasizes a search for security in a feudal-type military relationship. Cf. Hermann Mau's stress on the SA as a "soldierly" symbol: "30. Juni 1934—Zweite Revolution," *Vierteljahrshefte für Zeitgeschichte,* I (1953), 125.

34. See the articles by Louis R. Franck and Arthur Schweitzer in *The Third Reich,* pp. 539–594.

35. Godfrey Scheele, *The Weimar Republic: Overture to the Third Reich* (London, 1946), pp. 120–160.

36. F. Neumann, *Behemoth,* pp. 8–34. It might be observed that from an early date Hitler showed a genius for making temporary political combinations; cf. Bullock, *Hitler,* pp. 77–78, 85, 90, 103, 132. Perhaps the ability to convert an essentially weak position into new strength by temporary alliances vouchsafed by the Weimar system led National Socialism into its inner contractualism (temporary alliances among the leadership); cf. Neumann, *Behemoth,* p. 522.

37. Neumann, *Behemoth,* p. 5; E. Vermeil, *Germany's Three Reichs* (London, 1945), p. 258. Joseph Schumpeter wrote: "Whoever seeks to understand Europe must not overlook that even today [1919] its life, its ideology, its politics are greatly under the influence of the feudal 'substance.' . . ." *Imperialism and Social Classes* (New York, 1951), p. 122.

38. Cf. Heinz Pol, *The Hidden Enemy: The German Threat to Post-War Peace* (New York, 1943), pp. 23–27, 50–72, 234–241, 254–258.

39. G. F. W. Hallgarten, *Hitler, Reichswehr und Industrie. Zur Geschichte der Jahre 1918–1933* (2d ed., Frankfurt am Main, 1955), pp. 43–46. See also his "Adolf Hitler and German Heavy Industry 1931–1933," *The Journal of Economic History,* XII (1952), 222–246.

40. Richard Sasuly, *IG Farben* (New York, 1947), pp. 53–177; Judgment, case 10, *Trials of War Criminals,* IX, 1445–1446; NI-9981 and NI-3488, case 5, *ibid.,* VI, 244–245.

41. Rosenberg, *Memoirs,* p. 248. Max Weber wrote ". . . when enthusiasm and emotional response are rationally calculated *into* the equation of power, we are not dealing with genuine feudal and/or charismatic power" (*Essays in Sociology,* p. 254).

42. Neumann, *Behemoth.* pp. 350–356.

43. Schacht, for example, was an economic rationalist who tried to compromise with chaos; he managed quite successfully from 1933 to 1936. By 1937, how-

ever, he and the Nazis disagreed about *the degree* of lawfulness to be preserved (Beck, *Verdict on Schacht*, p. 92).

44. Coulborn suggests that feudalism ". . . appears in an age of failure of the high culture as a whole," also noting that "some feudal periods have been conspicuous also as 'ages of faith,'" *Feudalism*, p. 10. The effort to regard the inner circle of National Socialism as *merely* cynical nihilists results in half-truths: "It was a purely masculine Order, confined to initiates, to those with 'knowledge'—knowledge of nothing but the cynical nihilism that was the definition of their existence. In the presence of the masses they seemed to be performing pseudo-religious rites . . ." (Vermeil, *Third Reich*, pp. 297–298).

45. "Söhne des Chaos" (sons of chaos) are Hitler's own words to describe what Konrad Heiden has described as "the wreckage of dead classes," *Der Fuehrer*, p. 100; cf. Vermeil, *Third Reich*, p. 304. Toynbee's internal proletariat comes to mind here along with Erich Fromm's concept of "alienation": *A Study of History* (abridgment by D. C. Somervell of vols. I–VI [London and New York, 1956], pp. 393–403); *Escape from Freedom* (New York, 1941).

46. More revolutionary than a frontal attack on Germany's institutional integrity was National Socialism's tendency to plant seeds of disintegration in potential rivals: Mau, "30. Juni 1934," pp. 126, 136. Goebbels spoke of a "poison gas that penetrates the most solid objects" (opponents' institutions and faith), effecting their internal decomposition: Vermeil, *Third Reich*, p. 320.

7

T. W. MASON

The Primacy of Politics— Politics and Economics in National Socialist Germany

In 1933 the Nazis captured control of the organs of government in one of the most advanced capitalist nations of the world. Whether they subjugated the formidable economic vested interests of Germany or were themselves dominated by those interests has long been a matter of dispute. The latter interpretation still prevails in the writings of orthodox Marxist-Leninists throughout the world. The author of this selection, who teaches modern history at Oxford University, offers an original and provocative answer to the problem in the light of recent scholarship and his own research in the voluminous documentation now available on the subject. A version of this essay appeared in Das Argument— Berliner Hefte für Probleme der Gesellschaft, *No. 41 (1966), 473–494. It became the subject of a debate between the author and three Marxist-Leninist critics in the same periodical two years later: No. 47 (1968), 168–227. The English text which appears here, with emendations by the author, was first published in* The Nature of Fascism, *edited by S. J. Woolf (London, 1968), pp. 165–195. It is reprinted by permission of the author and The Graduate School of Contemporary European Studies, University of Reading.*

ONE OF THE main concerns of Marxist historiography is the question of the relationship between economics and politics in the capitalist epoch. Its central thesis can perhaps be outlined as follows: the sphere of politics represents, by and large, a superstructure of the specific economic and social system, and has the function of perpetuating that system. The existence of an autonomous political realm with its own self-determining laws is usually denied by Marxist historians, and passing tendencies toward the development of such an autonomous political realm are ascribed to a temporary balance between the various social and economic forces. Politics as such are held to remain incomprehensible until those forces of economic and social development are elucidated which determine the forms and substance of political life. All historical descriptions and analyses which do not attempt such an elucidation, or which deny the point of such an attempt, are considered to be at best unscientific, at worst ideologically motivated justifications of the social status quo. The view that the economy gets the system of government which it needs, is considered a better point of departure for historical inquiry than the saying that the people get the government which it deserves. It is not necessary to point out here that this Marxist approach has proved its value in the practice of historical research and writing.[1] But the overwhelming majority of works on the history of National Socialism which have appeared in the West are characterized precisely by a rejection of this approach; they are all too quick to apostrophize the economy as just one more sphere of public life alongside many others, all of which are supposed to have been subjected in like measure to the draconian coercion of an uninhibited political dictatorship.[2]

On the other hand, modern historical research in East Germany is still conducted in the light of Dimitroff's definition of fascism as "the openly terroristic dictatorship of the most reactionary, most chauvinistic and most imperialistic elements of Finance-Capital."[3] No doubt this definition had a function and a degree of plausibility in 1935, but today, in view of the later development of Nazi Germany, it can have only very limited use as a starting point for an investigation, and can certainly not be regarded as an answer to the problem of the relationship between politics and economics under National Socialism.

It is not that the truth lies somewhere in the middle, between these two interpretations (here almost caricatured). To anticipate the conclusion of this still very provisional study: it was apparently the case that both the domestic and the foreign policy of the National Socialist government became, from 1936 onward, increasingly independent of the influence of the economic ruling classes, and even in some essential aspects ran contrary to their collective interests. *This relationship is, however, unique in the history of modern bourgeois society and its governments; it is precisely this that must be explained.*[4] According to Marxist theory it cannot be explained *only* in terms of the establishment of an unlimited political despotism, that is with reference only to the impact of state controls; the autonomy of the laws governing the workings of the capitalist economic system is too strong for this to have been the case, and the significance of the economy for the political sphere too great. It is rather that far-reaching structural changes *must* have taken place both in the economy and in society before it became possible for the National Socialist state to assume a fully independent role, for the "primacy of politics" to assert itself. The methodological starting point, the approach, must therefore owe much to the insights gained from Marxist theory.

It is the aim of this essay to demonstrate the existence of a "primacy of politics" in Nazi Germany and to seek its roots in the economic history of the period. In order to avoid misunderstandings in advance, let it be emphasized that the question here is not what kind of an economic system existed at the time; whether it was a market economy, a centrally planned economy or a species of state-monopoly-capitalism.[5] Equally, it would exceed the bounds of this essay to portray in detail the structure of the governmental machine and to examine systematically the mainsprings of its policies and aims. The preliminary studies toward the clarification of this latter question do not yet permit more than suppositions to be made.[6] Even within these limits the present essay is highly speculative. The wide-ranging theoretical discussion of the 1930's about the nature and structure of National Socialist rule was not really taken up again after 1945;[7] the work of integrating the immense quantities of newly available documentary evidence into an interpretative framework will involve a high degree of cooperation among specialist historians and social scientists from a wide range of disciplines. The task has hardly begun to be faced and thus what is presented here is essentially a set of working hypotheses.

THE TRANSITION

National Socialist leaders constantly maintained that they had restored the "primacy of politics." In the place of the weak governments of the Weimar Republic, which had acted largely under the influence of the interest groups with which they were connected, they had introduced, so the claim ran, a politically independent and energetic state leadership which was no longer forced to take into account the selfish, shortsighted wishes of special interests in the social or economic sphere when it had to make important decisions. As a slogan the "primacy of politics" was undoubtedly very effective, since it promised to put an end to the apparently interminable economic and national distress of the years before 1933.

For the forces on which the Weimar Republic rested, this distress was rooted in the failure of the Republic to achieve any lasting compromises among its constituent social classes and interests and their political groupings. In the structure of the Republic a basic contradiction had been institutionalized: the working classes had the possibility of gaining political power but no social guarantees, and the propertied classes possessed social power but no political guarantees. Of greater, and directly political significance was the fact that the propertied classes were not united among themselves: the political and social structure of bourgeois Germany, already shaken to its foundations by the First World War and the inflation, fell apart completely under the pressure of the world economic crisis. The causal relationship between the world economic crisis and the seizure of power by the National Socialists needs more detailed examination;[8] but the economic crisis can safely be said to have contributed in two decisive ways to the seizure of power: it deprived industry of the only political alternative left open to it by making economic cooperation with the USA impracticable. Thereupon the propertied classes distintegrated both economically and politically into their basically divergent groupings; the new rapprochement with the Western powers in July 1932 came too late to reverse this process. Second, mass unemployment meant that class conflict again came to be expressed in immediately political terms—which had been denied to it by the basic agreement which had obtained between the bourgeois parties, social democracy, and the trade unions after 1924. The fundamental structural weakness of the Weimar Republic again became apparent in a politically intensified form; this time it entailed a marked growth in the power of the Communist Party (KPD) and a radicalization of the employers' organizations. The accumulated problems arising out of the nonviable structure of German society were even less amenable to solution during the world economic crisis than at any other time. Faced with these problems, the propertied classes, the old and the new petty bourgeoisie, and the rural population all sought their salvation in an unthinking flight into "pure politics": politics-as-propaganda, national exaltation, the cult of the leader, anti-Semitism and anti-Communism, a yearning for an idealized preindustrial community all served as political pseudosolutions to the structural problems of the social order of Weimar Germany. The National Socialist movement was the vehicle of this flight from reality into the fancy-free world of affective racial-national harmony and unity, but the various social groups which joined it during the years 1930–1933 saw no incompatibility between the new political style and the vigorous prosecution of their special (and incompatible) social and economic interests *within* the movement.

In the years between 1924 and 1929 the economic situation gave the various bourgeois coalition governments a certain freedom of action which permitted on the whole a conciliation of opposing class and group economic interests seriously endangering the position of capital.[9] The growing economic crisis accentuated the struggles between classes and among interest groups and thus deprived the state of this latitude. For the same reason the freedom which the party leaders had had vis-à-vis their own supporters (especially that of the Social Democratic leadership) also disappeared, and with it the possibility of forming parliamentary coalition governments. In these circumstances the relative autonomy of the state, indeed its very existence, could only be preserved by the formation of presidential cabinets which promised to divorce government from the sphere of political interest-group conflicts. Although Brüning's cabinet brought about a significant reduction in the standard of living of the working population, it was incapable of solving the great problems of domestic, economic, and foreign policy and of thereby giving bourgeois society a new structure and a new direction in which to develop. And during the "unpolitical" rule of Brüning, public concern about the structure and aims of society had necessarily become more urgent and hysterical. In the year 1932 all political organizations, with the exception of the Social Democratic Party, were convinced that a completely new system of government was called for, whether a Catholic corporative state, a Bonapartist autocracy (Schleicher), a National Socialist state based on the leader-principle, or a dictatorship of the proletariat. The machinery of state had admittedly increased its independence of social pressures during these years—Brüning's deflationary policy damaged the short-term material interests of every class of society and of every entrenched pressure group—but it had for this reason ceased to function as a representation of the propertied classes in general, let alone of the whole people: and public opinion in Germany was very much aware of this.[10]

"Civil Society" was no longer able to reproduce itself. The basic precondition for overcoming this situation was the recovery of the economy. Capital could not bring this about by itself, principally because of the power of the heavy industrial cartels.[11] An economic recovery in the interests of the middle classes could only be implemented by a government that was strong enough to: (a) mediate between the contrary interests of the heavy and consumer goods sectors of industry, and protect the special interests of agriculture; (b) bring about general domestic "peace and quiet" for industry;[12] (c) prevent the standard of living of the majority of the population from rising for some time above the crisis level—which meant effectively the elimination of the trade unions; (d) secure a strict control and management of foreign exchange resources, which had become very scarce; (e) effectively combat the deeply rooted fear of inflation and so make possible a state-sponsored expansion of credit.

In short, the reproduction of society could only be guaranteed through radical political means.[13] Early in 1933 it was only National Socialism which fulfilled these minimum conditions. Its uncertainty and opportunism in many specific questions, the socially heterogeneous character of its following, the ruthlessness with which decisions, once taken, were implemented, and the proven success of its propaganda methods all contributed to make it appear the vehicle best suited for a regeneration of civil society. At the latest when Chancellor Schleicher began to negotiate with the trade unions and the SA, heavy industry drew the necessary conclusions.

It is the main function of politics in a stable, liberal democracy to reconcile the interests of the dominant social groups with each other, to interpret their common needs, and to cater for them by the most suitable means in their domestic and foreign policy aspects. This harmonious cooperation between the economy and the state demands in the long run the recognition, in a form which is acceptable to business, of the basic social and economic interests of the working class, and a consensus of the most powerful organs of opinion in matters of political principle. These are, generally speaking, functions of civil society rather than results of public policy. In Germany, on the other hand, it became the function of National Socialism to create a new social and economic compromise, a new public consensus, in fact a new general representation of the people, *by political means;* and in the context of 1933 that necessarily meant the open use of force. The "primacy of politics," which was undeniable in 1933—the creation of a dictatorship, terrorism, political and cultural *Gleichschaltung*—was the result of a social disintegration which it was the function of National Socialism to repair. Accordingly, Schacht, Papen, groups in the *Reichswehr* and industry expected that it would be possible to push the National Socialists out again, at least to limit them to a decorative function in the state, as soon as the rebuilding of a viable civil society permitted a new bid for political power on the part of its traditional ruling classes. These groups expected to be able to secure their own social supremacy, which was based on private property and threatened by the KPD, by *temporarily* giving up the *direct* execution of political power. This hope was, of course, not fulfilled. From a historical point of view, the incapacity of the political representatives of the propertied classes to formulate and implement their own policies, their abdication in favor of National Socialism—even if partly marked by unconcerned fellow-traveling— represented a great historical defeat. The political leadership of the Third Reich was able, through means unforeseen by anyone, to maintain the independence from the old ruling classes which it had gained in the crisis, 1930–1933. It did not fulfil its function of becoming obsolete.

THE DISTRIBUTION OF POWER IN THE MACHINERY
OF NATIONAL SOCIALIST GOVERNMENT

One fundamental condition of the primacy of politics was in any case a matter of course for National Socialism—a strong concentration of power in the hands of a leader who wholly dominated even his closest associates. For reasons of tactics as well as of disposition and character, Hitler largely kept out of routine governmental work; his function in the system of government of the Third Reich was, with the exception of foreign policy (later strategy) and of his personal hobbies (military weapons and architecture), chiefly that of a supreme arbiter. All important drafts of proposals by heads of departments and party leaders required his personal approval; there was never any collective responsibility within the government; after the event, Hitler's decisions could hardly ever be frustrated or changed by those responsible for their implementation. This should not of course be understood to imply that Hitler alone bears the historical responsibility for all National Socialist policies; it is rather that, in important questions, the various ruling groups within the Third Reich could only assert their interests through this one channel; and the approval of the Führer was no mere formality.[14] A supreme political arbiter was glorified whose understanding of politics was predominantly aesthetic, who tended to see politics in terms of will, spectacle, enjoyment of power and tactical finesse, and who left all substantial problems in domestic policy to "experts," but who either could not or would not take decisions about the contradictory solutions proposed to him by these experts. Thinking in economic terms was totally alien to the members of the old guard in the leadership of the National Socialist system, that is to those who had most ready access to Hitler.[15] By economics Hitler understood only *what was produced*. His memorandum on the second Four Year Plan demanded repeatedly and exclusively the simple accumulation of goods and armaments;[16] and his speech before the Reichstag on February 20, 1938—probably his only one on this subject—consisted solely of a boastful list of the figures for the increases in production in Germany since the seizure of power. He had no grasp of the question of *how* things were done in economic policy, and there is hardly any indication that he ever worried about the economic consequences of his political goals or of the decisions he made in foreign policy.[17]

Until 1942 no economic expert worthy of mention was a member of the inner circle of Hitler's advisers. Of the first men who created links between the party and industry, Funk went to the Ministry of Propaganda, Kessler turned out to be incapable, and Keppler's influence never matched his ambition.[18] As early as mid-1933 Thyssen's position as Hitler's favorite industrialist was undermined—his support of a guild system of social organization of the type advocated by Othmar Spann was irreconcilable with the claims of the NSDAP for a leading role in all spheres. In 1934 and 1935 Schacht, at once President of the Reichsbank and Minister of Economics, was allowed to make economic policy almost without hindrance. His contacts with banks, large firms, and economic organizations were extremely close, but he never enjoyed the full confidence of the party or of the Führer. This system could only last as long as there were no signs of crisis in the domestic economic situation. By 1936 this was no longer the case. From the start of that year fundamental decisions had to be taken which constantly demanded reference to Hitler. For this reason, if for no other, it was necessary to appoint to the direction of economic policy a member of the old guard who enjoyed Hitler's confidence. This role suited Göring, the Prussian Minister-President and Colonel-General of the Air Force, and suited him well inasmuch as his ideological interests were much less marked than those of most other top party functionaries; he seemed quite open to the pragmatic arguments of the civil service. However Göring was in no way up to the twofold task of forcing through necessary but unpopular measures of economic planning and of compelling some consideration of the interests of the economy in the formulation and execution of foreign policy. Whenever the civil service and representatives of industry thought they had him in their grasp, he would tend to relapse and to sacrifice pragmatic arguments to his loyalty to the movement and to his fear of the Führer.[19] Not until February 1942, when Speer was appointed Minister of Armaments and Munitions, did the effective scope of economic considerations extend to the antechamber of the political arbiter of the Third Reich.

Thus the political structure and the personality of the Führer provided a favorable basis for the maintenance of a "primacy of politics," and it is in fact very difficult to demonstrate the participation of economic leaders or organizations, even in an indirect way, in the formation of overall policy in the Third Reich. One very important reason for this was the changed position of Germany in world trade and in the international capital market. During the Weimar Republic economic and foreign policy had been closely interwoven, but this relationship was largely dissolved by the termination of reparations payments. For this reason and also thanks to the extensive control of all foreign currency transactions which was a result of Schacht's "New Plan," German foreign policy was no longer impeded by the possibility of economic sanctions on the part of the Western powers. So it is not surprising that pressure from economic interest groups played no significant role in the decisions to leave the League of Nations (November 1933), to reintroduce military service (March 1935), and to reoccupy the Rhineland in March 1936. It seems that they were not even consulted. From 1933 until 1936 economic policy, and in part also social policy, was left to the propertied classes, but they were not permitted to play any directly political role beyond these spheres. This division of labor and the approval given in economic circles to the aggressive moves in foreign policy in these years was based on the belief that industry and the NSDAP shared a common imperialist program. This apparent consensus of opinion is not only evident in the cooperation between heavy industry, the military, the party, and the civil service in the question of rearmament:[20] as far as resistance to Hitler is concerned, there were no doubt many managers and industrialists who regarded the new foreign policy as "a bit risky," and the persecution of Communists and Jews as "unnecessary" or even wrong; but the fact remains that no effective resistance whatsoever was offered by these circles during the years in question, and that they were the very groups whose social position gave them the greatest scope for such action. This apparent harmony in the aims of the ruling groups had one by-product which at first sight looks paradoxical: the *direct* links between the economic and political elites became weaker than they had been in the Weimar Republic. During the years of relatively unproblematic economic and military reconstruction, industry had neglected to maintain and safeguard its power at the political level. Hugenberg had resigned as Minister of Economics; all parties except the NSDAP had been prohibited; Seldte, the Minister of Labor, had simply looked on and done nothing as the *Stahlhelm,* which he had controlled, was taken out of his charge and handed over to the SA; and Papen had been relegated in autumn 1934 from Vice-Chancellor to Special Ambassador in Vienna—after these changes, the only representative of the old bourgeoisie left in the government was Schacht.[21] Much was made to depend on his influence. In 1936 Schacht reconstructed the former employers' organizations, chambers of trade, and industrial groups into a comprehensive "Organization of Industry" and, in the shape of the *Reichswirtschaftskammer,* created a new summit organization for it. His aim was, on the one hand to enable the state to manipulate the economy more easily in technical matters (allocation of foreign exchange, etc.), on the other, to consolidate the position and power of industry within the overall system.[22] In a liberal or in an authoritarian state, profitable and lasting cooperation between the state and the economy might perhaps have been possible on the basis of this modern corporativism, to the end of achieving a gradual imperialist expansion, *without* further extending the political power of industry. But the consequences of the forced rearmament drive eliminated this possibility.

THE DISINTEGRATION OF THE INDUSTRIAL
POWER BLOC

Since 1879 heavy industry had been the determining factor in the political economy of Germany. It had been—in contrast with British experience—the vehicle of the industrial revolution, and in the many confrontations with the consumer goods sector, handicraft organizations, and trading interests about protective tariffs, price agreements, and most recently over civilian work-creation measures (1932–1933), heavy industry had always got its own way. The seizure of power by the National Socialists would hardly have been possible without the support of considerable circles in heavy industry during the years of crisis. But in 1936 a great change in the structure of the German economy became apparent, which, although inherent in the system, was not apparently foreseen by any of the ruling groups. Whereas under the Weimar Republic industrial expansion had been inhibited by a lack of liquid capital, now, as a result of the rearmament boom, more tangible limits on production became apparent—shortages of raw materials from abroad, and of labor. These became the two decisive factors in the German arms and war economy and resulted in a far-reaching transformation of the economic power structure; and hence in a change in the relationship between economics and politics, industry and the state.

First, the lack of foreign exchange: rearmament demanded increasingly large imports of raw materials but did not contribute to a corresponding increase in exports;[23] added to this was the necessity of importing increased quantities of foodstuffs for a population whose overall purchasing power slowly rose with the disappearance of unemployment. If rearmament was not to be scaled down, the only way to avoid a repetition of the foreign trade crisis of 1936 was to bring about an immense increase in the domestic production of raw materials.[24] But to curtail rearmament was a *political* impossibility for National Socialism. Schacht vainly urged this course of action, and the leaders of the iron and steel industries gave him objective if not deliberate support by opposing the exploitation of low-grade German iron ores. The chemical industry (i.e. IG Farben) became the new economic pillar of the Third Reich; it urged the large-scale synthetic production of vital raw materials such as rubber and petrol. The decision in its favor by the state leadership and the announcement of the second Four Year Plan in September 1936—in its final phase a personal decision by Hitler—finally broke the economic and political supremacy of heavy industry. At the same time this meant an end to the formation of any general and unified political will or representation of interests on the part of German capital, such as the Industrial Association (*Reichsverband*) had achieved under the Weimar Republic. In the forced rearmament of the last years before the war, the top industrial organizations lost their overall vision and control of the general economic development—all that was left were the special interests of individual firms, at most of certain branches of the economy. Heavy industry could no longer maintain that its interests were identical with those of German imperialism in general, let alone make good this claim. As a result of technological developments, rearmament, for which heavy industry had fought so bitterly and doggedly since 1919, marked the start of its own downfall. Heavy industry became the victim of its own expansionism. The direction and the dynamic of National Socialist economic and foreign policy after 1936 rested upon the domestic production of raw materials. Without the accelerated expansion of the chemical industry a European war could never have been risked in 1939.[25]

These structural changes were strengthened and speeded up by developments in the labor market. In this period of rapidly advancing rearmament, the public purse became the decisive factor in the shaping of the German economy. In 1939 the share of Reich expenditure in the gross social product was 34 to 35 percent, of which two-thirds went toward preparation for war. Armaments expenditure had increased fifteenfold in seven years.[26] Up to January 1939, public contracts were not subject to the price-freeze—on the contrary, most were calculated on a "costs plus" basis. To increase his own profits, every contractor tried to obtain these orders and to fulfil them as punctually as possible, so that he would be taken into consideration when contracts were next distributed. In conjunction with the shortage of labor and raw materials brought about by the rearmament drive, this led to ruthless competition between firms, not for markets, which were well-nigh unlimited for the industries concerned, but for the basic factors of production. The firms which produced goods needed in the armaments drive had an advantageous position in the struggle for raw materials, and were, by virtue of the generously calculated estimates, able to attract workers by increased wages, to poach them from other firms. So a second rift was added to the division in the economy caused by the rise of the chemical industry: that between firms primarily engaged in the armaments drive and those working mainly for civilian or export markets. Although the coal mines, for example, were indispensable to the war economy as a whole, this industry exported about one-sixth of its production and did not deliver direct to the armed forces; consequently, wages remained low and miners left in increasing numbers for other branches of industry; the per capita productivity of the miners decreased and, at the outbreak of war, there was a shortage of coal which presented a severe threat to the army's rail transport program. The same factors threatened agricultural production too, whereas the building, chemical, and engineering industries enjoyed an unprecedented prosperity.[27]

This intensification and change in the character of capitalist competition contributed further to the disintegration of the political power of industry. Once freed by the terrorist methods of the Gestapo from the necessity of defending themselves against an organized working class, and relieved by the armaments boom from the necessity of planning and limiting production on a cartel basis, the propertied classes lost their sense of common interest. The collective interest of the capitalistic economic system dissolved progressively from 1936 to 1939 into a mere agglomeration of the short-term interests of individual firms, which, to reverse a dictum of Lenin, marched separately and fell together. It is not a gross oversimplification to say that they were bought by the government.[28] The public purse—that is, a part of the same institution which determined foreign policy—became the interpreter of the interests of the economy, by sole virtue of its enormous financial resources. The *Reichswirtschaftskammer,* which had been called into being in 1936 to head the new and strengthened Organization of Industry, in fact carried out only technical and administrative tasks for the Reich government and was incapable of making itself felt in high politics.

As far as the distribution of raw materials was concerned, the state did not succeed in curbing the competition among the firms and the growing number of public agencies issuing contracts until 1941–1942. On the other hand, the state had, for political reasons, only a limited interest in regulating the labor market to the advantage of industry. By the autumn of 1936 the shortage of labor in the building and metal industries had led to considerable pay increases, partly forced by strikes, and to the widespread practice of firms poaching skilled workers from one another by the offer of improved working conditions. It ought to have been clear at this juncture that these were not merely temporary phenomena, but rather the necessary consequences of a rearmament program which was itself only in its initial stages. Three measures were necessary to forestall the spread of these conditions to the entire labor market, and to prevent them from having a harmful effect on the course of rearmament through lowering productivity and increasing the purchasing power of the population: a general limitation of the freedom of movement of labor, the fixing of maximum wages, and a more stringent allocation of economic resources to priority tasks. The National Socialist leadership deliberately omitted to take these steps, which were advocated by several ministries, until the international crisis over the Sudetenland came to a head in the summer of 1938 and not only provided the pretext for them (which considerations of morale demanded), but also made such state controls quite unavoidable.[29] By that time the shortage of labor had long become general—shop assistants and hairdressers were in as short supply as lathe hands. The reasons for this inaction by the government were quite obvious and at the same time throw a clear light on the problem of the primacy of politics: all the above-mentioned measures were rejected for two years by the political leadership because such radical steps against the material interests of workers and consumers were not reconcilable with the *political* task of "educating" them in National Socialism. It was absolutely necessary for the National Socialist system, at least until well into the war years, to be quite sure of the active sympathy and agreement of the mass of the population with its ideology, goals, and policies. The attempt to achieve this through pseudo-egalitarian demagogy, by improving social amenities in the factories, and through "Strength through Joy," etc., had clearly failed —so the workers' approval of the system had to be bought by high wages, paid holidays, and the like[30]—although such measures were in direct contradiction to the demands of the rearmament drive, which the government was, at the same time, determined to speed up. For the same reason the political leaders obstructed the efforts of industry (led by the *Reichswirtschaftskammer*) to limit the growing power of the Labor Front. This organization had been given the task of winning over the workers to National Socialism and nothing, not even the smooth running of the arms economy, was allowed to impede its efforts, even though the Labor Front acted, in a disguised form but after 1936 in increasing measure, as bearer of the economic interests of the working classes.[31]

The old contradiction between the potential political power and the economic impotence of the working classes had apparently been "solved" when the National Socialists destroyed the workers' organizations in 1933, but the plebiscitary elements of the system, which necessarily came more to the forefront after full employment had been reached, made the political and economic repression of the working class more difficult and necessitated the sanctioning of material improvements to mobilize their support. The contradiction between demagogy ("Strength through Joy") and political practice (forced rearmament) reproduced the contradiction between the mass basis necessary to National Socialism and the unchanged structure of property relationships. Labor exploited its own growing scarcity and the government had to acquiesce in this.

While the suggestion that the freedom of the workers to change their jobs should be curtailed met with hardly any resistance among employers,[32] their reaction to the proposal that an upper limit to wages should be fixed was different. Those firms which were directly or indirectly involved with rearmament needed more and more labor. A reserve army of unemployed workers "capable of being used anywhere"[33] had effectively ceased to exist since early 1937. Additional workers thus had to be poached from other firms and the decisive means of achieving this was the offer of higher pay. Until an efficient form of state-controlled labor deployment had been developed late in 1939, which was able to direct workers into the armaments sector and force them to stay there, a wage-freeze was by no means in the interests of all employers. The maximum-wage scales which were introduced in the last twelve months before the outbreak of war were in practice circumvented by many employers by means of gifts and concealed bonuses to their workers.[34] There was also the further problem of the generally declining productivity of labor; this was a consequence in part of the physical overtaxation of the workers (too much overtime), in part of inadequate food (shortage of fats), but also of the new job-security resulting from full employment, and of the sullen indifference of most industrial workers toward the whole social and political system of National Socialism. The only countermeasure and inducement to higher output which many employers could think of was an increase in wages. This line of argument, which was still implemented in a more modest way during the war, rested as far as the employers were concerned on an extraordinary indifference to the wider economic consequences of such a policy (inflation) and on a neglect, which was determined by the generosity of the public purse, of normal procedures of economic calculation within the firm. The historically typical behavior-patterns of capitalist economic policy and management had, thanks to the forced rearmament drive, become largely irrelevant; all that was left were the primitive and short-term interests of each and every firm.

In these conditions the large firms became larger still. For various reasons rearmament necessarily accelerated the process of concentration in the German economy. This tendency was particularly obvious in the electrical industry (Siemens), in the chemical industry (IG Farben), and in the iron and metal industries (Reichswerke Hermann Göring). By virtue of their position as monopolies and of the importance of their products for the war economy, these firms maintained close and direct contacts with the machinery of state and with the military; sometimes they even achieved through their personnel the equation of the interests of the state with those of their firms—leading managers were seconded to public economic agencies.[35] But rearmament also meant that the *direct* relationships with the agencies distributing contracts became more important for most big firms than *collective* dealings with the state through the channels of the economic and industrial organizations. Once the problem of the allocation of raw materials and labor had become crucial, this traditional form of collaboration between industry and the state became secondary. For all these reasons, which were inherent in the political and economic system, the capitalist economic structure largely disintegrated into its component parts. It was easy for the huge armaments firms to prosecute their immediate material interests, but, in the process, the responsibility for the overall economic system was left to a political leadership whose final arbiter, Hitler, saw in the economy merely a means for attaining certain vaguely outlined, yet in principle quite unattainable, political goals—goals which, though certainly of great incidental benefit to German industry, were not determined by economic considerations. Even the fact that Speer called in "Leaders of the Economy" in 1942–1944, to help with the distribution of public contracts and raw materials, did little to alter this situation. The "rings" and committees in his system of the "self-government of German industry" were indeed run by industrialists, but they were responsible, in accordance with the *Führerprinzip,* only for ensuring that the rulings and plans made by Speer's ministry were carried out. They were given considerable freedom of action in this sphere, but on decisive questions of strategy, foreign policy, and war aims their opinion was not sought. Their competence was limited entirely to the question of *how* things were done.[36]

INDUSTRY AND THE WORLD WAR

All the important foreign policy decisions in 1938 and 1939 were taken by Hitler personally. It is not yet possible to state with any degree of certainty how far he may have taken economic factors into consideration in these decisions. As yet there are hardly any positive proofs that he did.[37] Göring and General Thomas, who were both in close contact with industrial leaders and may well have been influenced by them, concluded from Germany's shortage of almost all strategic economic reserves that Hitler's foreign policy was rash and that the great war would have to be postponed. Their doubts were dismissed by Hitler. The fact that their pessimistic economic prognoses were not fulfilled until later was largely owing to the military inactivity and weakness of the Western powers in 1939–1940 (a factor which Hitler had at least in part reckoned with in his plans for a *Blitzkrieg*), to deliveries of goods from the Soviet Union under the Non-Aggression Pact in 1939–1941, and to the plundering of occupied territories. "Rearmament in depth" as demanded by Thomas remained, for the plebiscitary reasons noted above, a political impossibility for National Socialism until the defeat at Stalingrad; it would have demanded a drastic lowering of the standard of living. The domestic-political function of the *Blitzkrieg* plans resided in their promise of bringing the war to a swift and successful conclusion *without* demanding any undue sacrifices of the German people; and thereby providing a basis of tangible social and economic privilege for the alleged racial superiority of the German people in Europe.

Although the lack of raw materials and of labor therefore can still not be cited as a direct or immediate cause of the war of 1939, the war, once started, of necessity turned into an ever more intensive economic exploitation of the whole of Europe.[38] The war made plunder possible —and also essential. In this connection the Second World War differed in two decisive respects from earlier imperialist wars: the economic need which was to be satisfied by military expansion was by no means of an autonomous economic nature (lack of markets or openings for investment), but was heavily determined by political factors. It was only the forced rearmament drive of 1936–1939 which brought about the shortages of the basic factors of production; these were in turn intensified by the war, but could at the same time through war be alleviated in the most brutal way. Wartime plunder thus had its roots in political considerations: rearmament, the rapid extension by force of the German sphere of influence. These considerations had appeared to be based on a consensus of opinion between the Nazi leadership and industry, but the course of their translation into practice changed the terms of the partnership; control had largely slipped from the hands of industry from 1936 onward, partly as a result of the political structure of the Third Reich, but also partly because of the inevitable changes in the structure of the economy. The high taxation rates and the control exercised by the state over the capital market did not trouble industry because it got the money back again in the form of public contracts. Thus the pursuit of war and the pursuit of profit became under National Socialism a closed system, a vicious circle of almost complete mutual dependence. What this closed system was for remained unclear.

This was the second peculiarity of German policy in 1939–1945. National Socialism lacked concrete war aims; accordingly there was no conception of a new imperial order in Europe which was based on the needs of the economy—extensive plundering simply permitted the war to be continued. German industrialists certainly took advantage of the victories of the *Wehrmacht* to eliminate or take over foreign competitors and to extend the interests of their firms into France and eastern Europe; they sometimes took the initiative in submitting takeover plans to the government.[39] Yet it cannot be said that this was what the war was really about; no compelling economic necessity lay behind such private industrial annexations. Final victory would have brought German industry dominance over the whole European economy—which would obviously have been welcome (though it must be doubted whether the NSDAP and the SS would have left the pickings to industry alone). It is however very hard to underpin such a statement with examples of preconquest expansionist designs either from within industry or at the level of government economic policy, and it is even harder to build bridges from "economic imperialism" in this sense to the crucial decisions of high policy which were taken in 1939–1941. It may be misplaced to look for such designs and interconnections; perhaps the various elites of Nazi Germany all had their own different views of what the war was about, views which remained roughly compatible with each other as long as the war continued. The question requires more systematic investigation, but it is difficult to detect any coherent economic vision of empire behind the conquests and occupations of the period 1938–1942. Neither in a political nor in an economic sense did the Nazi system produce a realistic conception of an ultimate status quo. For this reason, if for no other, a *victory* of National Socialism in the usual sense, which presupposes the goal of a postwar order, is unthinkable. Furthermore, by 1942 the armaments drive had brought about such a great change in the industrial structure, in favor of the production of basic materials and capital goods, that a peacetime market economy could scarcely be visualized. Even the gradual termination of the state's demand for military goods would have entailed a radical change in the economic and political system.[40] In all respects war had become an end in itself; the boundless expansionism of National Socialism gave rise to an international alliance which was bound to bring about its destruction.

SUMMARY

From 1936 onward the framework of economic action in Germany was increasingly defined by the political leadership. The needs of the economy were determined by political decisions, principally by decisions in foreign policy, and the satisfaction of these needs was provided for by military victories. The fact that numerous industrialists not only passively cooperated in the "Aryanization" of the economy, in the confiscation of firms in occupied territory, in the enslavement of many million people from eastern Europe, and in the employment of concentration camp prisoners, but indeed often took the initiative in these actions, constitutes a damning judgment on the economic system whose essential organizing principle (competition) gave rise to such conduct. But it cannot be maintained that even these actions had an important formative influence on the history of the Third Reich; rather, they filled out in a barbaric manner a framework which was already given. The large firms identified themselves with National Socialism for the sake of their own further economic development. Their desire for profit and expansion, which was fully met by the political system, together with the stubborn nationalism of their leaders did, however, bind them to a government on whose aims, inasmuch as they were subject to control at all, they had virtually no influence.

Only between 1934 and 1936 was there a degree of elastic cooperation between the economy and the state to the advantage of the economic system, and that only in a simulated form, for it was not based on a stable balance between the various class interests but on the terroristic suppression of the workers' organizations and on totalitarian propaganda. The political leadership constructed for itself a position of supremacy which, in institutional terms, was autonomous and unshakable and which, through its control of foreign policy, determined the direction of the system as a whole.

The seizure of power by the National Socialists can be traced back to a fundamental disintegration of bourgeois society in Germany, and the "primacy of politics" in its mature form was based on a renewed disintegration in the years 1936–1938. This lack of unity and of coordination was by no means limited to the economy; on the contrary, it became the basic organizing principle of the National Socialist system of rule. A new stable and general representation of the people could not be achieved only by terror, propaganda, and successes in foreign policy (i.e., through politics). It would have required a rational restructuring of society, and neither in industry nor in the NSDAP was there the slightest inclination to attempt this. The old conflicts between agriculture and industry, capital and the working classes continued with the old intensity, though in new institutional forms. To these, new structural conflicts were added: *Gauleiter* against the central government, the party against the *Wehrmacht* and the civil service, the SS and the SD against everybody else. In 1938 General Keitel characterized the social and economic system as "a war of all against all."[41] It was no less warlike for being fought in silence. Debates in Germany as elsewhere about the social distribution of the national wealth had always been public and ideological. The monolithic front which National Socialism wished to present to the outside world fo bade such debate, and the ideology did not furnish a language in which it could be conducted. The differences between the various ruling groups were thus fought out behind closed doors and in the form of straightforward, unideological battles for power and economic resources. The constantly invoked "national community" of the propaganda concealed a reality in which the only acknowledged conformism was the cynical prosecution of one's own material interests; there developed as a result a broad, complex, and "modern" pluralism of political and economic interests which, until the military recovery of the Soviet Union in 1942, defeated most of the government's efforts to simplify and unify the power structure. Until 1942 the system was held together by two things: the frenetic, aimless dynamism of expansion, in which the constant setting of new tasks compelled the various organizations and interests to cooperate with each other—standstill would have meant decay; and second, by the function of the *Führerprinzip*. Hitler's supposed technique of extending his own sphere of influence by tactics of *divide et impera* was in practice a necessity dictated by the system, since the plurality of interests and organizations was already in existence.[42] Attempts to secure unitary structures of command foundered not so much on Hitler's desire to play the arbiter wherever he could, but on the power of those interest groups whose influence would have had to be curtailed if the various decisions on matters of principle were made. To decide between the rival claims of the Labor Front and industry, the contradictory interests of the farmers and the consumers, or the different views of Göring and the *Gauleiter* on the need for stringent war economy measures was a very delicate and thankless task, which Hitler usually preferred simply to avoid. Speer was one of the few who could force him to take such decisions. Loyalty to the Führer and the willingness of the leaders of state and party organs to accept Hitler's decisions often seemed to be the barrier standing between the "Thousand-Year Reich" and anarchy.[43]

The self-destructive measures of the National Socialist system can only be understood in the context of the primacy of politics and of the material plurality of the power structure from which the state derived its autonomy. Among the first Polish Jews who were gassed in the extermination camps were thousands of skilled metal workers from Polish armament factories. This was in the autumn of 1942, at the turning point in the campaign against the Soviet Union, which was to increase still further the demands made by the *Wehrmacht* on the German economy. The army emphasized the irrational nature of this action in view of the great shortage of skilled labor, but was unable to save the Jewish armament workers for industry. The general who made the formal complaint was relieved of his post.[44] The same internal power relationship lay behind the use of scarce railway installations for the deportation of persecuted Jews toward the end of the war, instead of for the provisioning of the forces on the Eastern Front. The SS was able, by virtue of its monopoly over the information services and the machinery of terror, of its position outside the legal framework, and lastly by virtue of Himmler's special relationship with Hitler, to execute its ideologically determined task of the destruction of the Jews to the material detriment of the whole system. The way in which the political sphere emancipated itself from all reference to the needs of society is nowhere clearer than in the example of the SS, where the translation of ideology into practice was in flat contradiction to the interests of the war economy and yet was allowed to continue.

Another slightly less crass example was the decision of March 1942 to enslave the populations of eastern Europe systematically and put them at the disposal of the German war economy. *Gauleiter* Sauckel, who was given control over all labor deployment at that time, suggested that the problem of labor shortage could be solved by rationalization of the methods of production and by conscripting German women to work in industry. Slave labor, he maintained, was politically and technically unreliable, unproductive, and represented a "racial danger" to the German people. His program was rejected by Hitler on the grounds that there was no time to rationalize the economy and that the German woman's place was in the home. After this a further five million "foreign and Russian workers" were brought forcibly into Germany, and Sauckel's doubts were confirmed.[45] Again an ideologically determined policy triumphed over economic calculation.

Any attempt to find a common denominator in this ideology, to interpret it as if it were systematic, is doomed to failure. Goebbels and his team tended to understand and use the ideology as an instrument of domination, the contents of which could be manipulated almost at will. But in the end, the racial-ethical Utopia at its core was taken so seriously by the political leadership, in particular by Hitler and by the SS, that in decisive questions even the urgent material needs of the system were sacrificed to it. Precisely in the case of the destruction of the Jews and in the question of conscripting women into industry, the ideology was *not* any longer a necessary pillar of the system—as it perhaps had been in the early years of the Third Reich. For the destruction of the Jews was carried out *in secret* in Poland; and, according to the reports of the security services on public opinion within Germany, the majority of the population would have approved of measures to compel women to work. What held the system together as late as 1944 was neither common interest nor a consensus, but fear—fear of "the Russian hordes," and of the now indiscriminate terror of the Gestapo.

Under the conditions of capitalist production, there is always something irrational about the assertion of a "primacy of politics," since that which alone can legitimate this primacy, a commonweal, can only be simulated. It is only possible to talk of a rational primacy of politics when the state can act as trustee of a homogeneous society and base its policies on the needs and resources of the society. The radical nature of the "primacy of politics" under National Socialism, however, was rooted in the specific historical disintegration of bourgeois German society (1929–1933), of German capitalism (1936–1938), and of international politics in the 1930's. The immense political scope of the National Socialist government was not based on the confidence of a politically and economically homogeneous society; on the contrary, it was a result precisely of the disintegration of society. The coincidence of this with the collapse of the international order in the 1930's enabled the National Socialist state to achieve a degree of independence of society which is unparalleled in history. The development of the National Socialist system of rule tended inevitably toward *self-destruction,* for a political system which is not based on the requirements of social reproduction is no longer in a position to set itself limited and rational aims. This autonomy of the political sphere led to a blind, goal-less activism in all spheres of public life—a tendency to which the capitalist economy, based as it was on competition and the maximization of profit, was particularly susceptible. The separation of the economic principle of competition from all institutional limitations designed to ensure the continued reproduction of society was part of the dialectic of National Socialism. The economic power of the state as an unlimited source of demand for armaments gave free rein to destructive tendencies in the economic system.

The fundamental irrationality of the National Socialist system had in part its origin and found its concrete expression in the specific irrationality of the ideology. This ideology was the product of a declining social class and came increasingly into conflict with the social realities created by National Socialist rule itself: the movement whose ideology had been directed toward the construction of a society of small traders, craftsmen, and smallholders, brought about a tremendous acceleration in the process of concentration in industry and trade, and intensified the drift of population from the countryside into the towns; industry was concentrated in central and western Germany and drew increasingly on the population of the poorer eastern regions as a source of labor, thus making nonsense of the policy of colonizing and settling eastern Europe with German farmers—the one attempt at this in western Poland was a signal failure. Likewise the attempt to educate the working classes to idealism—the workers had to be bought at a cost to military strength, and yet even this method did not suffice. In the end the ideology could only find a secure place in the "reality" of everyday life in and through the SS—and that only through terror and bureaucratic norms.

Fighting spirit and the willingness to make sacrifices on the one hand, and comprehensive military-economic planning on the other, were only realized under pressure of imminent defeat. Self-destruction was the preordained end of a system in which politics was synonymous with the boundless pursuit of political power; destruction its only achievement.[46]

NOTES

1. Franz Neumann, *Behemoth* (London and New York, 1944), remains the best single work on the Third Reich.

2. Thus Gerhard Schulz in Bracher, Sauer and Schulz, *Die nationalsozialistische Machtergreifung* (Cologne, 1960), Part 2, Chap. v; also Ingeborg Esenwein-Rothe, *Die Wirtschaftsverbände von 1933 bis 1945* (Berlin, 1965) and David Schoenbaum, *Hitler's Social Revolution* (New York, 1966). The controversy about totalitarianism rests on similar postulates. The only exceptions among the scholarly postwar works to have appeared in the West are Arthur Schweitzer, *Big Business in the Third Reich* (Bloomington, 1964), Dieter Petzina, *Autarkiepolitik im dritten Reich* (Stuttgart, 1968), and Berenice A. Carroll, *Design for Total War* (The Hague, 1968).

3. Quoted after Dietrich Eichholtz, "Probleme einer Wirtschaftsgeschichte des Faschismus in Deutschland," *Jahrbuch für Wirtschaftsgeschichte* (1963), Part III, 103. This essay brings some important refinements to the Marxist-Leninist concept of fascism and one awaits with interest the author's book on the German war economy 1939–1945; but he still writes of "the tasks allotted by finance-capital to its fascism." For a critical review of East German historiography, see B. Blanke, R. Reiche and J. Werth, "Die Faschismus-Theorie der DDR," *Das Argument—Berliner Hefte für Probleme der Gesellschaft*, No. 33 (May, 1965).

4. The New Deal in the USA, the Popular Front of 1936 in France, and the Labour Government of 1945 in Britain represented a different kind of variation from the norm—their limited reforms tended to strengthen the existing social order, the needs of which they understood better than the respective ruling classes

5. This question is of lesser importance; some light is thrown on it by J. S. Geer, *Der Markt der geschlossenen Nachfrage* (Berlin, 1961).

6. The recent works of Andreas Hillgruber, *Hitlers Strategie* (Frankfurt a.M., 1965) and Hans Mommsen, *Beamtentum im Dritten Reich* (Stuttgart, 1966) are suggestive in this connection.

7. Useful selections from the prewar literature have been edited and published by Wolfgang Abendroth, *O. Bauer, H. Marcuse, A. Rosenberg—Faschismus und Kapitalismus* (Frankfurt a.M.–Vienna, 1967) and Ernst Nolte, *Theorien über den Faschismus* (Cologne-Berlin, 1967). See also R. Griepenburg and K. H. Tjaden, "Faschismus und Bonapartismus," *Das Argument*, No. 41 (December, 1966).

8. Above all the social consequences of the crisis need detailed investigation. There was no simple correlation between mass unemployment and the rise of National Socialism; new, potentially fascist popular movements antedated the crisis by over a year—cf. Arthur Rosenberg, *A History of the German Republic* (London, 1936), Chap. IX, and Rudolf Heberle, *From Democracy to Nazism* (Baton Rouge, 1945).

9. For Stresemann's freedom of action vis-à-vis heavy industry, see Henry Ashby Turner, Jr., *Stresemann and the Politics of the Weimar Republic* (Princeton, 1963).

10. Bracher's concept of a "political power-vacuum" in the years 1930–1933 is useful, but needs to be underpinned by an analysis of the disintegration of social and economic power structures: cf. *Die Auflösung der Weimarer Republik* (Stuttgart, 1960), part 2, sec. B.

11. The cartels kept up the price of coal, iron, steel, etc., thus ruling out the type of economic revival predicated by classical economic theory.

12. *Ruhe und Ordnung* was the euphemism current among employers for the restoration of their managerial prerogatives, which were threatened by the working class organizations.

13. How exceptional this position was can be seen by comparison with the history of the Federal Republic since 1953—the sphere of high politics, though not that of administration, can be almost superfluous to the reproduction of society.

14. Hitler several times withheld his approval from draft laws signed by all interested ministers; some of these concerned economic policy and did not come into force in the form of the drafts—examples in *Bundesarchiv Koblenz*, R43 II, vols. 417a, 810a.

15. Darré (Minister of Agriculture) and *Gauleiter* Wagner (Price Commissar) were both increasingly forced to think in economic categories by the steadily growing difficulties in their respective spheres of competence; neither of them had easy access to Hitler; both fell from power early in the war.

16. Text of the memorandum in *Vierteljahrshefte für Zeitgeschichte*, III (1955), 204–210.

17. Excerpts from the speech in Max Domarus, ed., *Hitler: Reden und Proklamationen*, I (Würzburg, 1962), 793ff. A good example of Hitler's lack of concern for the economic consequences of his decisions is the hectic building of the Siegfried Line in the latter half of 1938, which brought the already overstrained building industry to the edge of chaos.

18. Before 1933 Funk was on the staff of the *Berliner Börsenzeitung;* he carried little weight as Minister of Economics from 1938 on. Kessler held the

position of "Leader of the Economy" very briefly, 1933–1934. Wilhelm Keppler was Hitler's personal economic adviser, held a post in the administration of the second Four Year Plan 1936–1938, and then became Secretary of State in the Foreign Office; his political role remains unclear. The importance of Goerdeler as economic adviser to the Chancellory 1933–1935 would bear further investigation.

19. Göring havered continually in the conflict between the Labor Front and industry (see below) and could reach no decisions on wage policy; he opposed Hitler's foreign policy, 1938–1939, but dared not force the issue. He too had little understanding of economics, as he proudly proclaimed at the 1938 party rally.

20. Apart from the working class organizations, the other victims of this alliance were sections of the Nazi movement itself—the handicraft and factory cell organizations and the SA, whose populistic and anti-industrial tendencies caused the business world a great deal of concern in 1933.

21. Neurath's position as Foreign Minister till early 1938 may have acted as a reassurance to some, and the army was not purged until this date either. There seem to have been no contacts between industry and the first oppositional groups within the army in 1938; it is noteworthy that industry has hardly claimed any role at all in the conservative resistance.

22. Esenwein-Rothe, *Die Wirtschaftsverbände*, p. 72.

23. So great was the shortage of foreign exchange that considerable quantities of weapons and machine tools for their production were exported.

24. For the crisis see Arthur Schweitzer, "The Foreign Exchange Crisis of 1936," *Zeitschrift für die gesamte Staatswissenschaft* (1962). The autarchy program needed time, and the continued acceleration of rearmament was in fact only made possible by the unforeseeable revival of international trade during 1937.

25. Hardly any of the production goals of the Four Year Plan were in fact reached, but the achievement was considerable in relation to the narrow margin of German reserves in September 1939—full figures in Petzina, *Autarkiepolitik*, p. 182.

26. Cf. T. W. Mason, "Some Origins of the Second World War," *Past & Present*, No. 29 (1964).

27. *Bundesarchiv Koblenz*, R43 II, vol. 528; R41 I, vol. 174; WiIF5, vols. 560/1 and 2; R22Gr. 5, vol. 1206.

28. The quarterly reports on the economy of Berlin 1938–1939 give a good picture of the process (*Bundesarchiv Koblenz*, R41, vols. 155–156). The role of the cartels in the 1930's has not yet been properly studied.

29. The measures were first considered in September 1936; the building of the Siegfried Line was the immediate cause of their introduction.

30. Memories of the November revolution of 1918 were in some measure responsible for the stress which the Nazi leadership placed on this problem.

31. Cf. T. W. Mason, "Labour in the Third Reich 1933–39," *Past & Present*, No. 33 (1966).

32. The controls were introduced gradually 1936–1939 and proved very difficult to enforce.

33. The unemployed were divided into categories; only those who were physically fit and in a position to take up work away from their homes qualified as *voll einsatzfähig* after 1936.

34. Reports of the Reich Trustees of Labor for June 1938–March 1939

(*Bundesarchiv Koblenz*, R43II, vol. 528). Average hourly wage rates in industry rose by twenty-five percent from January 1933 to mid-1943 (*ibid.*, R4I, vol. 60, p. 200).

35. On the trend towards concentration in industry, see the reports on the economy of Berlin, note 28 above. Dr. Karl Krauch of IG Farben was in charge of chemical production under the Four Year Plan; 30 percent of his staff in this office came from IG Farben (Petzina, *Autarkiepolitik*, p. 123).

36. Cf. Alan Milward, *The German Economy at War* (London, 1965), Chap. IV.

37. Hitler mentioned Germany's need to annex agricultural land at the so-called Hossbach conference of November 5, 1937, and there are many *post factum* utterances by political leaders on the economic functions of territorial expansion. The subject may not have been discussed before the war because such a justification for expansion implied a certain weakness on Germany's part, of a kind which Hitler always refused to acknowledge.

38. This subject has hardly been investigated by historians yet.

39. E.g., D. Eichholtz, "Die IG-Farben-'Friedensplanung,'" *Jahrbuch für Wirtschaftsgeschichte* Part III (1966), 271–332. Further examples cited by E. Czichon, "Das Primat der Industrie," in *Das Argument*, No. 47; but the discovery of such evidence alone does not prove the significance of industrial expansionism.

40. During 1941 and 1942, when final victory seemed near, the government gave some thought to this question; it was decided to solve it through a large-scale housing program—there was a shortage of some three million dwellings at the outbreak of war. But this solution would have been of no benefit to the chemical and engineering industries. The postwar plans of the Nazi leadership would repay detailed investigation.

41. "Kampf aller Bedarfsträger um menschliche Arbeitskräfte, Rohstoffe und Geld"; minutes of meeting of Reich Defense Committee, December 15, 1938 (*Bundesarchiv Koblenz*, WiIF5, vol. 560/2, pp. 5f.).

42. For the war period, there is evidence that Hitler *deliberately* created agencies with overlapping competences.

43. Not least important was his considerable personal popularity among the people at large, which went a long way toward countering the unpopularity of the "little Hitlers," the war, etc. Cf. Heinz Boberach, *Meldungen aus dem Reich* (Neuwied-Berlin, 1965).

44. Testimony of Dr. H. von Krannhals in the trial of SS-Obergruppenführer Karl Wolff, Munich, September 1964. For the background see Raul Hilberg, *The Destruction of the European Jews* (Chicago and London, 1961), pp. 236, 246f., 284ff.

45. Cf. trial of Fritz Sauckel before the International Military Tribunal at Nuremberg, protocol, esp. vol. XV. Russian workers (*Ostarbeiter*) were treated even worse than other foreign workers. The mobilization of female labor was more complete in Britain than in Germany.

46. Cf. Norman Cohn's illuminating discussion of the self-destructive elements in the psychology of the anti-Semite in *Warrant for Genocide* (London, 1967), "Conclusion," esp. pp. 265f. "Self-destruction" appears to be the only universal theme in the history of National Socialist Germany, but the universality may only be verbal: it is difficult to relate the various manifestations—political, economic, psychological—with one another.

8

EBERHARD JÄCKEL

The Evolution of
Hitler's Foreign Policy Aims*

[TRANSLATED BY JOYCE CRUMMEY]

One of the most fundamental controversies about Nazism and the Third Reich concerns the determinants of Hitler's actions. Was he simply an unprincipled, power-seeking demagogue acting pragmatically to exploit any and all opportunities for enhancing his own position and that of the country he came to control? Or was he firmly committed to the attainment of certain well-defined goals, from which all his policies were derived? The latter viewpoint is forcefully argued by the author of this selection, which appeared originally as the second chapter ("Das aussenpolitische Konzept") of his book, Hitlers Weltanschauung *(Tübingen, 1969). A Professor of History at the University of Stuttgart, he has also published the most important book on Nazi policy toward France:* Frankreich in Hitlers Europa *(Stuttgart, 1966). This selection is reprinted by permission of the author, of the Rainer Wun-*

*Quotations here from *Mein Kampf* follow the first edition, vol. 1 (1925), vol. 2 (1927). However, since this edition is not readily available, page numbers follow the one-volume popular edition of 1930, to the pagination of which later editions correspond almost exactly, whereas earlier editions differ from it in pagination. Thus the reader can become acquainted with the wording of the original, while at the same time he can easily locate a quotation and its context in the most widely circulated editions. Important later deviations from the first edition will be pointed out in footnotes. On the question of textual alterations, cf. Hermann Hammer, "Die deutschen Ausgaben von Hitlers 'Mein Kampf,'" *Vierteljahrshefte für Zeitgeschichte,* IV (1956), 161ff.

201

derlich Verlag Hermann Leins, and of Wesleyan University Press, which will publish a complete translation of Hitlers Weltanschauung in the near future.

For a long time it was difficult to generate even so much as a discussion of Hitler's political goals because of the widespread acceptance of the view that explained his actions solely in terms of nihilistic opportunism. The field was completely dominated by interpretations placing primary emphasis on the instrumental nature of Hitler's policies and on the overriding importance to him of acquiring and holding power for its own sake.

If, as was long maintained, Hitler had no political goals, there was no need to inquire into their nature. To pose the problem in spite of all discouragements was to invite the suspicion that one wished to give the portrait of the tyrant grander features than it deserved. The liberating breakthrough to an undistorted look at reality originated with British historical research, to which scholars the world over were already indebted for the first major biography of Hitler. As early as 1952 the author of that biography, Alan Bullock, acknowledged that Hitler's program showed substantial consistency. In 1953 and 1959 Hugh R. Trevor-Roper, author of a masterful study of Hitler's last days[1] and, like Bullock, an Oxford historian, resolutely pushed beyond the cautious beginning made by Bullock, publishing two short but pioneering works.[2]

Trevor-Roper criticized the view of some historians "who feel so repelled by Hitler's vulgar, inhumane nature that they simply refuse to grant him such positive traits as clear thinking and purposeful action." The Oxford historian pointed out the error of "extrapolating low intelligence from moral degradation"[3] and outlined an impressive picture, at least as far as Hitler's concept of history and his foreign policy aims were concerned. He was the first to maintain that the future dictator's view of history had been formulated at the latest by 1923, after which time it had found expression in Hitler's actions "with absolute clarity and logic."[4] Hitler is portrayed by Trevor-Roper as acting—and thinking—like a statesman.[5] He had a vision, abhorrent but grandiose, of how the polities of this world rise and fall throughout history, and he resolved to resurrect a great German Empire through conquest of the East. This was his lifelong dream, the raison d'être of National Socialism.[6]

Since these beginnings were made, historians, their work confirmed repeatedly by new documentary discoveries, have reconstructed the genesis of Hitler's foreign and military policy with increasing clarity and, for the most part, with verifiable dates.[7] It has been established that Hitler began his political career after the First World War as a revisionist, like the majority of Germans. The term "revisionist" can, however, be applied here only with the reservation that in its strictest sense it is inapplicable to Hitler. From the very beginning, his revisionism was colored by his particular way of thinking. He demanded not merely a revision but the complete annulment of the Treaty of Versailles and the restoration of Germany to its borders of 1914. Nor did this revisionism call for peaceful negotiations; Hitler advocated use of force from the start. In one of the first of his speeches for which a transcript survives, that of November 13, 1919, Hitler said that "Germany's misery must be shattered by German iron. This time must come."[8] It is clear from a remark on September 5, 1920, that he meant by this not only internal violence but in fact a new European war: "We are muzzled, but, defenseless as we are, we will not shy away from a war with France."[9] Indeed, from that time on, Hitler considered war one of the most natural means for achieving political goals. The goals might be altered, but the means remained unchanged, like an axiom. Since the aim was now revision of the defeat of 1918, war was to be directed primarily against France.

But how was Germany, in its miserable condition, to carry on a war against the strongest military power on the continent, which was, moreover, supported by the League of Nations? For Germany to do it alone was impossible, as Hitler knew from the beginning. At an early date, therefore, he turned his attention not only to a radical change in domestic politics—the second prerequisite for a new assertion of German power—but also to Germany's remaining possible foreign allies. Since the hostile alliance was closely knit, a substantial measure of support abroad could be found only by discovering and exploiting differences among the Allies themselves. This did not take Hitler long. He had been observing the friction between France and Italy since 1920, first at the peace conference and then in the Fiume incident, for example. At once he concluded firmly, "For us, the enemy lies beyond the Rhine, not in Italy or any other place."[10] To these words of July 6, 1920, he added, on August 1 of the same year, "The essential demand is: Do away with the peace treaty! We must do everything possible to this end, especially exploiting the differences between France and Italy so that Italy comes over to our side."[11]

From this time on Hitler's calculations included the possibility of that alliance with Italy which was later to be of such significance. Hitler, it might be remarked, did not forget the origin of this idea, referring to it repeatedly even years later.[12] Significantly, it was not motivated by any ideological common ground with Mussolini's Fascism, nor could it have been, for in 1920 Hitler was not even aware of that movement so similar to his own.[13] Moreover, the politics of alliance were for him always simple power politics. Franco-Italian hostility was the crucial factor; yet to exploit this hostility ruled out any protest against Italian control in South Tyrol. Hitler did not balk at this tactic, even though it meant opposing a considerable sector of German public opinion, of which his Nazi comrades made up a not unimportant part. For the Nazi party program as of February 24, 1920, demanded in the first of its twenty-five points "the unification—based on the right of peoples to self-determination—of all Germans into a Greater Germany." Hitler, with noteworthy independence, disregarded that demand: "Germany must go forward beside Italy, which has experienced its own national rebirth and has a great future. What is necessary is a clear and binding renunciation by Germany of any claim to Germans living in South Tyrol. Idle talk about South Tyrol and empty protests against the Fascists will only harm us by alienating Italy. In politics, there can be no sentimentality, but only cold-blooded calculation."[14]

By itself, of course, the alliance with Italy did not amount to much. Still, it suggested the outline of a foreign policy which could be pursued further. The other most likely allies among the European powers were the Soviet Union and Great Britain. Hitler seems to have considered both possibilities. Legitimacy for a German-Soviet alliance could be found in the Bismarckian tradition; the Weimar Republic would soon adopt this course. Hitler rejected it: "An alliance between Russia and Germany," he said on July 27, 1920, "can only come about when Jewry has been dethroned."[15] This view derived from the repeatedly expressed belief that the Jews had come into power with the Bolshevik Revolution in Russia and had caused hunger, disorder, and misery there. Indeed, the Soviet Union did not appear to be a potentially useful ally, but Hitler admitted this with a certain reluctance. On the other hand he felt great respect for the British early in his career. Disregarding wartime enmity, he said on December 10, 1919: "The English as a people have reason to be proud."[16] Without doubt, what especially impressed Hitler was the British Empire.[17] But how could England be won over? No alliance seemed more firm than that between Britain and France.

Only in 1923 did the occupation of the Rhineland, from which Britain unmistakably dissociated herself, make Hitler aware of a friction which he could exploit. In any case, from then on the idea of a German-British alliance recurred constantly in his speeches and was always justified by references to the British policy of maintaining the balance of power on the continent. "For 140 years, England and France have struggled for hegemony. Despite a joint war of conquest, the old embittered rivalry has persisted to the present day."[18] Moreover, since 1918 and particularly since 1923, the British resolve to preserve a balance of power faced the challenge of renewed French striving for hegemony. Hitler argued on August 21, 1923, that the occupation of the Ruhr should have been met with armed resistance. Then the world would have understood that Germany had come to herself and "the first consequence would have been a reorientation of British policy, natural and welcome in London. Not out of love for us. No, because British policy has always been determined by one factor: that of maintaining an approximate balance of power on the continent for the sake of her own security and tranquility."[19]

However one may evaluate this plan of anti-French revisionism supported by an Italian and a British alliance, one can hardly call it vague or lacking in substance. In any event, the formation of Hitler's views on foreign policy by no means ended there. In 1924 he augmented and modified his views decisively in the course of considering Germany's relationship to the last remaining great power of Europe by introducing into his plan the idea of a war of conquest against the Soviet Union. Only further research—some of which has already been completed[20]—can establish how Hitler arrived at this capstone to his program. Previously, there was wide support for the view that the change must have taken place during his imprisonment at Landsberg, where, as he was writing the first volume of *Mein Kampf*, he allegedly came under the influence of certain ideas—possibly geopolitical in nature. This view has never been convincingly documented or even plausibly substantiated. It has proved impossible to establish any definite influence of the thought of others upon Hitler. And, whatever the objections to it, his plan was not without a certain incontestable originality. Therefore the more convincing thesis is that which attributes the change to a more or less logical extension of Hitler's previous thinking on the subject of alliances.

To be sure, after the alliance with Great Britain had first been called for, the Soviet Union came to the foreground. What place was it to occupy in this plan? More exactly—and more urgently—what role should or would it play in the suggested war of revision between France and Germany? As he had done so often before, Hitler referred back to prewar German diplomacy in dealing with this problem. He began uncertainly in a magazine article in April 1924: "In foreign policy, Germany had to choose. She could on the one hand resolve to gain more farmland, which would mean renouncing commercial shipping and colonies as well as refraining from overindustrialization, etc. In such a case, the German governments would have to recognize that this goal could be attained only in a league with England against Russia. On the other hand, if sea power and world trade were the goals, only an alliance with Russia against England was feasible."[21] For the time being, Hitler's only criticism was that Imperial Germany had chosen neither course, and he left the alternatives open.

The most conspicuous aspect of this choice between sea power and farmland (as Hitler put it, "to acquire soil for the annual population increase") was the relegation to the background of the revisionist policy he had previously advocated and its eclipse by more grandiose schemes. However indecisive Hitler may have been at that time, he took up the catchword "farmland," a theme that had recurred often in his earlier speeches. For instance, as early as December 10, 1919, he had questioned the justice "of there being eighteen times as much land per capita in Russia as in Germany."[22] And on April 17, 1923, he had demanded "land and soil for the nourishment of our nation."[23] But the formulation was vague, especially as to how and where soil could be acquired. Now, in 1924, in the course of considering alliances, Hitler seems to have come across the theme again. If a choice must be made, as he seemed to indicate it must, between England and Russia, then it must also be possible—or necessary—to choose between territorial, i.e., continental, expansion and maritime, commercial expansion. In any case, as the plan then stood it seemed impossible to exclude Russia from consideration. Closely connected with that problem were the questions of the two alternatives for alliance and, of course, of what to do with France. In view of the complexity of the matter, it would be futile to attempt to arrive at precise dates and motives for the changes that took place after 1924. Most probably, those changes were the result of the convergence of numerous and diverse considerations. What is important is to comprehend the solution arrived at by Hitler. It has long been well known to historians.

In the first volume of *Mein Kampf*, which appeared on July 18, 1925, seven months after Hitler's release from prison, this solution was presented in final form. Hitler had decided on the farmland solution and—

as before—on an alliance with Great Britain. Significantly, he referred on the very first page to "the moral right to the acquisition of foreign land and soil" and continued, "the plow will then be the sword and, from seeds watered by the tears of war, daily bread will spring forth for posterity."[24] The detailed exposition following in Chapter Four takes as point of departure a very simple fact: "Germany has an annual increase in population of nearly 900,000 persons."[25] It would of necessity become increasingly difficult to support this "army of new citizens" and, if no remedy were found, the consequence would be the "misery of hunger." Four different courses of action were conceivable: birth control, internal colonization, expansion of the export industry, or "acquisition of new land and soil." Hitler decisively rejected the first three possibilities in favor of the fourth, the policy of acquiring new territory. "To be sure," he added, "such a territorial policy cannot be carried out in a place like the Cameroun; today it is possible almost exclusively in Europe." He became even more specific: "If we desire the acquisition of land and soil in Europe, then this could only come about at the expense of Russia; thus the new Reich would have to follow in the footsteps of the old Teutonic knights in order to give soil to the German plow, to the nation its daily bread." Given this policy, only one European ally was possible, and that was of course England. "To win England's support, no sacrifice would be too great. It would be necessary to renounce colonies and sea power in order to avoid competing with British industry." Even a German battle fleet should be renounced in favor of "concentrating the entire instrument of state power on the army."

However sharply the alternatives between an English or a Russian alliance, territorial acquisition or world trade, land or sea power, were presented here, the plan as a whole had gained little in clarity. The fact that Hitler couched all his observations in the guise of criticisms of prewar German policy is of no significance, since he no longer concealed that his choice had been made. But what about the revisionist war against France; what about the alliance with Italy? How should or would France react if England supported a war of conquest against Russia? The first volume of *Mein Kampf* was silent on all these counts, and it almost seems as though Hitler was so overwhelmed by his discovery of the British-Russian alternative that he had forgotten about his previous plan. It is, however, more probable that the two plans, developed independently up to this time, still stood opposed in a severe conflict which Hitler had not as yet resolved. Obviously, France had now to return to the focal point of his calculations.

This happened in the second volume of *Mein Kampf*. The chapter of interest to us here is the thirteenth, entitled "German Alliance Policy after the War." In 1925, during work on the second volume, this chapter seemed so important to Hitler that he published it in advance as a brochure, with a foreword dated February 12, 1926.[26] The appropriate goal for German policy was, once again, the "strengthening of its continental power through gaining new land and soil in Europe."[27] The means to this end were war and alliances, for which England and Italy were considered potential partners. "The unrelenting deadly enemy of the German people is and will remain France." Russia was not mentioned at all. Had Hitler returned to his revisionist schemes of 1923? Evidence to the contrary is provided by the retention of the territorial policy, but in favor of this possibility there is the heavy emphasis on the Franco-German and Anglo-French conflicts, which in the first volume had been almost entirely omitted. Probably Hitler's resolution of the conflict in policy was expressed in the following sentence: "Today we are not fighting for a position of world power, but rather struggling for the very existence of the fatherland." Obviously, the emphasis is on "today"; in other words, this chapter presents only the short-term program.[28]

Long-term goals, on the other hand, were presented in the fourteenth chapter, entitled, "Eastward Orientation or Eastern Policy." Originally it too had been intended for separate publication, which, perhaps because of the publisher, never occurred. Thus it appeared on December 11, 1926, in the second volume of *Mein Kampf*.[29] This chapter was the most significant one for Hitler's projected foreign policy, for it contained for the first time all the previous elements in combination. Now Russia was in the foreground again. The relationship to Russia was "the most important foreign policy question."[30] For the primary goal of a National Socialist foreign policy was "to gather our people and its might for the advance along that road which leads this people forth from a strangling lack of living space to new land and soil," in other words, "to eliminate the disparity between our population and our land area—the latter regarded both as a source of nourishment and as a base for power politics." The war of revision was not now forgotten; instead it was radically rejected. "The demand for a restoration of the boundaries of 1914 is political folly of such proportions and consequences that it may be viewed as a crime." For those boundaries were illogical, irrational, inexpedient in terms of military geography, and above all, too narrow. To fight a new war for them (they could, of course, be reconquered "only with blood") would "in the name of God not be worth the effort." Indeed, the only action that could "make the shedding of blood seem justified to God and German posterity" was "to insure for the German people the land and soil to which they were entitled."

With this, the revisionism advocated since 1919 was abandoned in favor of the much more far-reaching policy of territorial acquisition. Since war must come in any case, it should be made as worthwhile as possible. But now France could be included in the calculations. The abandonment of revisionism by no means meant giving up the long-demanded military conflict with France. To be sure, to win this fight would be insufficient "in the larger context if the goals of our foreign policy should end there." Victory over France "can and will have meaning only insofar as it provides protection from the rear for an expansion of our people's living space in Europe." As Hitler wrote in the following chapter, "The eternal struggle, in and of itself so futile, between us and France" had made sense only "presupposing that Germany regarded the annihilation of France merely as a means to the ultimate end of giving our population room for growth in another place."[31] This other place was of course Russia, for "if we talk in Europe today about land and soil, we can only be thinking first and foremost about Russia and her subjugated border states." A war of conquest against Russia was a relatively easy task: "The gigantic realm in the East is on the verge of collapse."[32] In Hitler's eyes, that is, the October Revolution had meant nothing more than a change of rulers for the inherently passive Slavic masses, a replacement and extermination by the Jews of the previous, Germanic ruling class. Jews, however, were incapable of either organizing or preserving a state, and Hitler therefore concluded: "We have been elected by fate to witness a catastrophe which will prove most forcefully the correctness of our theory of races and peoples."[33]

Of course, Germany would need allies under these changed circumstances. Hitler once more named England and Italy, referring back to the preceding chapter. There it had been stated that the fates of nations could be inseparably bound only by the prospect of common successes in the sense of "shared acquisitions or conquests, in short, by an aggrandizement of power for both parties."[34] By this it was not meant that Great Britain or Italy should take part in the conquest of Russian territory. Instead, the new Triple Alliance was based on the idea that each of the three partners should expand in a different direction: Germany, toward the Eastern part of the continent; England, overseas; and Italy, into the Mediterranean region. Their interests could be united precisely because no power would hinder another in extending its own boundaries. To facilitate this plan, Germany would have to abandon its rivalry with Italy over the South Tyrol, but would above all have to refrain from further competition with England overseas. The main advantage of the alliances was to be the isolation of France; after she had been conquered, the "Eastern policy" could be embarked upon "in the sense of acquiring land to support our German nation."[35]

With this chapter, Hitler had succeeded in bringing together in one self-contained program all of his previous reflections on foreign policy: the relationship to the four European great powers, the policy of territorial expansion, the revisionist policy, and even his racial policy. The program envisioned three different phases. In the first, the internal consolidation and rearmament of Germany, as well as the alliances with Italy and England, were to be effected. That would isolate France and at the same time make it possible "to proceed at a leisurely pace with those preparations which must, within the framework of such a coalition, be made for a reckoning with France."[36] In the second phase, war with France would come about, one way or another. The resultant blow to France's dominant position in Europe would eliminate a threat from the rear to German eastward expansion and would moreover fulfill automatically the demands by Germany for a revision of the Versailles settlement, at least insofar as these could be met on the European continent. In the third and final phase, the great war of conquest could then be waged against Russia. While a mere bagatelle militarily (since the only obstacle was the disorganized land of the Jewish Bolsheviks and the incompetent Slavs), this would be politically of epoch-making significance: living space for generations of Germans would be conquered and at the same time a new position of world power won for Germany.

Hitler had taken seven years to formulate these views on foreign policy. He had not proceeded very systematically, but rather according to his own description of the art of reading.[37] Here and there in his reading he had run across a "fragment of a mosaic," and had given it "its appropriate place in the total world-view," so that a discernible mosaic slowly took shape. Just as Hitler had not proceeded systematically, his effort to present his plan systematically was unsuccessful. But he made a second attempt: in the summer of 1928 he wrote another book about "basic National Socialist principles for a genuinely German foreign policy." Probably for reasons other than that of its content, this book was not published until its posthumous appearance in 1961.[38] This time, Hitler's presentation was much better. His argumentation was, without question, more tightly organized, perhaps for the very reason that he had not altered his basic plan at all. New thoughts appeared only as nuances in peripheral matters, and there was much word-for-word repetition from *Mein Kampf*. Hitler's "second book" contains the most precise and the most carefully reasoned delineation of his program and represents the ordering of it into a broad historical context.

Hitler's foreign policy plan was now complete. To be sure, it did not lack contradictions and inconsistencies. For instance, were there not Anglo-Italian conflicts of interest in the Mediterranean and in Africa which were bound to jeopardize the new Triple Alliance? In expanding into this sphere, Italy would without doubt be opposed by Great Britain as well as by France. Was an alliance between the two possible? And further, was not the Anglo-French alliance in reality much firmer than Hitler assumed? Above all, was it true that the British balance-of-power policy permitted an Anglo-German alliance? Certainly history might teach that Britain had often opposed attempts to establish a continental hegemony; Hitler knew the relevant examples quite well.[39] Now, completely apart from the fact that it was very doubtful whether France still aspired to hegemony, Hitler's plan clearly aimed at German hegemony, even demanded it. Thus, if his assumptions about British policy were correct, the result of Hitler's program would be conflict, not an alliance, between Germany and Britain.

Hitler saw this dilemma, but in 1928 argued his way out of it with a characteristically far-fetched line of reasoning. In the second book, he added to his previous ideas a single new one: it was erroneous to assume that England would naturally oppose any nation's attaining preponderance in Europe. Rather, he continued, history taught that England acted only to counteract competition in overseas areas but not as long as the goals of the currently dominant European power were "manifestly purely continental in scope."[40] Thus, a power enjoying European hegemony could maintain an alliance with Great Britain provided it abstained from threatening her as a rival overseas and limited itself strictly to the continent. Although Hitler was prepared to take this course of action, it was very doubtful whether he correctly interpreted the British principle of maintaining the balance of power. As we know, he was subsequently proven wrong. And this incorrect assessment of Britain imperiled the realization of his plan more severely than any other resistance he faced.[41]

Along with its inner contradictions, which have by no means been presented in full here, Hitler's plan was characterized by astounding gaps. He concerned himself only with the great powers, and therefore he never had anything to say about how the war for living space was to be carried to Russia, considering the fact that there was no common German-Soviet border. In other words, the measures subsequently taken against Czechoslovakia and Poland were in no way foreseen in the plan, however necessary as first steps they might have proven to be. Nor was there any mention whatever of how Germany's surplus population could settle the regions to be conquered in Russia. These regions were already inhabited, and by no means as thinly as Hitler sought to prove—with statistics which were dubious by virtue of being based on the Soviet Union as a whole. This gap was later filled by gigantic projects for expulsion of the native population, such as later found expression in the so-called General Plan for the East.[42] On the other hand, the familiar objection that Hitler did not take the USA into account sufficiently is not entirely justified. Hitler must have known from the First World War that the preponderance of American power was decisive. But the USA had after all waited out three years of the First World War. And moreover, Hitler presupposed an Anglo-American conflict so severe as to prevent a second US intervention.[43] Undoubtedly, however, Hitler's plan was defective because of its one-sided focus on Europe.

Leaving aside these and other contradictions, inconsistencies, and weaknesses, as well as any moral judgments, there can be no denying that this plan for foreign policy revealed at an early date a high degree of purposefulness, consistency, and coherence. Political ends were clearly defined and the means specified by which they could be pursued and perhaps even attained. . . . Hitler's views may be called opportunistic, but his opportunism, insofar as it had goals, was not nihilistic. Hitler's policy may be called power politics for the sake of power politics, yet he had an obvious purpose apart from the sheer enjoyment of power. His views may be called unprincipled, yet they did not lack deliberate consideration of principles and tactics. They might have been madness, but, as Polonius put it, there was method in it.

For the purpose of such judgments, it is of considerable importance whether Hitler immediately abandoned or revised this plan for opportunistic reasons, or whether he held to it. The answer is clear. Any examination of the diplomatic and military history of the Third Reich shows that the plan subsequently provided the guidelines for German policy under Hitler.

It is of course impossible to give here even a compressed survey of the years from 1933 to 1945, especially since a large number of general surveys and treatments of special topics are already available. Unfortunately, however, the connection between Nazi foreign policy as a whole and Hitler's views has yet to be examined thoroughly. It is therefore worthwhile to point out, at least by way of suggestion, a few important underlying features and problems revealed by the subsequent development of Hitler's foreign policy.[44]

As early as his government declaration of March 23, 1933, Hitler laid greater stress on Britain and Italy than on any of the other powers.[45] After Germany had cast off the bonds of multilateral involvement by withdrawing from the League of Nations on October 19, 1933, Hitler's first visit abroad as Chancellor was that paid to the prospective ally Mussolini. Rapprochement was, however, delayed by the Austrian question. Instead, he achieved the Anglo-German Naval Treaty of June 18, 1935, which represented the most significant breach of the terms of the Versailles Alliance to date, and which was at the same time regarded as a step toward alliance. But whereas Italo-German rapprochement made steady progress from 1936 on, Great Britain resisted closer ties to Germany. In this connection, the conclusion of the Anticomintern pact with Japan on November 25, 1936, served, as Ribbentrop stated in a basic policy memorandum of January 2, 1938, "so to mold alliance politics that a German constellation confronts an English one from an equal or even superior position," so that "England will after all prefer to seek a compromise."[46] That is, persuasion was replaced by intimidation in pursuit of the unchanging goal of achieving a free hand on the continent.

After the alignment with Japan had proved to have little effect on British policy, and after the occupation of Prague on March 15, 1939, had in fact led to the British guarantee of Polish security, Hitler expected this intimidation to be effected by, first, the conclusion of a pact with the Soviet Union on August 23, 1939, and then, when even that did not prevent Britain's entry into the war, the defeat of France. The extent to which Hitler was here guided by old concepts is revealed in his explanation of the German-Soviet treaty to Mussolini on March 18, 1940. "As early as *Mein Kampf*," he said, "he had demonstrated that Germany could either side with England against Russia or with Russia against England. He had always wanted," he continued, "to cooperate with England, as long as England did not limit Germany's living space, especially toward the East."[47] Unaccountably, Ribbentrop had this reference to *Mein Kampf* sent to Moscow in a communiqué to the

Soviet government.[48] Although the Soviet reaction is not known, one can imagine that concern arose in the Kremlin when the leaders of the Third Reich still referred to a book in which many other features of Germany's Eastern policy were discussed as well.

When France fell in the summer of 1940 and Britain, against all expectations, still did not yield, despite her expulsion from the continent, Hitler was confronted with the greatest test of his policy and, at the same time, the greatest dilemma to arise from it. He had now fulfilled all the prerequisites of the great war for living space except one: Great Britain still refused to accept German hegemony on the continent. There was thus the threat that in the midst of the German advance into the Soviet Union—about which Hitler had thought even at the height of his triumphs in the West and before the final English rejection of a compromise—that danger would materialize which he had always warned against: the necessity for Germany to fight against two great powers simultaneously. Hitler found a way out of this dilemma with a very characteristic synthesis. In July 1940 he decided to attack the Soviet Union without delay, hoping thus to achieve with one blow his two remaining military goals. These were, on the one hand, the final intimidation of Great Britain before the United States was ready for war, and, on the other hand, the realization of his plan to acquire living space. Once victory over the Soviet Union had been achieved, Great Britain would lose all hope; but, if she continued to hold out, Germany would have a base from which to continue the war almost indefinitely. The dilemma even gave Hitler an argument to use against his hesitant generals; he maintained that, in conquering Russia, Germany could strike the last weapon from England's hand by entirely removing her mainland support.

The underestimation of Great Britain had proven—and would continue to be—the decisive error in Hitler's calculations. Because of Britain, Hitler was forced repeatedly to modify his plan, especially in concluding the Soviet-German Non-Aggression Pact of 1939. Nevertheless, the plan remained the guide to all of his foreign policy decisions. Seldom has a statesman pursued his goals with greater persistence and perseverance. In using the term opportunistic for Hitler's innumerable treaty violations and broken promises, one must not forget two facts. First, this opportunism of cunning and mendacity was a matter of principle. Politics was for Hitler, as he repeatedly stated, a primitive struggle for survival in which only the law of the jungle counted. Second, his opportunism had concretely defined goals arrived at independently of the opportunities offered by the course of events. These goals remained unflinchingly those which had been developed in the 1920's and brought together, at the latest by 1926, into a coherent plan for foreign policy.

NOTES

1. H. R. Trevor-Roper, *The Last Days of Hitler* (London, 1947; rev. ed. 1962).

2. H. R. Trevor-Roper, "The Mind of Adolf Hitler," introduction to *Hitler's Table Talk,* ed. H. R. Trevor-Roper (London, 1953); also H. R. Trevor-Roper, "Hitlers Kriegsziele," *Vierteljahrshefte für Zeitgeschichte,* VIII (1960), 121ff. (lecture given on November 24, 1959). The author wishes at this time to thank Mr. Trevor-Roper for an informative conversation.

3. "Hitlers Kriegsziele," p. 122.

4. Trevor-Roper, "The Mind of Adolf Hitler," pp. xvii, xxxv.

5. Trevor-Roper referred expressly to Hitler's distinction between a "political philosopher" and a "practical politician," *ibid.,* p. xvi.

6. Trevor-Roper, "Hitlers Kriegsziele," p. 133.

7. Cf. especially Günter Schubert, *Anfänge nationalsozialistischer Aussenpolitik* (Cologne, 1963), and Fritz Dickmann, "Machtwille und Ideologie in Hitlers aussenpolitischen Zielsetzungen vor 1933," in *Spiegel der Geschichte. Festschrift für Max Braubach zum 10. 4. 1964,* ed. K. Reppen and S. Skalweit (Münster, 1964), pp. 915ff. The author bases the conclusions which follow largely on the introduction to his book, *Frankreich in Hitlers Europa* (Stuttgart, 1966).

8. Ernst Deuerlein, ed., "Hitlers Eintritt in die Politik und die Reichswehr," *Vierteljahrshefte für Zeitgeschichte,* VII (1959), 207.

9. Reginald H. Phelps, ed., "Hitler als Parteiredner im Jahre 1920," *ibid.,* XI (1963), 314.

10. *Ibid.,* p. 305.

11. Heinz Preiss, ed., *Adolf Hitler in Franken. Reden aus der Kampfzeit* (1939), p. 11. Cf. Walter Werner Pese, "Hitler und Italien 1920–1926," *Vierteljahrshefte für Zeitgeschichte,* III (1955), 113ff.

12. Thus he wrote to Colonel von Reichenau on December 4, 1932, that he had suggested, "for about the last twelve years," that closer ties to Italy be sought: *Vierteljahrshefte für Zeitgeschichte,* VII (1959), 435. On July 1, 1940, he explained to the Italian ambassador, Alfieri, that he had foreseen the alignment of Italy and Germany "as early as twenty years ago"; *Akten zur deutschen auswärtigen Politik 1918–1945,* series D, X (1963), 68. These examples, two of many which could be cited, demonstrate the remarkable exactness, at times, of Hitler's dating.

13. He brought up the ideological argument only just before the March on Rome, on August 17, 1922: Pese, "Hitler und Italien," p. 116. He later said he had heard of Fascism for the first time in 1921: Trevor-Roper, *Hitler's Table Talk,* p. 266.

14. The statement must have been made at the end of 1922 or the beginning of 1923; quoted in Schubert, *Anfänge,* p. 77. Cf. Pese, "Hitler und Italien," pp. 121ff.

15. Phelps, "Hitler als Parteiredner," p. 308.

16. *Ibid.*, p. 290.

17. See for example the speech of April 17, 1920, *ibid.* pp. 297f.

18. Ernst Boepple, ed., *Adolf Hitlers Reden* (Munich, 1925), pp. 55f. The date could refer to the Peace of Paris (September 3, 1783); cf. *Mein Kampf,* p. 692.

19. Boepple, *Hitlers Reden,* pp. 93f.

20. Alex Kuhn, *Hitlers aussenpolitisches Programm* (Stuttgart, 1970). The author is indebted to Dr. Kuhn for help in various ways and for stimulating exchanges of ideas.

21. Adolf Hitler, "Warum musste ein 8. November kommen?" *Deutschlands Erneuerung,* VII (1924), 199. Cf. Wolfgang Horn, "Ein unbekannter Aufsatz Hitlers aus dem Fruhjahr 1924," *Vierteljahrshefte für Zeitgeschichte,* XVI (1968), 280ff.

22. Phelps, "Hitler als Parteiredner," p. 289.

23. Boepple, *Hitlers Reden,* p. 66.

24. *Mein Kampf,* p. 1. Hitler's often repeated plow and sword imagery is a reversal of the well-known peace metaphor from Isaiah 2:4, which had, to be sure, already been turned about to its bellicose opposite in Joel 4:10.

25. For this and the following, see *Mein Kampf,* pp. 143ff.

26. Cf. Gerhard L. Weinberg, Introduction to *Hitlers Zweites Buch* (Stuttgart, 1961), pp. 21f.

27. For this and the following see *Mein Kampf,* pp. 689ff.

28. The rest of the chapter will be treated below in another connection.

29. 1927 had already been designated as the year of publication, the epilogue having been written in November 1926.

30. For this and the following see *Mein Kampf,* pp. 727ff.

31. *Ibid.*, pp. 766f.

32. *Ibid.*, p. 743. Here, as an exception, we quote from the 1930 edition; in the first edition this sentence, in an otherwise identical context, reads: "The Persian Empire, once so powerful, is also on the verge of collapse today; . . ." Later, Hitler omitted the figurative historical analogy for the sake of greater clarity.

33. *Ibid.*

34. *Mein Kampf,* p. 697.

35. *Ibid.*, p. 757.

36. *Ibid.*, p. 755.

37. *Ibid.*, p. 36.

38. Weinberg, ed., *Hitlers Zweites Buch,* p. 45.

39. Cf. *Mein Kampf,* pp. 691ff.

40. *Zweites Buch,* pp. 167ff.

41. Hitler explained this with other arguments, already introduced in *Mein Kampf,* which followed from his theories on race; cf. Jäckel, *Hitlers Weltanschauung,* pp. 69ff.

42. Cf. Helmut Heiber, ed., "Der Generalplan Ost," *Vierteljahrshefte für Zeitgeschichte,* VI (1958), 281ff.; cf. *ibid.,* VIII (1960), 119.

43. *Zweites Buch,* p. 173.

44. The notes are restricted to very brief source citations and as a matter of principle list none of the abundant secondary literature.

45. Max Domarus, ed., *Hitler. Reden und Proklamationen 1932–1945*, I (Neustadt an der Aisch, 1962), 235ff.

46. *Akten zur deutschen auswärtigen Politik 1918–1945*, Series D, I (1950), 135.

47. *Ibid.*, IX (1962), 6.

48. *Ibid.*, pp. 16f.

9

ALAN BULLOCK

Hitler and the Origins of the Second World War

The controversy about the determinants of Hitler's actions has been most hotly debated in connection with the question of responsibility for the outbreak of the Second World War. In this selection, the author of the major biography of Hitler supplements his analysis of the origins of the war in that volume with new observations and proposes a resolution of the dispute about whether Hitler was motivated by fanaticism or opportunism. The author is Vice-Chancellor of Oxford University. This selection, which was the Raleigh Lecture on History of the British Academy for 1967, originally appeared in the Proceedings of the British Academy, LIII (1967), 259–287. *It is reprinted by permission of the author and the British Academy.*

I

IN THE TWENTY years since the end of the war and the Nuremberg Trials, historical controversy has been largely concerned with the share of the other powers in the responsibility for allowing war to break out in 1939. Thus, the British and French Governments of the 1930's have been blamed for their policy of appeasement and for failing to secure an agreement with Russia; Mussolini for his alliance with Hitler; Stalin for the Nazi-Soviet Pact; the Poles for the illusions which encouraged them to believe that they could hold Russia as well as Germany at arm's length. Taking a wider sweep, historians have turned for an explanation of the origins of the Second World War to the mistakes made in the peace settlement that followed the First; to the inadequacies of British and French policy between the wars; the retreat of the United States into isolation; the exclusion of the Soviet Union; the social effects of the Great Depression, and so on.

All this is necessary work, in order to establish the historical situation in which the war began, but as the catalogue grows, I find myself asking what is left of the belief universally held outside Germany twenty years ago that the primary responsibility for the war rested on Hitler and the Nazis?

No one suggests that theirs was the sole responsibility. Hitler would never have got as near to success as he did if it had not been for the weakness, the divisions, the opportunism of the other governments, which allowed him to build up such power that he could not be prevented from conquering Europe without a major war. Still, there is a lot of difference between failing to stop aggression, even hoping to derive side profits from it—and aggression itself. Indeed, much of the criticism directed at the other powers for their failure to stop Hitler in time would fall to the ground if there proved to have been nothing to stop.

Is the effect of filling in the historical picture to reduce this difference to the point where it no longer appears so important, where the responsibility for the war becomes dispersed, or is shifted on to the shortcomings of an anarchical system of international relations, or of militarism or of capitalism, as happened after the First World War? Is Mr. A. J. P. Taylor[1] the harbinger of a new generation of revisionist historians who will find it as anachronistic to hold Hitler—or anyone else—responsible for the outbreak of the Second World War as to hold the Kaiser responsible for the outbreak of the First?

The question is an important one, for to an extent which we only begin to realize when it is questioned, the accepted version of European history in the years between 1933 and 1945 has been built round a particular view of Hitler and of the character of German foreign policy, and if the centerpiece were removed, far more than our view of Hitler and German foreign policy would have to be revised—our view of the foreign policies of all the powers and of the substantiality of the dangers which the other governments, and their critics, believed they confronted.

It occurred to me, therefore, that it would be interesting to take a fresh look at Hitler's foreign policy in the light of the new evidence that has become available in the twenty years since the Nuremberg Trials (and, no less important, of new ways of looking at familiar evidence), and then to go on and ask, in what sense, if at all, it is still possible to speak of Hitler's and the Nazis' responsibility for what became a Second World War.

II

There are two contrasted versions of Hitler's foreign policy which for convenience's sake I will call the fanatic and the opportunist.

The first[2] fastens upon Hitler's racist views and his insistence that the future of the German people could be secured neither by economic development nor by overseas colonization, not even by the restoration of Germany's 1914 frontiers, but only by the conquest of living space (*Lebensraum*) in Eastern Europe. Here the scattered populations of Germans living outside the Reich could be concentrated, together with the surplus population of the homeland, and a Germanic empire established, racially homogeneous, economically self-sufficient, and militarily impregnable. Such *Lebensraum* could only be obtained at the expense of Russia and the states bordering on her and could only be won and cleared of its existing population by force, a view which coincided with Hitler's belief in struggle as the law of life, and war as the test of a people's racial superiority.

Hitler first set these views down in *Mein Kampf*, elaborated them in his so-called *Zweites Buch*,[3] and repeated them on almost every occasion when we have a record of him talking privately and not in public, down to the Table Talk of the 1940's[4] and his final conversations with Bormann in the early months of 1945[5] when his defeat could no longer be disguised. Not only did he consistently hold and express these views over twenty years, but in 1941 he set to work to put them into practice in the most literal way, by attacking Russia and by giving full rein to his plans, which the SS had already begun to carry out in Poland, for the resettlement of huge areas of Eastern Europe.

The alternative version[6] treats Hitler's talk of *Lebensraum* and a racist empire in the East as an expression of the fantasy side of his personality and fastens on the opportunism of Hitler's actual conduct of foreign policy. In practice—so this version runs—Hitler was an astute and cynical politician who took advantage of the mistakes and illusions of others to extend German power along lines entirely familiar from the previous century of German history. So little did he take his own professions seriously that he actually concluded a pact with the Bolsheviks whom he had denounced, and when Hitler belatedly began to put his so-called program into practice, it marked the point at which he lost the capacity to distinguish between fantasy and reality and, with it, the opportunist's touch which had been responsible for his long run of successes. Thereafter he suffered nothing but one disaster after another.

These two versions of Hitler's foreign policy correspond to alternative versions of his personality. The first stresses his insistence on a fanatical will, force, and brutality of purpose, his conviction that he was a man of destiny, his reliance on intuition, his scorn for compromise, his declaration after the occupation of the Rhineland: "I go the way that Providence dictates with the assurance of a sleepwalker."[7]

The second takes this no more seriously than the rest of Nazi and Fascist rhetoric and insists that in practice Hitler relied for his success upon calculation, total lack of scruple, and remarkable gifts as an actor. The suggestion that his opponents had to deal with a man who was fanatical in his purposes and would stop at nothing to accomplish them was part of the act, and a very successful part. His threats were carefully timed as part of a war of nerves, his ungovernable rages turned on or off as the occasion demanded, his hypnotic stare and loss of control part of a public *persona* skilfully and cynically manipulated. And when Hitler, carried away by his triumphs, himself began to believe in his own myth, and no longer to manipulate it, success deserted him.

It is a mistake, however, I believe, to treat these two contrasting views as alternatives, for if that is done, then, whichever alternative is adopted, a great deal of evidence has to be ignored. The truth is, I submit, that they have to be combined and that Hitler can only be understood if it is realized that he was at once both fanatical *and* cynical; unyielding in his assertion of will-power *and* cunning in calculation; convinced of his role as a man of destiny *and* prepared to use all the actor's arts in playing it. To leave out either side, the irrational or the calculating, is to fail to grasp the combination which marks Hitler out from all his imitators.

The same argument, I believe, applies to Hitler's foreign policy, which combined consistency of aim with complete opportunism in method and tactics. This is, after all, a classical receipt for success in foreign affairs. It was precisely because he knew where he wanted to go that Hitler could afford to be opportunistic and saw how to take advantage of the mistakes and fears of others. Consistency of aim on

Hitler's part has been confused with a timetable, blueprint, or plan of action fixed in advance, as if it were pinned up on the wall of the General Staff offices and ticked off as one item succeeded another. Nothing of the sort. Hitler frequently improvised, kept his options open to the last possible moment, and was never sure until he got there which of several courses of action he would choose. But this does not alter the fact that his moves followed a logical (though not a predetermined) course—in contrast to Mussolini, an opportunist who snatched eagerly at any chance that was going but never succeeded in combining even his successes into a coherent policy.

III

Hitler had established his power inside Germany by the late summer of 1934. By securing the succession to President Hindenburg, he became Head of State and Commander-in-Chief of the Armed Forces as well as leader of the only party in the country and head of a government in which no one dared to oppose him. From now on, apart from the one thing which he put before everything else, his own supremacy, Hitler took no great interest in internal affairs or administration. He turned his attention almost wholly to foreign policy and rearmament.

Shortly after he became Chancellor, on February 3, 1933, Hitler had met the leaders of the armed forces privately and told them that, once his political power was secure, his most important task would be to rearm Germany and then move from the revision of the Versailles Treaty to the conquest of *Lebensraum* in the East.[8]

Just over a year later, on February 28, 1934, Hitler repeated this at a conference of Army and SA leaders, declaring that here was a decisive reason for rejecting Röhm's plan for a national militia and for rebuilding the German Army. The Western powers would never allow Germany to conquer *Lebensraum* in the East. "Therefore, short decisive blows to the West and then to the East could be necessary," tasks which could only be carried out by an army rigorously trained and equipped with the most modern weapons.[9]

None the less, in the first two years, 1933 and 1934, Hitler's foreign policy was cautious. Politically, he had still to establish his own supremacy at home. Diplomatically, Germany was isolated and watched with suspicion by all her neighbors. Militarily, she was weak and unable to offer much resistance if the French or the Poles should take preventive action against the new regime.

These were all excellent reasons for Hitler to protest his love of peace and innocence of aggressive intentions. As he told Rauschning, now that Germany had left Geneva, he would more than ever speak "the language of the League."[10] There is, in fact, a striking parallel between his conduct of foreign policy in this early period and the tactics of "legality" which he had pursued in his struggle for power inside Germany. By observing the forms of legality, staying within the framework of the constitution, and refusing to make a putsch—which would have brought the Nazis into open conflict with the Army—Hitler was able to turn the weapons of democracy against democracy itself. His appeal to Wilsonian principles of national self-determination and equality of rights had precisely the same effect—and those who believed him were to be as sharply disillusioned as those who supposed Hitler would continue to observe the limits of legality in Germany once he had acquired the power to ignore them.

Although Nazi propaganda made the most of them, none of Hitler's foreign policy moves in his first two years did much to improve Germany's position. Leaving the Disarmament Conference and the League was a gesture; the Pact with Poland clever but unconvincing, and more than counterbalanced by Russia's agreement to join the League and start negotiations for an alliance with France. The hurried repudiation of the Austrian Nazis in 1934 was humiliating, and the Saar plebiscite in January 1935 was largely a foregone conclusion. When Hitler announced the reintroduction of conscription in March 1935, Germany's action was condemned by the British, French, and Italian governments meeting at Stresa, as well as by the League Council, and was answered by the conclusion of pacts between Russia and France, and Russia and France's most reliable ally Czechoslovakia.[11]

Between 1935 and 1937, however, the situation changed to Hitler's advantage, and he was able not only to remove the limitations of the Versailles Treaty on Germany's freedom of action but to break out of Germany's diplomatic isolation.

It is true that the opportunities for this were provided by the other powers: for example, by Mussolini's Abyssinian adventure and the quarrel to which this led between Italy and the Western powers. But Hitler showed skill in using the opportunities which others provided, for example, in Spain where he reduced the policy of nonintervention to a farce and exploited the civil war for his own purposes with only a minimum commitment to Franco. He also provided his own opportunities: for example, the offer of a naval treaty to Britain in 1935 and the military reoccupation of the Rhineland in 1936. This was a bold and risky stroke of bluff, taken against the advice of his generals, without anything like sufficient forces to resist the French if they had marched, and accompanied by a brilliantly contrived diversion in the form of the new peace pacts which he offered simultaneously to the other Locarno powers.

Of course, there were failures—above all, Ribbentrop's failure to get an alliance with Britain. But between April 1935, when the powers, meeting at Stresa, had unanimously condemned German rearmament, and Mussolini's state visit to Germany as a prospective ally in September 1937, Hitler could claim with some justification to have transformed Germany's diplomatic position and ended her isolation.

IV

The German Foreign Ministry and diplomatic service were well suited to the international equivalent of the policy of "legality," but Hitler soon began to develop instruments of his own for a new style of foreign policy.[12] One was the Nazi groups among the Volksdeutsche living abroad. The two most obvious examples are the Nazi Party in Austria and Henlein's *Sudetendeutsche Partei* in Czechoslovakia. The former had to be hastily disavowed in the summer of 1934, when the putsch against Dollfuss failed, but the subsidies to the Austrian Nazis continued and so did the many links across the frontier from Munich and Berlin. Henlein's Sudeten Party was also secretly in receipt of subsidies from Germany from early 1935,[13] and was to play a key role in the campaign against Czechoslovakia. These links were maintained outside the regular Foreign Ministry system and there were a number of Nazi agencies—Bohle's *Auslandsorganisation*, Rosenberg's *Außenpolitisches Amt*, VOMI (*Volksdeutsche Mittelstelle*) competing with each other, and with the Foreign Ministry, to organize the German-speaking groups living abroad.

At the same time Hitler began to make use of envoys from outside the foreign service for the most important diplomatic negotiations: Göring, for instance, who frequently undertook special missions to Italy, Poland, and the Balkans, and Ribbentrop whose Büro, originally set up to deal with disarmament questions in 1933, soon moved into direct competition with the *Auswärtiges Amt*. It was Ribbentrop who negotiated the naval treaty with London; Ribbentrop who was given the key post of ambassador in London in order to secure a British alliance; Ribbentrop who represented Germany on the Non-Intervention Committee, who negotiated and signed the Anti-Comintern Pact with Japan in 1936 and a year later brought in Italy as well.

It was not until the beginning of 1938 that Hitler appointed Ribbentrop as Foreign Minister: until then he left the German Foreign Ministry and diplomatic service as a respectable façade but increasingly took the discussion of policy and the decisions out of their hands and used other agents to carry them out. In Hitler's eyes the diplomats—like the generals, as he came to feel during the war—were too conservative, too preoccupied with the conventional rules of the game to see the advantages of scrapping rules altogether and taking opponents by surprise. Hitler's radicalism required a new style in the conduct of foreign affairs as different from old style diplomacy as the Nazi Party was from the old style political parties of the Weimar Republic.

This new style did not emerge clearly until 1938–1939, but there were unmistakable signs of it before then in the changed tone in which Hitler and German propaganda were speaking by 1937. Hitler receiving Mussolini and showing off the strength of the new Germany,[14] Hitler beginning to talk of Germany's "demands," was speaking a very different language from that of the man who only three or four years before had used all his gifts as an orator to convince the world of Germany's will to peace. German national pride and self-confidence had been restored, and, instead of trying to conceal, Nazi propaganda now boasted of her growing military strength.

V

The Nazis' claims about German rearmament were widely believed. Phrases like "Guns before butter"—"total war"—"a war economy in peacetime" made a deep impression. When Göring was appointed Plenipotentiary for the Four Year Plan in October 1936, this was taken to mean the speeding up of rearmament, and Hitler's secret memorandum to Göring found among Speer's papers after the war confirms this view.[15] Irritated by Schacht's opposition to his demands, he declared that the shortage of raw materials was "not an economic problem, but solely a question of will." A clash with Bolshevik Russia was unavoidable: "No State will be able to withdraw or even remain at a distance from this historical conflict. . . . We cannot escape this destiny."

Hitler concluded his memorandum to Göring with the words:

I thus set the following task:
1. The German Army must be operational (*einsatzfähig*) within 4 years.
2. The German economy must be fit for war (*kriegsfähig*) within 4 years.

Yet the evidence now available does not bear out the widespread belief in Germany's all-out rearmament before 1939.[16]   The figures show that the rearmament program took a long time to get under way and did not really begin to produce the results Hitler wanted until 1939. Even then Germany's military superiority was not as great as both public opinion and the Allies' intelligence services assumed.

The really surprising fact, however, is the scale of German rearmament in relation to Germany's economic resources. At no time before September 1939 was anything like the full capacity of the German economy devoted to war production. The figures are well below what German industry could have achieved if fully mobilized, below what German industry had achieved in 1914–1918, and below what was achieved by the British when they set about rearmament in earnest.

The immediate conclusion which one might well draw from these facts is that they provide powerful support for the argument that Hitler was not deliberately preparing for war but was thinking in terms of an armed diplomacy in which he relied on bluff and the *threat* of war to blackmail or frighten the other powers into giving way to his demands.

Before we accept this conclusion, however, it is worth while to carry the examination of the rearmament figures beyond the date of September 1, 1939. The attack on Poland may or may not have been due to mistaken calculation on Hitler's part (I shall come back to this later), but no one can doubt that the German attack on France and the Low Countries on May 10, 1940, was deliberate, not hastily improvised but prepared for over a six months' period. And this time it was an attack not on a second-class power like Poland but on two major powers, France and Britain. Yet the interesting fact is that the proportion of Germany's economic resources devoted to the war hardly went up at all. Even more striking, the same is true of the attack on Russia in 1941. In preparation for Operation Barbarossa, the Army was built up to 180 divisions, but this was not accompanied by an all-out armaments drive and on the very eve of the invasion of Russia (June 20, 1941) Hitler actually ordered a reduction in the level of arms production. This was put into effect and by December 1941, when the German Army was halted before Moscow, the overall level of weapons production had fallen by 29 percent from its peak in July of that year.[17]

In fact, it was not until 1942, the year in which Hitler lost the initiative and Germany was pushed on to the defensive, that Hitler was persuaded to commit the full resources of the German economy to an all-out effort.

This puts the facts I have mentioned in a different light. For, if Hitler believed that he could defeat the Western powers, subdue the Balkans, and conquer Russia without demanding more than a partial mobilization from the German people, then the fact that German rearmament before the war had limited rather than total objectives is no proof that his plans at that time did not include war.

The truth is that, both before and after September 1939, Hitler was thinking in terms of a very different sort of war from that which Germany had lost in 1914–1918 or was to lose again between 1942 and 1945. With a shrewder judgment than many of his military critics, Hitler realized that Germany, with limited resources of her own and subject to a blockade, was always going to be at a disadvantage in a long-drawn-out general war. The sort of war she could win was a series of short campaigns in which surprise and the overwhelming force of the initial blow would settle the issue before the victim had time to mobilize his full resources or the other powers to intervene. This was the sort of war the German Army was trained as well as equipped to fight, and all the German campaigns between 1939 and 1941 conformed to this pattern—Poland, four weeks; Norway, two months; Holland, five days, Belgium, seventeen; France, six weeks; Yugoslavia, eleven days; Greece, three weeks. The most interesting case of all is that of Russia. The explanation of why the German Army was allowed to invade Russia without winter clothing or equipment is Hitler's belief that even Russia could be knocked out by a blitzkrieg in four to five months, before the winter set in. And so convinced was Hitler that he had actually achieved this that in his directive of July 14, 1941,[18] he spoke confidently of reducing the size of the Army, the Navy, and the armaments program in the near future.

This pattern of warfare, very well adapted both to Germany's economic position and the advantages of secrecy and surprise enjoyed by a dictatorship, fits perfectly the pattern of German rearmament. What was required was not armament in depth, the long-term conversion of the whole economy to a war footing which (as in Britain) would only begin to produce results in two to three years, but a war economy of a different sort geared (like German strategy) to the concept of the blitzkrieg. It was an economy which concentrated on a short-term superiority and the weapons which could give a quick victory, even when this meant neglecting the proper balance of a long-term armament program. What mattered, as Hitler said in his 1936 memorandum, was not stocks of raw materials or building up productive capacity, but armaments ready for use, plus the will to use them. How near the gamble came to success is shown by the history of the years 1939–1941, when Hitler's limited rearmament program produced an army capable of overrunning the greater part of Europe, and very nearly defeating the Russians as well as the French.

VI

But we must not run ahead of the argument. The fact that Germany was better prepared for war, and when it began proceeded to win a remarkable series of victories, does not prove that Hitler intended to start the war which actually broke out in September 1939. We have still to relate Hitler's long-term plans for expansion in the East and his rearmament program to the actual course of events in 1938 and 1939.

A starting-point is Colonel Hossbach's record of Hitler's conference with his three Commanders-in-Chief, War Minister, and Foreign Minister on November 5, 1937.[19] It was an unusual occasion, since Hitler rarely talked to more than one Commander-in-Chief or minister at a time, and he came nearer to laying down a program than he ever had before. Once again he named *Lebensraum* in the East and the need to provide for Germany's future by continental expansion as the objective, but instead of leaving it at that, he went on to discuss how this was to be achieved.

The obstacles in the way were Britain and France, Germany's two "hate-inspired antagonists." Neither was as strong as she seemed: still, "Germany's problems could only be solved by force and this was never without attendant risk."

The peak of German power would be reached in 1943–1945: after that, their lead in armaments would be reduced. "It was while the rest of the world was preparing its defenses that we were obliged to take the offensive." Whatever happened, he was resolved to solve Germany's problem of space by 1943–1945 at the latest. Hitler then discussed two possible cases in which action might be taken earlier—one was civil strife in France, disabling the French Army: the other, war in the Mediterranean which might allow Germany to act as early as 1938. The first objective in either case "must be to overthrow Czechoslovakia and Austria simultaneously in order to remove the threat to our flank in any possible operation against the West." Hitler added the comment that almost certainly Britain and probably France as well had already tacitly written off the Czechs.

To speak of this November meeting as a turning-point in Hitler's foreign policy at which Hitler made an irreversible decision in favor of war seems to me as wide of the target as talking about timetables and blueprints of aggression. Hitler was far too skillful a politician to make irreversible decisions in advance of events: no decisions were taken or called for.

But to brush the Hossbach meeting aside and say that this was just Hitler talking for effect and not to be taken seriously seems to me equally wide of the mark. The hypotheses Hitler outlined—civil strife in France, a Mediterranean war—did not materialize, but when Hitler spoke of his determination to overthrow Czechoslovakia and Austria, as early as 1938 if an opportunity offered, and when both countries *were* overthrown within less than eighteen months, it is stretching incredulity rather far to ignore the fact that he had stated this as his immediate program in November 1937.

The next stage was left open, but Hitler foresaw quite correctly that everything would depend upon the extent to which Britain and France were prepared to intervene by force to prevent Germany's continental expansion, and he clearly contemplated war if they did. Only when the obstacle which they represented had been removed would it be possible for Germany to carry out her eastward expansion.

This was a better forecast of the direction of events in 1938–1941 than any other European leader including Stalin made at the end of 1937—for the very good reason that Hitler, however opportunist in his tactics, knew where he wanted to go, was almost alone among European leaders in knowing this, and so kept the initiative in his hands.

The importance of the Hossbach conference, I repeat, is not in recording a decision, but in reflecting the change in Hitler's attitude. If the interpretation offered of his policy in 1933–1937 is correct, it was not a sudden but a gradual change, and a change not in the objectives of foreign policy but in Hitler's estimate of the risks he could afford to take in moving more rapidly and openly toward them. As he told the Nazi Old Guard at Augsburg a fortnight later: "I am convinced that the most difficult part of the preparatory work has already been achieved. . . . To-day we are faced with new tasks, for the *Lebensraum* of our people is too narrow."[20]

There is another point to be made about the Hossbach conference. Of the five men present besides Hitler and his adjutant Hossbach, Göring was certainly not surprised by what he heard and Raeder said nothing. But the other three, the two generals and Neurath, the Foreign Minister, showed some alarm and expressed doubts. It is surely another remarkable coincidence if this had nothing to do with the fact that within three months all three men had been turned out of office—the two generals, Blomberg and Fritsch, on barefaced pretexts. There is no need to suppose that Hitler himself took the initiative in framing Blomberg or Fritsch. The initiative seems more likely to have come from Göring and Himmler, but it was Hitler who turned both Blomberg's *mésalliance* and the allegations against Fritsch to his own political advantage. Blomberg, the Minister of War, was replaced by Hitler himself who suppressed the office altogether, took over the OKW, the High Command of the armed forces, as his own staff and very soon made clear that neither the OKW nor the OKH, the High Command of the Army, would be allowed the independent position of the old General Staff. Fritsch, long regarded by Hitler as too stiff, conservative, and out of sympathy with Nazi ideas, was replaced by the much more pliable Brauchitsch as Commander-in-Chief of the Army, and Neurath, a survivor from the original coalition, by Ribbentrop who made it as clear to the staff of the Foreign Ministry as Hitler did to the generals that they were there to carry out orders, not to discuss, still less question the Führer's policy.

VII

I find nothing at all inconsistent with what I have just said in the fact that the timing for the first of Hitler's moves, the annexation of Austria, should have been fortuitous and the preparations for it improvised on the spur of the moment in a matter of days, almost of hours. On the contrary, the Anschluss seems to me to provide, almost in caricature, a striking example of that extraordinary combination of consistency in aim, calculation, and patience in preparation with opportunism, impulse, and improvisation in execution which I regard as characteristic of Hitler's policy.

The aim in this case was never in doubt: the demand for the incorporation of Austria in the Reich appears on the first page of *Mein Kampf*. After the Austrian Nazis' unsuccessful putsch of 1934, Hitler showed both patience and skill in his relations with Austria: he gradually disengaged Mussolini from his commitment to maintain Austrian independence and at the same time steadily undermined that independence from within. By the beginning of 1938 he was ready to put on the pressure, but the invitation to Schuschnigg to come to Berchtesgaden was made on the spur of the moment as the result of a suggestion by an anxious Papen trying hard to find some pretext to defer his own recall from Vienna. When Schuschnigg appeared on February 12, Hitler put on an elaborate act to frighten him into maximum concessions with the threat of invasion, but there is no reason to believe that either Hitler or the generals he summoned to act as "stage extras" regarded these threats as anything other than bluff. Hitler was confident that he would secure Austria, without moving a man, simply by the appointment of his nominee Seyss-Inquart as Minister of the Interior and the legalization of the Austrian Nazis—to both of which Schuschnigg agreed.

When the Austrian Chancellor, in desperation, announced a plebiscite on March 9, Hitler was taken completely by surprise. Furious at being crossed, he decided at once to intervene before the plebiscite could be held. But no plans for action had been prepared: they had to be improvised in the course of a single day, and everything done in such a hurry and confusion that 70 percent of the tanks and lorries, according to General Jodl, broke down on the road to Vienna. The confusion was even greater in the Reich Chancellery: when Schuschnigg called off the plebiscite, Hitler hesitated, then was persuaded by Göring to let the march in continue, but without any clear idea of what was to follow. Only when he reached Linz did Hitler, by then in a state of self-intoxication, suddenly decide to annex Austria instead of making it a satellite state, and his effusive messages of relief to Mussolini show how unsure he was of the consequences of his action.

No doubt the Anschluss is an exceptional case. On later occasions the plans were ready: dates by which both the Czech and the Polish crises must be brought to a solution were fixed well in advance, and nothing like the same degree of improvisation was necessary. But in all the major crises of Hitler's career there is the same strong impression of confusion at the top, springing directly (as his generals and aides complained) from his own hesitations and indecision. It is to be found in his handling of domestic as well as foreign crises—as witness his long hesitation before the Röhm purge of 1934—and in war as well as peacetime.

The paradox is that out of all this confusion and hesitation there should emerge a series of remarkably bold decisions, just as, out of Hitler's opportunism in action, there emerges a pattern which conforms to objectives stated years before.

VIII

The next crisis, directed against Czechoslovakia, was more deliberately staged. This time Hitler gave preliminary instructions to his staff on April 21, 1938,[21] and issued a revised directive on May 30.[22] Its first sentence read: "It is my unalterable decision to smash Czechoslovakia by military action in the near future." It was essential, Hitler declared, to create a situation within the first two or three days which would make intervention by other powers hopeless: the Army and the Air Force were to concentrate all their strength for a knockout blow and leave only minimum forces to hold Germany's other frontiers.

It is perfectly true that for a long time in the summer Hitler kept out of the way and left the other powers to make the running, but this was only part of the game. Through Henlein and the Sudeten Party, who played the same role of fifth column as did the Austrian Nazis, Hitler was able to manipulate the dispute between the Sudeten Germans and the Czech Government, which was the ostensible cause of the crisis, from within. At a secret meeting with Hitler on March 28, Henlein summarized his policy in the words: "We must always demand so much that we can never be satisfied." The Führer, says the official minute, approved this view.[23]

At the same time through a variety of devices—full-scale press and radio campaigns, the manufacture of incidents, troop movements, carefully circulated rumors, and diplomatic leaks, a steadily mounting pressure was built up, timed to culminate in Hitler's long-awaited speech at the Nuremberg Party Congress. Those who study only the diplomatic documents get a very meager impression of the war of nerves which was maintained throughout the summer and which was skilfully directed to play on the fear of war in Britain and France and to heighten the Czechs' sense of isolation. It was under the pressure of this political warfare, something very different from diplomacy as it had been traditionally practiced, that the British and French governments felt themselves impelled to act.

What was Hitler's objective? The answer has been much confused by the ambiguous use of the word "war."

Western opinion made a clear-cut distinction between peace and war: Hitler did not, he blurred the distinction. Reversing Clausewitz, he treated politics as a continuation of war by other means, at one stage of which (formally still called peace) he employed methods of political warfare—subversion, propaganda, diplomatic and economic pressure, the war of nerves—at the next, the threat of war, and so on to localized war and up the scale to general war—a continuum of force in which the different stages ran into each other. Familiar enough now since the time of the Cold War, this strategy (which was all of a piece with Hitler's radical new style in foreign policy) was as confusing in its novelty as the tactics of the Trojan horse, the fifth column, and the "volunteers" to those who still thought in terms of a traditionally decisive break between a state of peace and a state of war.

So far as the events of 1938 go, there seem to be two possible answers to the question: What was in Hitler's mind?

The first is that his object was to destroy the Czech State by the sort of blitzkrieg for which he had rearmed Germany and which he was to carry out a year later against Poland. This was to come at the end of a six months' political, diplomatic, and propaganda campaign designed to isolate and undermine the Czechs, and to maneuver the Western powers into abandoning them to their fate rather than risk a European war. The evidence for this view consists in the series of secret directives and the military preparations to which they led, plus Hitler's declaration on several occasions to the generals and his other collaborators that he meant to settle the matter by force, with October 1 as D-day. On this view, he was only prevented from carrying out his attack by the intervention of Chamberlain which, however great the cost to the Czechs, prevented war or at least postponed it for a year.

The other view is that Hitler never intended to go to war, that his objective was from the beginning a political settlement such as was offered to him at Munich, that his military preparations were not intended seriously but were designed as threats to increase the pressure.

The choice between these two alternatives, however—*either* the one *or* the other—seems to me unreal. The obvious course for Hitler to pursue was to keep both possibilities open to the very last possible moment, the more so since they did not conflict. The more seriously the military preparations were carried out, the more effective was the pressure in favor of a political settlement if at the last moment he decided not to take the risks involved in a military operation. If we adopt this view, then we remove all the difficulties in interpreting the evidence which are created either by attempting to pin Hitler down on any particular declaration and say *now,* at this point, he had decided on war—or by the dogmatic assumption that Hitler *never* seriously contemplated the use of force, with the consequent need to dismiss his military directives as bluff.

Neither in 1938 nor in 1939 did Hitler deliberately plan to start a general European war. But this was a risk which could not be ignored, and in 1938 it was decisive. The generals were unanimous that Germany's rearmament had not yet reached the point where she could face a war with France and Britain. The Czech frontier defenses were formidable. Their army on mobilization was hardly inferior at all, either in numbers or training, to the thirty-seven divisions which the Germans could deploy and it was backed by a first-class armaments industry.[24] To overcome these would require a concentration of force which left the German commander in the West with totally inadequate strength to hold back the French Army.

While the generals, however, added up divisions and struck an unfavorable balance in terms of material forces, Hitler was convinced that the decisive question was a matter of will, the balance between his determination to take the *risk* of a general war and the determination of the Western powers, if pushed far enough, to take the *actual decision* of starting one. For, however much the responsibility for such a war might be Hitler's, by isolating the issue and limiting his demands to the Sudetenland, he placed the onus of actually starting a general war on the British and the French. How far was Hitler prepared to drive such an argument? The answer is, I believe, that while he had set a date by which he knew he must decide, until the very last moment he had not made up his mind and that it is this alternation between screwing up his demands, as he did at his second meeting with Chamberlain in Godesberg, and still evading an irrevocable decision, which accounts both for the zigzag course of German diplomacy and for the strain on Hitler.

In the end he decided, or was persuaded, to stop short of military operations against Czechoslovakia and "cash" his military preparations for the maximum of political concessions.

No sooner had he agreed to this, however, than Hitler started to regret that he had not held on, marched his army in, then and there, and broken up the Czechoslovak State, not just annexed the Sudetenland. His regret sprang from the belief, confirmed by his meeting with the Western leaders at Munich, that he could have got away with a localized war carried out in a matter of days, and then confronted the British and French with a *fait accompli* while they were still hesitating whether to attack in the West—exactly as happened a year later over Poland.

Almost immediately after Munich, therefore, Hitler began to think about ways in which he could complete his original purpose. Every sort of excuse, however transparent, was found for delaying the international guarantee which had been an essential part of the Munich agreement. At the same time, the ground was carefully prepared with the Hungarians, who were eager to recover Ruthenia and at least part of Slovakia, and with the Slovaks themselves who were cast for the same role the

Sudeten Germans had played the year before. The actual moment at which the crisis broke was not determined by Hitler and took him by surprise, but that was all. The Slovaks were at once prodded into declaring their independence and putting themselves in Hitler's hands. The Czech Government, after Hitler had threatened President Hacha in Berlin, did the same. The "legality" of German intervention was unimpeachable: Hitler had been invited to intervene by both the rebels and the government. War had been avoided, no shots exchanged, peace preserved—yet the independent state of Czechoslovakia had been wiped off the map.

IX

Within less than eighteen months, then, Hitler had successfully achieved both the immediate objectives, Austria and Czechoslovakia, which he had laid down in the Hossbach meeting. He had not foreseen the way in which this would happen, in fact he had been wrong about it, but this had not stopped him from getting both.

This had been true at every stage of Hitler's career. He had no fixed idea in 1930, even in 1932, about how he would become Chancellor, only that he would; no fixed idea in 1934–1935 how he would break out of Germany's diplomatic isolation, again only that he would. So the same now. Fixity of aim by itself, or opportunism by itself, would have produced nothing like the same results.

It is entirely in keeping with this view of Hitler that, after Czechoslovakia, he should not have made up his mind what to do next. Various possibilities were in the air. Another move was likely in 1939, if only because the rearmament program was now beginning to reach the period when it would give Germany a maximum advantage and Hitler had never believed that time was on his side. This advantage, he said in November 1937, would only last at the most until 1943–1945; then the other powers with greater resources would begin to catch up. He had therefore to act quickly if he wanted to achieve his objectives.

Objectives, yes; a sense of urgency in carrying them out, and growing means to do so in German rearmament, but no timetable or precise plan of action for the next stage.

Ribbentrop had already raised with the Poles, immediately after Munich, the question of Danzig and the Corridor. But there is no evidence that Hitler had committed himself to war to obtain these, or to the dismemberment of Poland. If the Poles had been willing to give him what he wanted, Hitler might well have treated them, for a time at any rate, as a satellite—in much the same way as he treated Hungary—and there were strong hints from Ribbentrop that the Germans and the Poles could find a common objective in action against Russia. Another possibility, if Danzig and the Corridor could be settled by agreement, was to turn west and remove the principal obstacle to German expansion, the British and French claim to intervene in Eastern Europe.

After Prague, the German-Polish exchanges became a good deal sharper and, given the Poles' determination not to be put in the same position as the Czechs, but to say "No" and refuse to compromise, it is likely that a breach between Warsaw and Berlin would have come soon in any case. But what precipitated it was the British offer, and Polish acceptance, of a guarantee of Poland's independence. In this sense the British offer is a turning-point in the history of 1939. But here comes the crux of the matter. If Mr. Taylor is right in believing that Hitler was simply an opportunist who reacted to the initiative of others, then he is justified in calling the British offer to Poland a revolutionary event.[25] But if the view I have suggested is right, namely, that Hitler, although an opportunist in his tactics, was an opportunist who had from the beginning a clear objective in view, then it is very much less than that: an event which certainly helped—if you like, forced—Hitler to make up his mind between the various possibilities he had been revolving, but which certainly did not provoke him into an expansionist program he would not otherwise have entertained, or generate the force behind it which the Nazis had been building up ever since they came to power. On this view it was Hitler who still held the initiative, as he had since the Anschluss, and the British who were reacting to it, not the other way round: the most the British guarantee did was to give Hitler the answer to the question he had been asking since Munich: Where next?

The answer, then, was Poland, the most probable in any event in view of the demands the Nazis had already tabled, and now a certainty. But this did not necessarily mean war—yet.

Hitler expressed his anger by denouncing Germany's Non-Aggression Pact with Poland and the Anglo-German Naval Treaty, and went on to sign a secret directive ordering the Army to be ready to attack Poland by September 1.[26] The military preparations were not bluff: they were designed to give Hitler the option of a military solution if he finally decided this way, or to strengthen the pressures for a political solution—either direct with Warsaw, or by the intervention of the other powers in a Polish Munich. Just as in 1938 so in 1939, Hitler kept the options open literally to the last, and until the troops actually crossed the Polish frontier on September 1 none of his generals was certain that the orders might not be changed. Both options, however: there is no more reason to say dogmatically that Hitler was aiming all the time at a political solution than there is to say that he ruled it out and had made up his mind in favor of war.

Hitler's inclination, I believe, was always toward a solution by force, the sort of localized blitzkrieg with which in the end he did destroy Poland. What he had to weigh was the risk of a war which could not be localized. There were several reasons why he was more ready to take this risk than the year before.

The first was the progress of German rearmament—which was coming to a peak in the autumn of 1939. By then it represented an eighteenfold expansion of the German armed forces since 1933.[27] In economists' terms this was not the maximum of which Germany was capable, at least in the long run, but in military terms it was more than adequate, as 1940 showed, not just to defeat the Poles but to deal with the Western powers as well. The new German Army had been designed to achieve the maximum effect at the outset of a campaign and Hitler calculated—quite rightly—that, even if the British formally maintained their guarantee to Poland, the war would be over and Poland crushed before they could do anything about it.[28]

A second reason was Hitler's increased confidence, his conviction that his opponents were simply not his equal either in daring or in skill. The very fact that he had drawn back at Munich and then regretted it made it all the more likely that a man with his gambler's temperament would be powerfully drawn to stake all next time.

Finally, Hitler believed that he could remove the danger of Western intervention, or at least render the British guarantee meaningless, by outbidding the Western powers in Moscow.

In moments of exaltation, e.g., in his talks to his generals after the signature of the Pact with Italy (May 23) and at the conference of August 22 which followed the news that Stalin would sign, Hitler spoke as if the matter were settled, war with Poland inevitable, and all possibility of a political settlement—on his terms—excluded. I believe that this was, as I have said, his real inclination, but I do not believe that he finally made up his mind until the last minute. Why should he? Just as in 1938, Hitler refused to make in advance the choice to which historians have tried to pin him down, the either/or of war or a settlement dictated under the threat of war. He fixed the date by which the choice would have to be made but pursued a course which would leave him with the maximum of maneuver to the last possible moment. And again one may well ask: Why not—since the preparations to be made for either eventuality—war or a political settlement under the threat of war—were the same?

Much has been made of the fact that for the greater part of the summer Hitler retired to Berchtesgaden and made no public pronouncement. But this is misleading. The initiative remained in Hitler's hands. The propaganda campaign went ahead exactly as planned, building up to a crisis by late August and hammering on the question: Is Danzig worth a war? So did the military preparations which were complete by the date fixed, August 26. German diplomacy was mobilized to isolate Poland and, if the pact with Italy proved to be of very little value in the event, and the Japanese failed to come up to scratch, the pact with Stalin was a major coup. For a summer of "inactivity" it was not a bad result.

Hitler's reaction when the Nazi-Soviet Pact was signed shows clearly enough where his first choice lay. Convinced that the Western powers would now give up any idea of intervention in defense of Poland, he ordered the German Army to attack at dawn on August 26: i.e., a solution by force, but localized and without risk of a general European war, the sort of operation for which German rearmament had been designed from the beginning.

The unexpected British reaction, the confirmation instead of the abandonment of the guarantee to Poland—this, plus Mussolini's defection (and Mussolini at any rate had no doubt that Hitler was bent on a solution by force) upset Hitler's plans and forced him to think again. What was he to do? Keep up the pressure and hope that the Poles would crack and accept his terms? Keep up the pressure and hope that, if not the Poles, then the British would crack and either press the Poles to come to terms (another Munich) or abandon them? Or go ahead and take the risk of a general war, calculating that Western intervention, if it ever took place, would come too late to affect the outcome.

It is conceivable that if Hitler had been offered a Polish Munich, on terms that would by now have amounted to capitulation, he would still have accepted it. But I find it hard to believe that any of the moves he made, or sanctioned, between August 25 and September 1 were seriously directed to starting negotiations. A far more obvious and simple explanation is to say that, having failed to remove the threat of British intervention by the Nazi-Soviet Pact, as he had expected, Hitler postponed the order to march and allowed a few extra days to see, not if war could be avoided, but whether under the strain a split might not develop between the Western powers and Poland and so leave the Poles isolated after all.

Now the crisis had come, Hitler himself did little to resolve or control it. Characteristically, he left it to others to make proposals, seeing the situation, not in terms of diplomacy and negotiation, but as a contest of wills. If his opponents' will cracked first, then the way was open for him to do what he wanted and march into Poland without fear that the Western powers would intervene. To achieve this he was prepared to hold on and bluff up to the very last minute, but if the bluff did not come off within the time he had set, then this time he steeled his will to go through with the attack on Poland even if it meant running the risk of war with Britain and France as well. All the accounts agree on the strain which Hitler showed and which found expression in his haggard appearance and temperamental outbursts. But his will held. This was no stumbling into war. It was neither misunderstanding nor miscalculation which sent the German Army over the frontier into Poland, but a calculated risk, the gambler's bid—the only bid, Hitler once told Göring, he ever made, *va banque,* the bid he made when he reoccupied the Rhineland in 1936 and when he marched into Austria, the bid he had failed to make when he agreed to the Munich conference, only to regret it immediately afterwards.

X

Most accounts of the origins of the war stop in September 1939. Formally, this is correct: from September 3, 1939, Germany was in a state of war with Britain and France as well as Poland, and the Second World War had begun. But this formal statement is misleading. In fact, Hitler's gamble came off. The campaign in which the German Army defeated the Poles remained a localized war and no hostilities worth speaking of had taken place between Germany and the Western powers by the time the Poles had been defeated and the state whose independence they had guaranteed had ceased to exist.

If Hitler had miscalculated at the beginning of September or stumbled into war without meaning to, here was the opportunity to avoid the worst consequences of what had happened. It is an interesting speculation what the Western powers would have done, if he had really made an effort to secure peace once the Poles were defeated. But it is a pointless speculation. For Hitler did nothing of the sort. The so-called peace offer in his speech of October 6 was hardly meant to be taken seriously. Instead of limiting his demands, Hitler proceeded to destroy the Polish state and to set in train (in 1939, not in 1941) the ruthless resettlement program which he had always declared he would carry out in Eastern Europe.

Even more to the point, it was Hitler who took the initiative in turning the formal state of war between Germany and the Western powers into a real war. On October 9 he produced a memorandum in which he argued that, instead of waiting to see whether the Western powers would back their formal declaration of war with effective force, Germany should seize the initiative and make an all-out attack on the French and the British, thereby removing once and for all the limitations on Germany's freedom of action.

The German generals saw clearly what this meant: far from being content with and trying to exploit the good luck which had enabled him to avoid a clash with the Western powers so far, Hitler was deliberately setting out to turn the localized campaign he had won in Poland into a general war. Their doubts did not deter him for a moment and, although they managed on one pretext or another to delay operations, in May 1940 it was the German Army, without waiting for the French or the British, which launched the attack in the West and turned the *drôle de guerre* into a major war.

Even this is not the end of the story. Once again, Hitler proved to be a better judge than the experts. In the middle of events, his nerve faltered, he became hysterical, blamed everyone, behaved in short in exactly the opposite way to the copy-book picture of the man of destiny; but when the battle was over he had inflicted a greater and swifter defeat upon France than any in history. And it is no good saying that it was "the machine" that did this, not Hitler. Hitler was never the prisoner of "the machine." If "the machine" had been left to decide things, it would never have taken the risk of attacking in the West, and, if it had, would never have adopted the Ardennes plan which was the key to victory. Pushing the argument further back, one can add that, if it had been left to "the machine," German rearmament would never have been carried out at the pace on which Hitler insisted, or on the blitzkrieg pattern which proved to be as applicable to war with the Western powers as to the limited Polish campaign.

Once again, the obvious question presents itself: what would have happened if Hitler, now as much master of continental Europe as

Napoleon had been, had halted at this point, turned to organizing a continental New Order in Europe, and left to the British the decision whether to accept the situation—if not in 1940, then perhaps in 1941—or to continue a war in which they had as yet neither American nor Russian allies, were highly vulnerable to attack, and could never hope by themselves to overcome the disparity between their own and Hitler's continental resources. Once again—this is my point—it was thanks to Hitler, and no one else that this question was never posed. It was Hitler who decided that enough was not enough, that the war must go on—Hitler, not the German military leaders or the German people, many of whom would have been content to stop at this point, enjoy the fruits of victory, and risk nothing more.

If the war had to continue, then the obvious course was to concentrate all Germany's—and Europe's—resources on the one opponent left, Britain. If invasion was too difficult and dangerous an operation, there were other means—a Mediterranean campaign with something more than the limited forces reluctantly made available to Rommel, or intensification of the air and submarine war, as Raeder urged. The one thing no one thought of except Hitler was to attack Russia, a country whose government had shown itself painfully anxious to avoid conflict and give every economic assistance to Germany. There was nothing improvised about Hitler's attack on Russia. Of all his decisions it was the one taken furthest in advance and most carefully prepared for, the one over which he hesitated least and which he approached with so much confidence that he even risked a five-week delay in starting in order to punish the Yugoslavs and settle the Balkans.[29]

Nor was it conceived of solely as a military operation. The plans were ready to extend to the newly captured territory the monstrous program of uprooting whole populations which the SS—including Eichmann—had already put into effect in Poland.[30] Finally, of all Hitler's decisions it is the one which most clearly bears his own personal stamp, the culmination (as he saw it) of his whole career.

XI

It will now be evident why I have carried my account beyond the conventional date of September 1939. Between that date and June 1941, the scope of the war was steadily enlarged from the original limited Polish campaign to a conflict which, with the attack on Russia, was now on as great a scale as the war of 1914–1918. The initiative at each stage—except in the Balkans where he was reluctant to become involved—had been Hitler's. Of course he could not have done this without the military machine and skill in using it which the German armed forces put at his disposal, but the evidence leaves no doubt that the decision where and when to use that machine was in every case Hitler's, not his staff's, still less that all Hitler was doing was to react to the initiative of his opponents.

Now, it may be that the Hitler who took these increasingly bold decisions after September 1939 was a different person from the Hitler who conducted German foreign policy before that date, but this is surely implausible. It seems to me far more likely that the pattern which is unmistakable after September 1939, using each victory as the basis for raising the stakes in a still bolder gamble next time, is the correct interpretation of his conduct of foreign policy before that date. And this interpretation is reinforced by the fact that at the same time Hitler was carrying out the rearmament and expansion of the German armed forces on a pattern which exactly corresponds to the kind of war which he proceeded to wage after September 1939.

Let me repeat and underline what I said earlier: this has nothing to do with timetables and blueprints of aggression. Throughout his career Hitler was an opportunist, prepared to seize on and exploit any opportunity that was offered to him. There was nothing inevitable about the way or the order in which events developed, either before or after September 1939. The annexation of Austria and the attempt to eliminate Czechoslovakia, by one means or another, were predictable, but after the occupation of Prague, there were other possibilities which might have produced a quite different sequence of events—as there were after the fall of France. Of what wars or other major events in history is this not true?

But Hitler's opportunism was doubly effective because it was allied with unusual consistency of purpose. This found expression in three things:

First, in his aims—to restore German military power, expand her frontiers, gather together the scattered populations of Volksdeutsche, and found a new German empire in Eastern Europe, the inhabitants of which would either be driven out, exterminated, or retained as slave-labor.

Second, in the firmness with which he grasped from the beginning what such aims entailed—the conquest of power in Germany on terms that would leave him with a free hand, the risk of preemptive intervention by other powers, the need to shape German rearmament in such a way as to enable him to win a quick advantage within a limited time by surprise and concentration of force, the certainty that to carry out his program would mean war.

Third, in the strength of will which underlay all his hesitations, opportunism, and temperamental outbursts, and in his readiness to take risks and constantly to increase these by raising the stakes—from the reoccupation of the Rhineland to the invasion of Russia (with Britain still undefeated in his rear) within the space of no more than five years.

Given such an attitude on the part of a man who controlled one of the most powerful nations in the world, the majority of whose people were prepared to believe what he told them about their racial superiority and to greet his satisfaction of their nationalist ambitions with enthusiasm—given this, I cannot see how a clash between Germany and the other powers could have been avoided. Except on the assumption that Britain and France were prepared to disinterest themselves in what happened east of the Rhine and accept the risk of seeing him create a German hegemony over the rest of Europe. There was nothing inevitable about either the date or the issue on which the clash actually came. It half came over Czechoslovakia in 1938; it might have come over another issue than Poland. But I cannot see how it could have been avoided some time, somewhere, unless the other powers were prepared to stand by and watch Hitler pursue his tactics of one-at-a-time to the point where they would no longer have the power to stop him.

If the Western powers had recognized the threat earlier and shown greater resolution in resisting Hitler's (and Mussolini's) demands, it is possible that the clash might not have led to war, or at any rate not to a war on the scale on which it had finally to be fought. The longer they hesitated, the higher the price of resistance. This is their share of the responsibility for the war: that they were reluctant to recognize what was happening, reluctant to give a lead in opposing it, reluctant to act in time. Hitler understood their state of mind perfectly and played on it with skill. None of the Great Powers comes well out of the history of the 1930's, but this sort of responsibility—even when it runs to appeasement, as in the case of Britain and France, or complicity as in the case of Russia—is still recognizably different from that of a government which deliberately creates the threat of war and sets out to exploit it.

In the Europe of the 1930's there were several leaders—Mussolini, for instance—who would have liked to follow such a policy, but lacked the toughness of will and the means to carry it through. Hitler alone possessed the will and had provided himself with the means. Not only did he create the threat of war and exploit it, but when it came to the point he was prepared to take the risk and go to war and then, when he had won the Polish campaign, to redouble the stakes and attack again, first in the West, then in the East. For this reason, despite all that we have learned since of the irresolution, shabbiness, and chicanery of other governments' policies, Hitler and the nation which followed him still bear, not the sole, but the primary responsibility for the war which began in 1939 and which, before Hitler was prepared to admit defeat, cost the lives of more than 25 million human beings in Europe alone.

NOTES

1. In *The Origins of the Second World War* (rev. ed., Greenwich, Conn., 1963). See also the article by T. W. Mason, "Some Origins of the Second World War," in *Past and Present*, No. 29 (1964), and Mr. Taylor's reply in the same journal, 30 (1965). For a German view of Mr. Taylor's book, see the review article by Gotthard Jasper in *Vierteljahrshefte für Zeitgeschichte*, X (1962), 311–340.

2. This view is well stated by Professor H. R. Trevor-Roper in an article "Hitlers Kriegsziele," *ibid.*, VIII (1960).

3. Written in 1928 but not published until 1961. An English translation has been published by Grove Press Inc., N.Y., *Hitler's Secret Book*. This book is almost entirely concerned with foreign policy.

4. An English version, *Hitler's Table Talk 1941–44*, was published in 1953, with an introduction by H. R. Trevor-Roper.

5. *The Testament of Adolf Hitler. The Hitler–Bormann Documents* (London, 1961).

6. For this view, see Taylor, *The Origins of the Second World War*.

7. March 14, 1936, in a speech at Munich. For the context, cf. Max Domarus, *Hitler, Reden und Proklamationen*, I (Würzburg, 1962), 606.

8. General Liebmann's note of Hitler's speech on this occasion is reprinted in *Vierteljahrshefte für Zeitgeschichte*, II (1954), 434–435. Cf. K. D. Bracher, W. Sauer, and G. Schulz, *Die Nationalsozialistische Machtergreifung* (Cologne, 1960), p. 748, and Robert J. O'Neill, *The German Army and the Nazi Party, 1933–1939* (London, 1966), pp. 125–126.

9. A report of Hitler's speech on this occasion, made by Field Marshal von Weichs, is printed by O'Neill, *ibid.*, pp. 39–42. For further discussion of the reliability of this report see Bracher, Sauer, and Schulz, *Die Nationalsozialistische Machtergreifung*, p. 749, n. 14.

10. Hermann Rauschning, *Hitler Speaks* (London, 1939), p. 116.

11. A critical review of Hitler's foreign policy in these years is made by K. D. Bracher in "Das Anfangsstadium der Hitlerschen Außenpolitik," *Vierteljahrshefte für Zeitgeschichte*, V (1957), 63–76.

12. I am indebted in this section to Dr. H. A. Jacobsen who allowed me to see a forthcoming article: "Programm und Struktur der nationalsozialistischen Außenpolitik 1919–1939."

13. *Documents on German Foreign Policy*, Series C, vol. 3, no. 509.

14. Mussolini's visit to Germany took place in the last ten days of September 1937 and left an indelible impression on the Italian dictator. A few weeks later, in November 1937, Mussolini agreed to sign the Anti-Comintern Pact, a further step in committing himself to an alliance with Hitler.

15. It is printed in *Documents on German Foreign Policy*, Series C, vol. 5, no. 490. Cf. Gerhard Meinck, *Hitler und die deutsche Aufrüstung*. (Wiesbaden, 1959), p. 164. Meinck's book is a valuable guide to the problems connected with German rearmament. Reference should also be made to Georg Tessin, *Formationsgeschichte der Wehrmacht 1933–39*, Schriften des Bundesarchivs, Bd. 7 (Boppard/Rhein, 1959). A convenient summary is provided by O'Neill, *The German Army*, Chap. 6.

16. The evidence has been admirably summarized and reviewed by Alan S. Milward in *The German Economy at War* (London, 1965). Further details are to be found in Burton H. Klein, *Germany's Economic Preparations for War* (Cambridge, Mass., 1959).

17. Klein, *Germany's Economic Preparations, pp.* 191–195; Milward, *German Economy,* pp. 43–45.

18. Reprinted in the English translation of Walter Hubatsch's *Hitlers Weisungen, Hitler's War Directives, 1939–45,* ed. H. R. Trevor-Roper (London, 1964), pp. 82–85.

19. Text in *Documents on German Foreign Policy*, Series D, vol. 1, no. 19. Cf. also Friedrich Hossbach, *Zwischen Wehrmacht und Hitler* (Hanover, 1949), pp. 207–220.

20. Speech at Augsburg, November 21, 1937. Domarus, *Hitler,* pp. 759–760.

21. *Documents on German Foreign Policy*, Series D, vol. 2, no. 133. Cf. also Series D, vol. 7, pp. 635–637.

22. Ibid., vol. 2, no. 221.

23. Ibid., vol. 2, no. 107.

24. For the strength of the Czech forces, see David Vital, "Czechoslovakia and the Powers," *Journal of Contemporary History*, I, no. 4 (1966).

25. Taylor, *The Origins of the Second World War,* Chap. 10.

26. International Military Tribunal Document C–120. Cf. also Walter Warlimont, *Inside Hitler's Headquarters* (London, 1964), p. 20.

27. O'Neill, *The German Army,* Chap. 6.

28. It is noticeable that there were far fewer doubts in the Army in 1939 than in 1938—and the major reason for this (apart from the fact that a war with Poland fitted in far better with the generals' traditionalist ideas than one with Czechoslovakia) was their belief that a war in 1939 involved fewer risks than in 1938.

29. See G. L. Weinberg, *Germany and the Soviet Union 1939–41* (The Hague, 1954).

30. See Robert L. Koehl, *RKFDV, German Resettlement and Population Policy 1939–45* (Cambridge, Mass., 1957), and Alexander Dallin, *German Rule in Russia, 1941–45* (London, 1957).

GUIDES TO OTHER STUDIES

So voluminous is the scholarly literature on Nazism and the Third Reich that only the most useful sources of bibliographical information can be cited here, along with references to a few of the most recent significant books.

An illuminating survey of the whole subject, as well as a thorough listing, by topics, of the major books and articles is provided by Karl Dietrich Bracher's *The German Dictatorship* (New York, 1970), originally published in Cologne in 1969 as *Die deutsche Diktatur*. Only a few essential books have been published since Bracher's bibliography was prepared. Included among these is the first attempt in more than thirty years at a comprehensive study of the NSDAP prior to the seizure of power, Dietrich Orlow's *The History of the Nazi Party: 1919–1933* (Pittsburgh, 1969). Also too recent for inclusion in Bracher's bibliography are two studies of the early years of Nazi foreign policy, Hans-Adolf Jacobsen's *Nationalsozialistische Aussenpolitik, 1933–1938* (Frankfurt and Berlin, 1968), and Gerhard L. Weinberg's *The Foreign Policy of Hitler's Germany. Diplomatic Revolution in Europe, 1933–36* (Chicago, 1970). Missing for the same reason are two new examinations of Nazi methods of rule, Peter Diehl-Thiele's *Partei und Staat im Dritten Reich* (Munich, 1969) and Edward N. Peterson's *The Limits of Hitler's Power* (Princeton, 1969), as well as the first major study in English of the fate of the Christian churches in the Third Reich, John S. Conway's *The Nazi Persecution of the Churches* (New York, 1968).

The best comprehensive guide for keeping abreast of current books and articles is the *Bibliographie zur Zeitgeschichte*. It provides a systematic listing of publications dealing with twentieth-century politics in general but is most thorough with regard to Germany. Published quarterly as a supplement to the most important journal in the field, *Vierteljahrshefte für Zeitgeschichte* (Munich, 1953–), it is also issued separately for libraries.

A useful source of information about articles in scholarly journals is the periodical *Historical Abstracts* (Santa Barbara, 1955–). It offers a succinct summary of the contents of new articles appearing in all languages and frequently includes as well information on the sources used by the authors. Articles dealing with Nazism and the Third Reich can be found in the sections dealing with international relations, the Second World War, and Europe: North and Central. A summary but up-to-date listing of new journal articles is published several times a year in *The American Historical Review* in a section entitled "Recently Published Articles."

A complete record of dissertations completed at the universities of both West and East Germany may be found in the annual volumes of *Jahresverzeichnis der deutschen Hochschulschriften.* A selected listing of dissertations dealing with political topics and completed since 1956 has been published in yearly volumes, beginning in 1965, by the East German Institut für Zeitgeschichte under the title *Deutsche Dissertationen zur Zeitgeschichte.* Information about dissertations and other research projects under way on topics related to the working class and social problems in general can be found in the journal *Internationale Wissenschaftliche Korrespondenz zur Geschichte der deutschen Arbeiterbewegung* (1965–   ), issued under the auspices of the Historische Kommission zu Berlin of the Friedrich-Meinecke-Institut of the Free University of Berlin (address of the journal: 1 Berlin 45, Tietzenweg 79).

AIDS TO RESEARCH

Those who wish to undertake research on aspects of Nazism and the Third Reich have at their disposal a wealth of documentary materials. There are also numerous finding aids containing information that can greatly facilitate the location and use of relevant materials. The most important of these are cited here in the hope of encouraging further research.

PUBLISHED SOURCES

At the end of the Second World War, tons of German documents were captured by the victorious powers, and many of importance for the study of Nazism and the Third Reich were subsequently published. For a general survey, see John A. Bernbaum, "The Captured German Records. A Bibliographical Survey," *The Historian,* XXXII (1970), 564–575.

One of the major postwar documentary publications is *Documents on German Foreign Policy, 1918–1945,* Series C and D (18 vols., London and Washington, 1949–). Containing documents from the files of the German Foreign Ministry, this collection actually covers only the period 1933–1941. The period 1941–1945 will be covered in a German-language publication of which only one volume has appeared: *Akten zur Deutschen Auswärtigen Politik, 1918–1945,* Series E (Göttingen, 1969–). Another collection of Foreign Ministry documents has been published in *Nazi-Soviet Relations, 1939–1941,* ed. Raymond J. Sontag and James S. Beddie (Washington, 1948). Two collections of German documents relating to foreign policy captured by the Russians were published as *Dokumente und Materialien aus der Vorgeschichte des Zweiten Weltkrieges* by the Foreign Ministry of the USSR (2 vols., Moscow, 1949).

The international war crimes trial conducted by the victorious powers after the war resulted in the publication of much documentation. The most extensive of these publications is: International Military Tribunal, *Trial of the Major War Criminals before the International Military Tribunal, Nuremberg, 14 November 1945–1 October 1946* (42 vols, Nuremberg, 1947–49). Volumes 1–23 contain the complete proceedings of the tribunal, while the documents introduced as evidence by the prosecution can be found in volumes 24–42. Much of this same material, as well as some defense documents, was published by the U.S.

Government Printing Office under the title *Nazi Conspiracy and Aggression* (10 vols., Washington, 1946–48).

Following the international war crimes trial, the American and British governments conducted separate trials in their occupation zones. Excerpts from the American trials, along with selected documents, were published as: Nuernberg Military Tribunals, *Trials of War Criminals before the Nuernberg Military Tribunals under Control Council Law No. 10* (15 vols., Washington, 1949–53). The corresponding British publication appeared under the title *War Crimes Trials Series,* ed. David Maxwell Fyfe (15 vols., London, 1948–54).

Newspapers from the period 1919–1945 represent another valuable source of published information. A useful survey of those newspaper collections in Germany that survived the Second World War or have since been assembled can be found in the article by Kurt Koszyk, "Zeitungssammlungen in Deutschland," *Der Archivar,* XI (1958), cols. 149–158. One of the most important of these collections is at the Institut für Zeitungsforschung in Dortmund, which issues a catalogue of its holdings, many of which are available on microfilm: *Mikrofilm Archiv der deutschsprachigen Presse e.V. Bestandsverzeichnis* (address for copies: Institut für Zeitungsforschung, D–46 Dortmund, Wissstrasse 4). Information about the location of extant copies of particular newspapers can be obtained from: Gesamtkatalog der Deutschen Presse, 28 Bremen 1, Breitenweg 27. A guide to some German newspapers available in one part of the United States can be found in *Union List of Western European Newspapers in the Boston-Cambridge Area,* comp. Leonie Gordon (Cambridge, Mass., 1971). See also U.S. Library of Congress, *Newspapers on Microfilm* (Washington, 1967).

Additional published source material of value for researchers can be found in the diaries and memoirs of participants in the events between 1919 and 1945, in various political publications of that time, and in studies by contemporary analysts. Some of these materials have been catalogued by the Wiener Library of London (now part of The Institute for Contemporary History, 4 Devonshire St., London W1), in its Catalogue Series: No. 1, *Persecution and Resistance under the Nazis* (2nd ed., London, 1960); No. 2, *From Weimar to Hitler. Germany, 1918–1933* (2nd ed., London, 1964). See also H. R. Boeninger, *The Hoover Library Collection on Germany* (Stanford, 1955). References to many such publications for the pre-1933 period can be found in the excellent bibliography of Karl Dietrich Bracher's *Die Auflösung der Weimarer Republik* (3rd ed., Villingen, 1960). For the early phases of the Third Reich, see the bibliography in Karl Dietrich Bracher, Wolfgang Sauer, Gerhard Schulz, *Die nationalsozialistische Machtergreifung* (Cologne and Oplanden, 1962). For the period of the Third Reich, see also *Bibliographische Vierteljahrshefte der Weltkriegsbücherei* (40 vols., Stuttgart, 1934–44). Information on obscure publications can frequently be obtained by reference to the now printed catalogues of the library of the Institut für Zeitgeschichte: *Bibliothek des Instituts für Zeitgeschichte, München. Alphabetisches Katalog* (5 vols., Boston: G. K. Hall, 1967).

Indispensable sources of biographical information are: Erich Stockhorst, *Fünftausend Köpfe. Wer war was im Dritten Reich* (Velbert & Kettwig, 1967); H. A. L. Degener, ed., *Wer Ist's,* especially the 9th and 10th editions (Leipzig, 1928 and 1935); *Das Deutsche Führerlexikon 1934/1935* (Berlin, 1934). Much useful biographical, institutional, and chronological information can be found in Cuno Horkenbach, *Das Deutsche Reich von 1918 bis heute* (4 vols., Berlin, 1930–35).

MICROFILMED DOCUMENTS

In addition to those captured documents that were published in printed form, a far greater number have been microfilmed and are now available for purchase by individual researchers or institutions. Most of these were filmed under the auspices of a joint project conducted by the American Historical Association and the National Archives of the United States, and copies of the films may be purchased from the latter. For information on that project, see the article by Dagmar Horna Perman, "Microfilming of German Records in the National Archives," *The American Archivist,* XXII (1959), 443–444; also that by Wilhelm Rohr, "Mikrofilmung und Verzeichnung deutscher Akten in Alexandria, USA," *Der Archivar,* XIX (1966), cols. 251–259.

A series of more than sixty detailed guides to these microfilms has been issued to research institutions in mimeographed form by the National Archives and the American Historical Association, Committee for the Study of War Documents, under the title: *Guides to German Records Microfilmed at Alexandria, Va.* (Washington: The National Archives, 1958–   ). A convenient listing of the collections contained in these microfilms, with references to the appropriate volumes of *Guides . . . ,* can be found in the current issue of: National Archives and Records Service, *List of National Archives Microfilm Publications,* in the section, "Other Governments," under the heading, "World War II Collections of Seized Enemy Records, RG 242." Also listed there are microfilmed collections for which no guides have been prepared. References to earlier guides to microfilmed captured documents are contained in the article by Francis L. Loewenheim, "Guides to Microfilmed German Records: A Review," *The American Archivist*, XXII (1959), 445–449.

A separate catalogue has been prepared for the microfilms of the German Foreign Ministry: George O. Kent, ed., *A Catalog of Files and Microfilms of the German Foreign Ministry Archives, 1920–1945* (3 vols., Stanford, 1962–66). A fourth and final volume will soon be published.

Of special importance for research on Nazism and the Third Reich are the microfilms of the archive of the Nazi Party itself, called the "Hauptarchiv," which were captured at the end of the Second World War and later filmed by the Hoover Institution on War, Revolution, and Peace, of Stanford University. Under the auspices of the Institution's "Bibliographical Series" an analytical guide has been prepared: Grete Heinz and Agnes F. Peterson, eds., *NSDAP Hauptarchiv. Guide to the Hoover Institution Microfilm Collection* (Stanford, 1964). Reels of the collection may be purchased separately from the Hoover Institution (Stanford, California 94305).

ARCHIVAL SOURCES: FEDERAL REPUBLIC

Abundant quantities of documents useful for research on Nazism and the Third Reich can be found in the numerous archives of West Germany. For a general survey of the principal archives and research libraries, see the article by J. R. C. Wright, "Libraries and Archives for Historians: I. Germany," in *History*, LIII (1968), 385–388; also, the extensive information provided in *Archivum: Revue Internationale des Archives*, XV (1965), 9–72. For an up-to-date listing of all major archives, with complete addresses, see the latest edition of the publication of the Stifterverband für die Deutsche Wissenschaft, *Vademecum deutscher Lehr- und Forschungsstätten* (5th ed., Essen, 1968).

Many valuable documentary materials, as well as a rich research library, can be found at the Institut für Zeitgeschichte in Munich. See the article by Helmut Krausnick, "Zur Arbeit des Instituts für Zeitgeschichte," *Geschichte in Wissenschaft und Unterricht*, XIX (1968), 90–96. There is no published catalogue of its archival holdings, but inquiries may be addressed directly to: Archiv, Institut für Zeitgeschichte, 8 München 19, Leonrodstrasse 46b. A smaller institution of the same variety is the Forschungsstelle für die Geschichte des Nationalsozialismus in Hamburg, 2 Hamburg 13, Rothenbaumchaussee 5.

Much important documentation on the Nazi Party, particularly the official records of party members and other files relating to particular individuals, are maintained by the United States State Department at the Berlin Document Center. No catalogue of the Center's holdings has ever been published, but inquiries may be directed to: Berlin Document Center, 1 Berlin 37, Wasserkäfersteig 1. State Department clearance must be obtained before the records can be used.

Nonbiographical collections of Nazi Party materials such as the "Hauptarchiv" microfilmed by the Hoover Institution (see above) have now been transferred from the Berlin Document Center to the West German Federal Archives, or Bundesarchiv (54 Koblenz, am Wöllershof 12). So have most of the captured documents that were microfilmed by the victorious powers, as well as some that were not filmed. For information on these and other Nazi documents, see Heinz Boberach, "Das Schriftgut der staatlichen Verwaltung, der Wehrmacht und der NSDAP aus der Zeit von 1933–1945: Versuch einer Bilanz," *Der Archivar,* XXII (1969), cols. 137–152; Manfred Wolf and Hans Schmitz, "Quellen zur Geschichte der Jahre 1930 bis 1950 in den Archiven. Archivgut—Überlieferungslücken—Ergänzungsmöglichkeiten," *ibid.,* cols. 129–136.

Besides these materials, the Bundesarchiv contains large quantities of other documents of value for research on Nazism and the Third Reich. The best source of information about its holdings is the official catalogue, *Das Bundesarchiv und seine Bestände: Übersicht,* ed. Friedrich Facius, Hans Booms, and Heinz Boberach (2nd ed., Boppard am Rhein, 1968). The military documents of the Bundesarchiv are housed in a separate archive, the Bundesarchiv-Militärarchiv, in Freiburg (78 Freiburg i.B., Wiesentalstrasse 1). For information on its holdings, see Erich Murawski, "Das Bundesarchiv-Militärarchiv," *Der Archivar,* XIII (1960), cols. 187–198; Hans Booms, "Zusammenfassung des militärischen Archivgutes im Bundesarchiv," *ibid.,* XXI (1968), cols. 238–240.

The locations of papers of historically important individuals are being registered in a useful new publication of the Bundesarchiv: *Verzeichnis der schriftlichen Nachlässe in deutschen Archiven und Bibliotheken.* Thus far, two volumes have appeared. Volume I was edited by Wolfgang A. Mommsen and carries the subtitle "Die Nachlässe in den deutschen Archiven" (Boppard am Rhein, 1971). It includes information on collections of papers of individuals located in the archives of both East and West Germany as well as references to such collections missing since the Third Reich. Volume II (which appeared earlier) was edited by Ludwig Denecke and covers those collections located in the libraries of the Federal Republic: "Nachlässe in den Bibliotheken der Bundesrepublik" (Boppard am Rhein, 1969).

Foreign Ministry documents for the pre-Nazi and Nazi periods are not housed in the Bundesarchiv along with those of other government agencies but are instead kept in the Political Archive of the Federal Republic's Foreign Ministry in Bonn (Politisches Archiv des Auswärtigen Amts, 53 Bonn, Adenauerallee 99–103). Information on that archive is provided by two articles by Hans Philippi, "Das Politische Archiv des Auswärtigen Amtes," *Der Archivar*, xi (1958), cols. 139–148; and "Das Politische Archiv des Auswärtigen Amtes: Rückfuhrung und Übersicht über die Bestände," *ibid.*, xiii (1960), cols. 199–218.

Another important West German archive is the Geheimes Staatsarchiv in West Berlin (1 Berlin 33, Archivstrasse 12/14), which contains documents of the Prussian state government, as well as the papers of a number of important individuals. Its collections are recorded in two guides: Hans Branig, Winifried Bliss, and Werner Petermann, *Übersicht über die Bestände des geheimen Staatsarchivs in Berlin-Dahlem: Zentralbehörden, andere Institutionen, Sammlungen* (Berlin and Cologne, 1967); Hans Branig, Ruth Bliss, Winifried Bliss, *Übersicht über die Bestände des Geheimen Staatsarchivs in Berlin-Dahlen: Provinzial- und Lokalbehörden* (Berlin and Cologne, 1966).

Information on the archives of the federal states of West Germany can be obtained from the reports included in the survey, "Aufbau und Organisation des staatlichen Archivwesens in den Ländern der Bundesrepublik Deutschland," in *Der Archivar*, xiii (1960), cols. 219–270.

Nongovernmental archives in West Germany are also a source of documentation useful for the researcher. For descriptions of a number of such archives, see the following publications: Paul Mayer and Wilhelm Peters, "Die Archive der Sozialdemokratischen Partei Deutschlands," *Der Archivar*, xx (1967), cols. 375–382; "Das Ludwigstein-Archiv der deutschen Jugendbewegung," *ibid.*, xiv (1961), col. 260; "Das Wirtschaftsarchiv des Instituts für Weltwirtschaft an der Universität Kiel," *ibid.*, xxii (1969), cols. 310–312; Bernhard Brilling, "Das jüdische Archivwesen in Deutschland," *ibid.*, xiii (1960), cols. 271–290; Hans-Joachim Weinbrenner, "Das Deutsche Rundfunkarchiv in Frankfurt a.M.," *ibid.*, xxi (1968), cols. 405–418; Willi A. Boelcke, "Die archivalischen Grundlagen der deutschen Rundfunkgeschichte 1923–1945," *Rundfunk und Fernsehen*, xvi (1968), 161–179; Hans-Wolfgang Strätz, "Archiv der ehemaligen Reichsstudentenführung in Würzburg," *Vierteljahrshefte für Zeitgeschichte*, xv (1967), 106–107;

Berhard Stasiewski, "Archivgut in katholischen Archiven in Nordrhein-Westfalen," *Der Archivar,* XXII (1969), cols. 151–155; Hans Steinberg, "Archivgut in evangelischen Archiven," *ibid.,* XXII (1969), cols. 155–157; Karlheinrich Dumrath, Wolfgang Eger, Hans Steinberg, eds., *Handbuch des kirchlichen Archivwesens,* vol. I, "Die zentralen Archive in der evangelischen Kirche" (Neustadt a.d. Aisch, 1965).

Industrial archives have rarely been used for research on Nazism and the Third Reich, and the contents of most remain to be explored. An extensive listing of the most important industrial archives, with addresses, may be found in *Vademecum deutscher Lehr- und Forschungsstätten* (see above). For descriptions of three major industrial archives, see these articles: Kurt Busse, "Das Siemens-Archiv in München," *Das Archivar,* XIII (1960); Bodo Herzog, "30 Jahre Historisches Archiv der Gutehoffnungshütte (GHH) in Oberhausen/Rhld.," *ibid.,* XX (1967), cols. 373–376; and Ernst Schroeder, "Das Krupp-Archiv—Geschichte und Gegenwart," *ibid.,* XIII (1960), cols. 305–316.

Further information on the archival resources of West Germany can be found in the back volumes and current issues of *Der Archivar. Mitteilungsblatt für Deutsches Archivwesen* (1947–   ). References to publications about archival materials are registered periodically in the section, "Hilfsmittel," of the *Bibliographie zur Zeitgeschichte* (see above, under "Guides to other Studies").

ARCHIVAL SOURCES: GERMAN DEMOCRATIC REPUBLIC

An excellent guide to the archives of the GDR has been prepared by Gordon R. Mork: "The Archives of the German Democratic Republic," *Central European History,* II (1969), 273–284. It provides not only a comprehensive listing of the most important archives and a description of their holdings but also full information regarding the procedures necessary to submit applications to use those archives. In addition, the footnotes contain extensive references to published archival catalogues and to articles on archival holdings that have appeared in various journals, particularly the organ of professional archivists in the GDR, *Archivmitteilungen. Zeitschrift für Theorie und Praxis des Archivwesens* (1951–   ). Mork's article should be the starting-point for anyone contemplating research in the archives of the GDR.

ARCHIVAL RESOURCES OUTSIDE GERMANY

Much documentation relevant to the study of Nazism and the Third Reich has been gathered together in Israel. See the article by Bernhard

Brilling, "Die staatlichen und öffentlichen Archive in Israel," *Der Archivar,* XX (1967), cols. 398–406. Also that by Kurt Jakob Ball-Kaduri, "Testimonies and recollections about activities organized by German Jewry during the years 1933–1945. Catalog of manuscripts in the Yad Vashem Archives. Supplement for the years 1960–67," *Yad Vashem Studies,* VII (1968), 205–219.

Another important repository of documentation concerning the Jews of Germany and Nazism is the Leo Baeck Institute of New York (129 East 73rd Street, New York, N.Y. 10021). On its holdings, see Max Kreutzberger, ed., *Leo Baeck Institut New York. Bibliothek und Archiv. Katalog* (Tübingen, 1970). Also Ilse Blumenthal-Weiss, "Die Memoiren-Sammlung des Leo Baeck Instituts," *Tribüne,* III (1964), 945–951; E. G. Lowenthal, "Das Leo-Baeck-Institut," *Der Archivar,* XIX (1966), cols. 277–279.

Of importance for the fate of the Social Democratic Party and the trade unions under Nazism are the holdings of the International Institut voor sociale Geschiedenis in Amsterdam (Keizersgracht 264). For information, see its publication, *International Institute of Social History, Amsterdam. History and Activities* (Assen, 1968). The catalogue of its library has recently been printed: *Alphabetical Catalog of the Books and Pamphlets of the International Institute of Social History, Amsterdam* (12 vols., Boston: G. K. Hall, 1970).

Index

A NOTE ON THE EDITOR

Henry A. Turner, Jr., was born in Atlanta and studied at Washington & Lee University, the University of Munich, the Free University of Berlin, and Princeton University, where he received a Ph.D. He is the author of *Stresemann and the Politics of the Weimar Republic,* and is now Professor of History at Yale University.